W9-ASH-305

MAX AND SHIRMAX
MORE THAN A LOVE AFFAIR

MAX KONIGSBERG

MAX AND SHIRMAX
MORE THAN A LOVE AFFAIR

This Special Edition has been published in support of
The Max Konigsberg Breast Cancer Prevention Fund
at the
Sir Mortimer B. Davis – Jewish General Hospital,
Montreal.

Editorial and production co-ordination: The Colophon Group
Design Consultants: ArtPlus Design and Communications
Jacket Cover Design: Sarah Orr/ArtPlus Design
Printed and bound in Canada by Transcontinental Printing G.P.

ISBN 0-9781115-0-8

Canadian Cataloguing in Publication Data

1. Konigsberg, Max, 1935-. 2. Shirmax Organization--History.
3. Stores, Retail--Québec (Province)--Montréal--History--20th century.
4. Women's clothing industry--Québec (Province)--Montréal--History--
20th century. 5. Businessmen--Québec (Province)--Montréal--
Biography.
I. Shirley K. Holdings II. Title.

HF9940.C32K66 2006   338.7'613912092
C2006-904050-8

CONTENTS

DEDICATION
PREFACE
AUTHOR'S NOTE

PART ONE
MY STORY

PART TWO
BUILDING AN ORGANIZATION THAT WORKS

PART THREE
LIVING LIFE WITH POWER

EPILOGUE
ACKNOWLEDGEMENTS
APPENDICES

I dedicate this book
to
My wife Shirley, my inspiration and the love of my life,
and our very dear friends,
the late Myrna Forman
and June Melnik,

all of whom were afflicted with breast cancer.
Sadly, Myrna succumbed in 2001,
June was taken from us in 2003.

I also dedicate this book
to
Bernard Konigsberg, my father,
who gave me the foundation for an extraordinary life
and to
Esther, Philip and Rachelle, our children,
who are our three blessings.

PREFACE

I MET MAX KONIGSBERG NEARLY TWENTY-FIVE YEARS AGO. His intense commitment to Shirmax, HIS COMPANY, and his enormous drive to succeed in both his business and personal life made deep impressions on me. During those 25, I have shared many of his ups and downs. (I even lost some money when I purchased stock in Shirmax when it became a public company.) But I have witnessed no softening of his commitment or that drive that is visible in everything he does. There is no half way with Max. He sees black and white — NOT GREY.

Our real story began when Max and I were sitting beside the pool at our hotel in Taiwan during his first buying trip to Asia. (I was president of Carr Associates Inc., at the time.) Max was all business, talking about it from morning 'til night. I admit now that it exhausted me. He was a man possessed, searching for ways to better himself and therefore his company. He wanted the road map to the next level. I felt as though I was under interrogation by the CIA!

Max realized that he was a one-man show. It was "his way or the highway" and in him I saw much of myself. The main difference in 1982 was that I had already experienced some business failures — or at least I perceived them as flops. It was, therefore, easy for me to tell Max that he was not adequately prepared to take his business to the next higher level. At the time, he was still a "seat of the pants" executive in a retail and apparel-manufacturing world that was evolving quickly. I knew that more than anything else, he needed to learn how to plan and strategize for his business. To learn that standing still was suicidal. He needed exposure, and I urged him to enroll in the American Management Association "Presidents Course." I had taken the course a few years earlier and I believed that he, like me, would benefit from the exposure. Certainly, you become "educated" when you are surrounded by some of the best company presidents in the United

States. In my case, I gave a little and got back a lot. I wanted the same for Max and he got it — and more!

For the longest time, I thought of Max as the purest of "philosophers". But it was not until I started to write this foreword that I actually looked up the dictionary definition of the word "philosophy": Use of reason and argument in seeking truth and knowledge, esp. of ultimate reality; system for conduct of life. That's Max Konigsberg — the Philosopher.

Max has an overwhelming desire to learn. His mission has always been about teaching, and passing on his knowledge is an important component of his goal. But in my view, that is secondary to his perseverance and his drive to become "educated", as opposed to an "educator." Max is on an endless trip for learning. He learns from every experience, every person, and every moment in his life. Each course taken in class or in life has molded a part of his being. His book is far from the auto biography it pretends to be. Its essence is that of a textbook on life — family and friends — as well as a textbook on business – from success to failure to success. It is a book about values and truth, love and commitment. It is also about relationships and how they develop and are nurtured over time.

One person above all stands out as his raison d'être — his wife, Shirley. In my view there could never have been a Shirmax without her. This book tells of the silent part she played in everything in Max's life and everything he has accomplished.

Martin Richter
June 2006

AUTHOR'S NOTE

Having recently sold my business, I am now at the end of one journey and at the beginning of another. As I reflect on my life, it is clear to me that I have had an amazing and extraordinary range of adventures, trials and tribulations. Along the way I learned some very valuable lessons and made a number of discoveries. In this book I share my experiences and the lessons I have learned.

My wife Shirley and I opened a ladies wear shop in Montreal in 1957 and this was the beginning of what was to become the Shirmax Organization. Happily, the Shirmax story is one of success; the organization grew from one store to more than 200 stores on a roller coaster of good and bad times, profits and losses, as well as huge challenges and rewards. We went through one particularly rough period in 1993 when Shirmax was forced to file for bankruptcy protection.

I consider the story of how we accomplished our turn-around to be truly amazing, particularly because what we achieved was thought by many to be impossible. We not only survived the crisis of bankruptcy protection, we did so without any new money being invested, and without any change or loss of share ownership! Shirmax then went on to a period of record profitability that culminated in the recognition we received when I was nominated as CEO of the Year in 1995, and named Entrepreneur of the Year in Quebec in 1998 (in the Wholesaling, Retailing and Manufacturing category) and, ultimately, the sale of the company at a premium price five years later, to Reitmans, Canada's largest specialty store fashion retailer.

I believe the account of our 45-year adventure is a story worth telling, and that it will be of value to other retailers, business people and entrepreneurs.

In 1981 I had a transformational experience that awakened me to a world of new possibilities for both my business and my personal life. That experience started me on a journey of exploration and self-discovery. In the course of that journey, I became intrigued with the sources of personal power, achievement and personal satisfaction.

I have learned many life lessons beyond Shirmax. I made many discoveries and developed valuable formulas for workability in life and for managing my life successfully — as a son, a brother, a husband, a parent and grandparent, a friend, a student and as a teacher and mentor. I have also acquired some wisdom that I believe may contribute not only to entrepreneurs, but also to those who may be seeking access to a life of quality, power, integrity and fulfillment.

The purpose of this book is to document my life's accomplishments and to share my discoveries and lessons learned with a wide range of readers. I hope what I have to say will be useful to those who are traveling along a path similar to the one I traveled, and contribute — make a difference — to them.

I have met literally thousands of people over the course of the past sixty years and although I have an excellent memory, I know it is not infallible. Like many of my peers today, I, too, have occasional lapses of selective hearing and memory — especially when I tell the same story over and over again. Nonetheless, what I have presented in this book is the truth as I know it. If there are errors or anomalies in my tales and reminiscences, I take full responsibility for them. I offer no apology, however. They are the "facts" as I know them.

Max Konigsberg
August 2006

PART ONE

MY STORY

1

BEGINNINGS

I WAS BORN IN HOLLAND but my roots go back to where my parents came from — Poland.

My parents came from different villages so they hadn't known each other before they left Poland. Both families were very poor and had been subjected to racial persecution and pogroms after World War I.

My mother's early years were truly wretched. She received very little education and even less affection, given that her own mother had died when she was a little girl. Her father sent her away to live with relatives when she was twelve because he could not afford to support her. Although the people who took her in were family, they did not treat her as a member of their family. In fact, she was little more than a maid in their house. She had to prepare and serve the family's meals, but was not invited to eat with them. She had a little stool in the kitchen where she ate by herself. All of these factors affected her and shaped her life.

My mother's name was Ethel Schiffman. Mina Adler was her first cousin and closest friend when she was growing up and they remained best friends for as long as they lived. They left Poland and went to Holland together when they were both nineteen. I believe they chose Holland because it was more tolerant to Jews and they thought there was more opportunity to make a living there than there was in Poland. They ended up in the city of Leiden, where they survived by working in a factory as sewing-machine operators. Both women met their husbands-to-be in Leiden.

Like my mother, my father, Bernard Konigsberg, came from Poland. When my father was born, his family name was Spergel. After the First World War, Poland moved back and forth between being an independent state and part of the Austro-Hungarian Empire. Different laws applied under each regime. My grandparents were married in a religious ceremony, which was recognized by the state to be a legal marriage at the time. However, when my father applied for a passport, which he needed in order to leave Poland, the regime in power at the time raised some question as to the legality of his parents' marriage. So tracing his origins back to a great grandmother whose name was Konigsberg, he changed his name from Spergel to Konigsberg.

My father's mother, Miriam, died when he was thirteen. He had been very close to her and was devastated when she died. On the other hand, he had a strained relationship with his father who was very authoritarian, a cold, strict person who showed his son little affection. However, he made sure his son received a sound Jewish and Hebrew education. My father loved Judaic studies and was very serious about them, so much so that he became a *khazan* and officiated at religious services for most of his adult life.

Not long after my grandmother died, my grandfather married his wife's sister. Apparently my father found that very hard to accept so, when he was fourteen, he left his father's house and moved to another village where he got a job in a shoe store. Like my mother, he was nineteen when he set out for Holland.

My parents met at a Jewish social club and meetinghouse in Leiden where newcomers to Holland used to get together. They married when my dad was 23; mother was three years older. They lived in a small room with little more than the bare necessities. Their bed was a pile of straw on the floor. They both eked out an existence as peddlers until I was born on July 6th, 1935, about a year after they were married. My mother got a sewing machine in their room soon after I was born. She did home sewing for a manufacturer and stayed home with me while my father continued

▼

*Bernard and Ethel Konigsberg,
Barbados, 1940*

▶ *Me in Holland,
age 18 months*

to peddle. My mother often told me about breast feeding me for a long time, much longer time than was usual even in those days, because that was the only way she could feed me. She fed herself and so she was able to breastfeed me.

That was our life in Holland — barely getting by.

About the same time as my parents met, Mina met Jacob Zierler, who came from Germany. They also married and our two families were inseparable from then on. My tanta Mina and my uncle Jacob were my godparents.

In the late '20s Hitler began making a lot of worrying noises. And by the early '30s his threats were becoming ominous. My father and some of his friends were convinced that Hitler was dangerous, so they conceived a plan to leave Europe. It wasn't easy for a Jew to leave Europe in those days. There were few countries willing to accept Jews, and those that did, like countries in South America, were half a world away. By 1935 Canada and the United States were already closed to Jews. Leaving Europe at that time meant leaving family and friends behind with the real prospect of never seeing them again. That was not an easy thing to do!

None of my father's friends had much money, but one of them, Moishe Altman, decided to be a pioneer. In 1931 he and his eldest son, Hershel (Henry), left their family, boarded a ship and set out for South America. The ship made a stop in Barbados, by which time they had had enough of sea travel. They simply got off the ship and didn't get back on. Mr. Altman decided to make Barbados home and started peddling. In a short time he saw the prospects for making a living and, eventually, he was able to send for the rest of his family.

As the pioneer, Mr. Altman had agreed to keep in touch with the other members of the group and to let them know whether they should follow him or not. So, as soon as he was settled, he wrote to his friend, Yankle Bernstein, my father's best friend, and told him it was all right for him to come. So, Mr. Bernstein followed Mr. Altman to Barbados. After Mr. Bernstein was settled, he wrote letters to three people in Europe. One was to my father saying,

"I am peddling here and it's OK for you to come, so make your arrangements and come." He sent a similar letter to his brother-in-law in Poland, and also told him to come. The third letter was to his friend, Mr. Korn, which said, "Don't come, because if there are too many of us peddling here, none of us will make a living."

Several months went by, then my father arrived, and a while later Mr. Korn appeared. Understandably, Mr. Bernstein was surprised to see Mr. Korn, and he asked him, "How come you came? I wrote you not to come." And Mr. Korn answered, "Well, I didn't get the letter you wrote to me; I got the letter you wrote to your brother-in-law. It was in the envelope addressed to me. The letter said to come, and I assumed you meant the same for me, so I came." In the meantime, Mr. Bernstein's brother-in-law received the letter intended for Mr. Korn, telling him not to come and, like Mr. Korn, he assumed the message was the same for him, so he stayed where he was. In those days, it took a long time for a letter to travel from Barbados to Poland and even though Mr. Bernstein wrote to his brother-in-law immediately, it was too late for him to get himself and his family out of Poland. Soon after the war started, he and his entire family perished at Hitler's hands — all because of a mix-up in letters.

I was one year old in 1936 when my father left my mother and me in Holland and set out for Barbados. He was a young man of twenty-five. When I was a youngster I remember him telling me that he had only a few pennies to his name when it was time for him to board the ship. He was a smoker and he was hoping to use what little money he had to buy a few cigarettes on the voyage. But as he was going up the gangplank, he looked back at my mother on the dock with me in her arms and he took out his small packet of coins — literally all the money he had in the world — and threw it to her. I can only guess that he was overcome by the grim realization that he might never see us again. And so he set out, alone and penniless, for Barbados.

2

GROWING UP
IN BARBADOS

IN 1936, BARBADOS WAS NOT THE PLACE IT IS TODAY. The Island was relatively primitive, undeveloped and insulated from the outside world. Ninety-three per cent of the population was black and although the basic language was English, they had their own Bajan dialect, which was difficult even for an English-speaking person to understand. My father didn't speak English, let alone understand the Bajan dialect. He had no money, he had just arrived in Bridgetown, and I doubt that he had ever seen a black person before. Moreover, he had to make a living; in fact, he had to make an entirely new life for himself. When I think of my father at age 25, I often mistakenly compare him to myself at the same age. By comparison, he had lived a hundred years to my twenty-five, and his experience with life was even one hundred times greater.

Like those who came before him, my father became a peddler. He was desperate to get my mother and me out of Holland as soon as possible and it was very important that he book passage for us before I was two years old for the simple reason that, if we traveled before my second birthday, he would not have to pay a fare for me. Fortunately for us, the few Jewish men in Barbados at the time helped him to finance our passage. And so, my mother and I arrived in Bridgetown, Barbados in the spring of 1937, just before my second birthday.

Thinking back to my father being a peddler and what he had to do in order to survive, I still find it hard to reconcile what he did with the person I knew. My dad was not particularly strong, he always had two "left hands", and he was not at all mechanically inclined. As far back as I can remember he couldn't easily balance himself on a bicycle. Yet, he had a big heavy bike with a heavy metal carrier attached to the front in which he carried a suitcase filled with assorted items for sale. Barbados is very hilly and I can't for the life of me figure out how he managed to peddle that bicycle all over the island. But for a number of years he somehow managed to do that. It was a very hard way to make a living.

After a few years, my father stopped peddling and opened a small dry-goods store on Swan Street in Bridgetown. For the rest of the time he spent on the Island, he was able to make a modest living from that store.

About a year after my mother and I arrived in Bridgetown, my brother, Alex (who is three years my junior) was born. My sister Betty was born the following year and my younger sister, Ellen, was born eight years later.

While we were growing up my mother's influence was almost inconsequential in our lives. I think the fact that her mother had died when she was very young and that she was sent away from home at an early age had a profound effect on her. She never knew a parent's love, she was never nurtured, and she received no education. She had no role models, so she never had the opportunity to develop any of the feelings and skills a woman needs to become a nurturing and supportive mother. Where she was most comfortable, and most effective, was in the family business. My father relied heavily on her; he was the brains behind the business but my mother managed the store.

It was my father who exerted virtually all the influence in the family and we received most of our nurturing and support from him. But, like my mother, he was not very demonstrative. He was also very guarded with his affection. To add to this, neither of my parents was about showing sympathy and they were not receptive to our saying, "I'm tired." or "I don't feel well." Our parents didn't permit those feelings for themselves, so they didn't allow them for their children. They considered showing affection, being tired or not feeling well to be signs of weakness. I am not suggesting that we thought they didn't love us. We knew they loved us, and that they would take care of us. But having said that, there was very little show of sympathy. Perhaps one of my early experiences will put this into perspective.

When I was twelve, I had a very painful toothache. After I had suffered with it for a few days, my mother took me into town with her when she went to open the store and she sent me across the street to see a dentist. He decided to pull the tooth and, after filling me with what seemed like 50 shots of novocaine, he did just that. I didn't know it at the time, but I have a tendency to bleed when I have dental work done that affects the gums, so the hole in my jaw would not stop bleeding.

I went back to the store, dizzy from the novocaine and bleeding all the way. My mother didn't exactly ignore me, but she didn't pay much attention to me either. She was busy. I was in mild shock from the experience, and my head was spinning so that I could hardly keep it up. My mother told me to go and lie down in the show window with a bolt of cloth under my head and to stay there until I felt better. Meanwhile, she continued to look after business in the store.

I lay in the show window with people walking by looking at me in my misery. Eventually, she told me to catch a bus and go home. I had to walk about a half mile to the bus station. I was feeling very ill. When I got on the bus I sat next to a large black lady. I put my head on her shoulder and fell asleep. I eventually got home and went to bed.

Even though it was very painful experience and it took a long time for my jaw to heal, no one ever acknowledged my condition. Interestingly, at the time, I didn't see that as being anything out of the ordinary. We were expected to be strong and not to complain and feel sorry for ourselves. That was just the way it was.

We had a wonderful life in Barbados. Because I had nothing to compare it with, I probably did not appreciate it enough. Other than when I was in school, I lived as a beach boy, wearing only bathing suits and shorts, no shoes and enjoying the wonderful climate and the sea. We were part of a small, tight and caring Jewish community and I had a solid Jewish upbringing. I had good friends, both Jewish and non-Jewish, and my life revolved mostly around sports — cricket, soccer and water polo — as well as Sea Scouts and the Barbados Cadets. All in all, I was a true Bajan boy.

Some segregation between blacks and whites was a fact of life in Barbados at the time. Still, I had both black and white friends and I do not remember ever experiencing any anti-Semitism. In retrospect, I feel very privileged to have grown up in Barbados. Growing up there was an experience most young people today can only dream about.

Culturally, we had a very rich Jewish life in Barbados even though we were not very religious and were not kosher. It was impossible to be kosher because kosher foods were not available. However, we were very traditional. There were 25 Jewish families in our community and we all lived in the same neighbourhood close to each other. Most of the seniors had come from Europe and had similar traditional Jewish backgrounds, so everyone, young and old, kept the traditions and celebrated and enjoyed all of the Jewish holidays. Socially, the seniors kept to themselves; there was no assimilation with the non-Jewish community. But, of course, all of the children went to schools where they had non-Jewish friends.

We were certainly not well off financially, so as children we didn't have many luxuries or extras — but we never wanted for our basic needs. Most of our food was grown on the Island and it was not expensive. We did not need heating, we needed very little clothing and we had an excellent school system.

School Days

WE WERE TAUGHT UNDER THE BRITISH SYSTEM and we wrote the Oxford and Cambridge O-level exams in order to graduate from high school. As a youngster, I suffered from a serious lack of self-esteem. There were two reasons for this. First, I was not a good student. In fact, I was a very poor student. I even had the distinction of failing the same grade twice when I was 12 and 13 years old. I always sensed that something was wrong, but I did not know what it was. I figured I was just not very smart. Years later I discovered that I had a learning disability that caused me to have great difficulty reading. (When I looked at a page of small print or very tight writing, everything blurred and became a gray blob.) So, in order to internalize what I was reading, I had to concentrate very hard to see the words and read the same paragraph two or three times. It was hard, slow work. In those days people were not sensitive to learning disabilities, and nobody seemed to suspect that I might have had a problem. A youngster with difficulties just got passed over, and that is what happened to me. Most of my teachers paid little attention to me and just wrote me off. I think they just decided I wasn't very bright and I became known as a "dunce."

I had a close friend by the name of Harold Treyhane. We went through most of high school together in the same classes. We used to sit next to each other in class and it was difficult to tell which one of us was the poorer student. During class the teacher would ask a question, then go around the room asking students by name if they knew the answer. When he got to us he always said, "Oh, Konigsberg and Trehane, forget it! No chance!" He never allowed that we might know the answer.

Harold left school a year before I did, so he never finished high school. He went to work and we lost touch when I left the Island the next year. I have taken the liberty of mentioning Harold and his school days here because, as things turned out, Harold went on to become very successful — but I will get to that later.

The second reason for my low self-esteem was my relationship with my father. In many respects he was a very gifted man. He had a photographic memory and an amazing mind. He was mostly self-taught, but he was a scholar, nonetheless. He was very learned in Jewish history and the Torah, he had a beautiful singing voice, he was a *khazan* and was highly respected by his peers. In fact, he was one of the leaders of the Jewish community. But he also had his shortcomings.

My dad did not understand the concept of empowerment and he never looked for ways to make his children feel proud of themselves. He could always find reasons to put us down, especially me, his first-born — not that he did not have reason. It is interesting that the very things he complained about in his own father became his *modus operandi* with me. He often talked about how he never got a word of approval from his own father.

He was also inept as a mentor and a teacher. When the time came for me to prepare for my *Bar Mitzvah*, my father was my teacher. His teaching method consisted of coming to the table with a strap. and every time I made a mistake I got a whack! Unfortunately, my fluency in Hebrew was no greater than it was in English so, for me, instruction for my *Bar Mitzvah* was one whack after another. Somehow, I managed to muddle through what I had to do and say for the ceremony, and I got it over with.

For a European, especially a Jewish father, a good education was paramount. So, given my lack of scholastic ability, it was clear to me that I was a disappointment to him. He believed I would never amount to anything and he would often look at me, shake his head and ask, in Yiddish, "What ever is going to become of you?" Given these dynamics, I grew up without confidence in myself. I felt inadequate and I thought of myself as backward. Unfortunately, I could not shine in those areas that were closest to my father's heart and I felt I had no other way to prove myself.

There was, however, another side to my father. He could be very sensitive and kind. When I failed the same grade the second time and I had to bring home my report card. I didn't know how I could possibly face him. I was scared out of my mind. Then he showed his other side.

Many of my friends had bicycles and I wanted one, too. I had been asking my dad for a bike for months but he kept telling me he didn't have the money to buy me one. Anyhow, when I came home and showed him my report card, he looked at it but he said nothing. I knew he was very upset, but still he didn't say anything. Nothing! That night, before I went to sleep, he came to me and said, "I want you to come downtown with me tomorrow morning." I went to sleep thinking that he had decided to take me out of school and that he was taking me downtown to look for a job. I was petrified and it took me a long time to fall asleep. Next morning, we went downtown but instead of looking for a job for me, he took me to a bicycle shop and bought me a bicycle! Not even once did he ever acknowledge my failure. He knew I was hurting enough.

Although my father rarely displayed his affection, he had his way of letting me know he loved me. Having said that, I loved my father with all my being and there was nothing I wanted more than to please him and to make him proud of me. Today, I know that whatever I have achieved in this life was driven by my enormous desire to please my father and to gain his approval. And even though he passed away when I was forty-four, I continued to be driven by that same desire to win his approval. So I credit my dad and his unorthodox ways for all that I have accomplished, for giving me my "drivenness" and for inspiring me to excel.

I had a lucky break when I was fifteen. I was attending Harrisons College, an all boys' school, when the school authorities decided to put together a water polo team to compete in the Barbados Water Polo League. I had played some water polo when I was with the Sea Scouts, but I was not big or strong physically and I was

▼

*Alex, my Dad and me, on the occasion of
Alex's Bar Mitzvah, 1951*

▼

*Me, as an army cadet —
guarding Barbados!*

▼

My Bar Mitzvah photo

only a mediocre player. I was also very much afraid of getting hurt but, because I had played before, I was drafted onto the school team.

Two years before I finished school and left Barbados, the Barbados Water Police put a team together and joined the Island Water Polo League. One of their players was a policeman whose name was Lorenzo Best. He was a big, powerful black man, about six feet six inches tall, with a great body and broad shoulders. He was also a very strong swimmer and from the day he joined the League, water polo in Barbados changed.

Before Best, water polo was a game where scores were measured in single digits: 3-2, 2-1, and sometimes 4-3. It was not a game in which high scores were registered. Best didn't have much finesse, but he was so strong and so fast he could bulldoze his way through anyone. If he got his hands on the ball, the goalkeeper had little chance of stopping it. From his very first game, Best consistently scored a lot of goals. He was unstoppable, game after game.

Eventually, our Harrisons College team came up against the Water Police team. Everyone on our team was around 16 years old and we were all lightweights. Best played forward and so did I, so we were on opposite ends. Within no time he had scored four goals. It was humiliating and my teammate who was defending against him said, "I don't want anything more to do with him." So we decided to take turns playing defense, and every time Best scored a goal we'd exchange places. He soon scored four more goals and it was my turn to mark him. He was playing forward and I was now playing defense.

Best terrified me. Although I was marking him, I was staying as far away from him as possible because I didn't want to get hurt. No one in the league, other than Best, could hold the ball in one hand; no one had hands big enough to manage that. Before Best, our game plan was to flip the ball — bouncing it, and then flipping it in the direction we wanted it to go. We were fast, but Best, who could pick up the ball like a baseball, would grab it, wind up, bringing his arm all the way back, and fire it at the net. Suddenly, while I was thinking I was far enough away from him to be out of his way, he brought his arm all the way back and his hand — with the ball in it — was right in my face! So, I just put up my hand and tapped the ball out of his. This happened once...twice...three times! What can I say? Best scored eight goals in the first half but in the second half, when I was playing defense against him, he didn't score a single goal against me. It was the first time anyone had ever held him scoreless.

The next day, the headline on the sports page of the local newspaper read, "KONIGSBERG HOLDS BEST SCORELESS!" It was the first time my name ever appeared in a newspaper! As the season progressed, Best continued to score lots of goals in every game he played — except when he played against Harrisons College. For whatever reason, I psyched him out and, for the next two years, he never scored a goal against me.

My water polo career ended during my last month in Barbados. It so happened that Harrisons College and the Water Police were the finalists in the league that year, and the last game of the season was the final for the cup. At that time, water polo was played out in the ocean beside a pier which was packed with people who had come to watch the game. My father happened to be sitting next to the referee. Shortly before the game, Best came along the bridge yelling, "Where's Mr. Konigsberg?" The crowd made way for him and when he was face-to-face with my father he said, "If you let your son into the water today, I'm going to kill him!" Now, Best was not a hurtful or malicious person so I am sure he said this just for effect. But, of course, the referee witnessed the entire spectacle.

When the whistle blew, the teams swam toward the centre. Best always swam with his head down and his arms churning like a mix-master. I was swimming toward him from the opposite end, but I got too close and his hand came down over me and caught me in the eye. I put on a terrific show; I sank to the bottom, then I came up, and then I went down again! The referee ordered Best out of the game. We went on to win the game — and the cup. That was my last game for Harrisons College. It was not, however, my last encounter with Lorenzo Best.

Because of Lorenzo Best I had my first real taste of success and that was the beginning of a long journey toward raising my self-esteem.

In my last year at Harrisons College, I had another important learning experience. Our Sports Day was a big, big event; in fact, it was the highlight of the school year. Many of the students from other schools on the Island — both boys and girls — came to watch. Parents attended, too. Since it was my final year at Harrisons College, I wanted to do something special; I wanted to leave some kind of mark that I had been there. Since I certainly wasn't going to leave my mark scholastically, I decided to try to qualify for the 400-metre (quarter-mile) race, which was an important event on Sports Day. So I bought a pair of running shoes and I started running. That was my training. I used to get up in the morning and run and run and run. I did that all year. When the time came to qualify for the running events, I won my heat in the 400 metres and qualified to run in the event on Sports Day.

When the day came, there was a lot of excitement and anticipation in the air. A lot of attention was focused on two big races, which were the last two events of the day. The 400-metre race was scheduled just before the 800-metre (half-mile). My father made a special effort to attend because I was running. My girlfriend at the time was there, too, and I wanted both of them to see me win my race.

I mentioned earlier that I had been afraid of Best, because he was big, but I neglected to say I was also intimidated because he was black. The truth is I was intimidated because I *knew* — in fact, I think that most of us white guys knew — that black guys were much stronger and faster than white guys! I just knew that *as if it were really so.*

At the gun I got off to a good start. After 200 metres I was in third place. With 100 metres to go, I was in second place. The runner in front of me was black and, without any thought, I just cruised in behind him with no effort at all and I finished in second place. My teacher ran up to me when the race was over (I will never forget the expression on his face) and shouted at me, "Konigsberg, what did you do? You didn't even try!" I was absolutely stunned by what he said and the realization that because the guy in front of me was black, and given my absolute belief that black guys were stronger and faster, *I had let him win — I hadn't even tried!*

That experience had a huge effect on me and has haunted me for the rest of my life. It was truly a life-altering experience, and I learned a very important lesson from it. I promised myself that I would never *ever* again not give my best! That commitment became one of my prime motivators and is still with me. I am sure that that race and the decision I made afterward was another source of much of the drive and tenacity I have had over the years.

Uncle John

AFTER THE WAR IN EUROPE ENDED in 1945, my father made a special effort to track down one of his relatives, an uncle, whose name was Moishe Spergel, who he believed was living somewhere in the United States or Canada. It took my dad several years to locate him, but he eventually found him living in Montreal under the name of John Spergel. In 1951 my dad invited him to visit us in Barbados. I was sixteen years old when my great uncle John came to visit.

One evening, we were sitting at the dinner table and my uncle asked my dad, "What are your plans for Max when he finishes high school?"

My dad answered, "We're sending him to Israel." There was a war on in Israel at the time, so my Uncle John was surprised by my dad's answer.

"Why are you sending him to Israel with a war going on there?"

"The only thing Max can do is drive a truck." my father answered

"If he drives a truck in North America, he'll be a third-class citizen, but if he drives a truck in Israel, he'll be a first-class citizen — because everyone in Israel is equal. That's why we're sending him to Israel."

I knew that my father intended to send me to Israel when I finished school, but until that moment I had no idea why. For me, the message that "The only thing he can do is drive a truck!" was another powerful blow to my already poor self-esteem. Once again, my father's remark underlined what he thought of me.

My uncle suggested that my dad consider sending me to Montreal instead. He said that he had recently attended a graduation ceremony at McGill University in Montreal and that one of the Deans had made a speech in which he mentioned that there was a shortage of accountants in Canada.

My father's response to that was, "So what? School is not for Max. He can't be an accountant."

Anyway, as the evening went on, the two men continued talking and I went to bed. In the morning I learned that my father had reconsidered his decision to send me to Israel, and had decided instead to send me to Montreal to try to become an accountant. I don't believe he thought I would ever actually succeed in becoming an accountant, but I was finishing school and I had to move on — and for him, that was "moving on."

MY GUARDIAN ANGEL

OVER THE YEARS I HAVE COME TO BELIEVE that I have a guardian angel who watches over and takes care of me. This belief has had a profound effect on how I view and live my life. For me, it is only by crediting my guardian angel that I can explain why, throughout my entire life, I have been directed, or led — or even forced — to take a specific fork in the road, even though I could not see at the time that it was in my best interest to do so. Those "forks" have always turned out to be the right ones for me to take and have always led me in the direction I needed to go.

Now, I'm not talking about divine guidance or spirituality. I simply believe that my guardian angel has always manipulated events and circumstances that have caused my life to change direction when a change was called for. Sometimes the circumstances seemed unfavourable, even potentially disastrous, but whatever path I was forced to take, it always turned out to be exactly the path I needed to take. My belief in my guardian angel is very empowering and supportive, and has given me a great deal of confidence and strength. So, when I am forced to follow a particular path, I do not resist.

The occasion of my uncle's visit, and the resulting change in the direction my life took as a result of it, was only one of the many events I am aware of where my guardian angel redirected me. In that instance, I did not choose that course; it was her intervention that guided me to Montreal instead of to Israel. Given the way my life has turned out, I am truly grateful. It was only later in life that I realized that my guardian angel has been looking out for me since I was a child — in fact, before I was even two years old.

I mentioned earlier that I was born in Holland, and that my mother and I joined my father in Barbados in 1937, just before my second birthday and the beginning of World War II. The War had little impact on me growing up on the Island. It was only after I came to Canada that I learned about Anne Frank in Holland and what had happened to her and her family. But even in the early '50s when I first heard the Anne Frank story, it did not have much of an impact on me. Of course, it is a sad and frightening story, but I did not "connect" the coincidence of my coming from Holland and our being about the same age.

Even years later, when I went to Holland and visited the house where she had lived, I was moved only as much as any other tourist might have been. The story of her life and death did not register with me, that as a Jewish child living in Holland at that time I was potentially destined for the same fate!

A few years ago, I watched a movie on television about a boy of about 12 who was living like a rat in Stalingrad during the siege of 1941. He lived in the sewers and underground, barely surviving. Somehow, he makes contact with a German general and persuaded him that he believed in Germany and the idea of a super race, and that he wanted to be part of it. Certainly, he didn't want to be part of an old, dying country like Russia. The general believed him and, as proof of his loyalty, got him to spy on the Russians.

As it turned out, the boy was a double agent and was really spying for the Russians and feeding the Germans misinformation. It was heart-wrenching to watch that boy moving from one side of the city to the other through devastation and wreckage, with death all around him. The Germans eventually learned that he was a Russian spy and they killed him.

That movie brought everything into focus and made me realize that I, too, could have ended up just as Anne Frank did, or as did the boy in the movie. But I was spared all that. I was there, but luckily my parents had had the foresight and courage to get us out just in time. It was 1937 when my mother and I left. In another 18 months we would not have escaped. My dad saved us from almost certain death by getting us out of Holland at that crucial time.

I regret that I never talked to my parents about any of this, or thanked them for saving my life. I credit my guardian angel for manipulating the events and circumstances that caused my parents to make the decision to leave Holland when they did. So, I now know that my guardian angel has been with me since I was two years old; in fact, for all of my life. As I continue my story, I will refer many times to my guardian angel and the ways she has redirected me.

A NEW DIRECTION

HAVING MADE THE DECISION to send me to Montreal to study accounting, my father recognized that the foundation of my early schooling was not strong and that I needed help if I was going to pass my final exams. I needed an O-level School Certificate to be accepted at McGill University, and so he hired a tutor for me.

My tutor was amazing. He worked with me on all of my subjects, and he always found a way to explain things that I had never before been able to understand. His patience, encouragement and skill as a teacher were the crucial elements that contributed to my successfully passing my O-levels. Considering the important contribution my tutor made to me, I am embarrassed to say that today I do not remember his name. However, I do know that he was at Harrisons College for only a short time, but that was the time I needed him. My teachers had long ago given up on me and I certainly did not receive any support or encouragement from them. Chemistry was a case in point.

On the morning of my final chemistry exam, I was sitting on the steps outside the building where I was to write the exam and looking through my textbook before the classroom opened. My chemistry teacher came along and when he saw me with my head buried in the book he laughed and called out to me, "Konigsberg! Forget it! Don't even try! You can't do it!" But I did do it! In fact, I came close to the top of the class in chemistry and I did well enough over-all to get into McGill.

That is another example of my guardian angel at work. No one, including me, would have thought that with my academic history I would ever pass my O-level exams. And then, just when I needed it most, she delivered this particular tutor — a man able to get through to me in a way that no one had been able to do before. Although my guardian angel arranged to bring my uncle John into our lives at such a crucial time for me, that deed would have been for nothing had I not been able to pass those exams.

SOCIAL LIFE (ROMANCE)

THERE WAS ONE ASPECT OF GROWING UP in the Jewish community in Barbados that warrants telling. Socially, the entire Jewish community was very protective of its young people. By that I mean there was no social inter-mingling of Jewish children with non-Jews — especially those of the opposite sex.

Most of the community elders had lived in Europe before the War and had experienced extreme anti-Semitism. They had lived with both the experiences and the effects of the pogroms and the reality of the Holocaust during World War II, and were therefore wary of all non-Jews. So, the very thought of inter-marriage between Jews and non-Jews was merely intolerable, it was heresy! Obviously, we Jewish youngsters associated with non-Jews in school and in sports, but that was as far as it was allowed to go. A Jewish boy or girl having a non-Jewish girl-friend or boyfriend was absolutely forbidden. A couple of years before I left the Island this consorting-with-non-Jews got me into big, big trouble.

My father always knew that I socialized with girls and, although it concerned him from time to time, he generally turned a blind eye. However, when I was 16 years old I became involved with a young Christian girl whose name was Fleur. She became my girlfriend, and our relationship continued for two years, to the day I left Barbados. With the connivance and support of my brother Alex and sister Betty, I managed to keep my relationship with Fleur a secret from my father for quite awhile. However, when he finally found out that I was seeing the same girl all the time, all hell broke loose! I promised him I would stop seeing her and things calmed down. But I couldn't bring myself to break off the relationship. I kept promising him that I would, but I just couldn't do it — so I lied repeatedly. I used to tell him that I had broken up with Fleur and then somebody would spot me with her and, within minutes it seemed, my father would receive a report and trouble would start all over again.

In a nutshell, that was the nature of my relationship with my father for the last two years I was in Barbados, one blow-up after another. One of the reasons I broke my promise to my Dad was that, soon after I had made that promise, Fleur's father, who had been ill for some time, died and she was orphaned. (She had lost her mother several years earlier.) Under those circumstances, I just could not desert her.

Fleur had lived with her father in one part of the Island, but after he died, she went to live with her older brother in another part of the Island and word soon got around that I had started up with another girl. My father tolerated my rumored new interest. He was relieved that my one-year escapade was over. So things settled down for awhile. However, a few months before I was to leave the Island, he found out that my supposedly "new" girl was actually the same girl, and all hell broke loose again! From then on, my relationship with my father was a disaster. He refused to talk to me and the atmosphere for all of us at home became very strained. This continued even after I left the Island.

I remember the day I left Barbados like a scene from a Fellini movie.

(Scene 1) Background: To begin with, my father is not talking to me. In fact, he hasn't been talking to me for many months. And now I'm leaving the Island. Fleur and I had always known that when I finished high school I would be leaving the Island and that our relationship would end.

Action: The day begins very early. Before dawn, I get up and go over to say goodbye to Fleur.

Meanwhile, my father wakes up, discovers that I am not in the house and he goes berserk. I come home (keep in mind, he hasn't spoken to me in months) and he starts to rant and rave, accusing me of being his "final destruction" and about 101 other things along the same line. On that note, we go to the airport.

(Scene 2) Action: In those days when anybody left or arrived on the Island, it was a big event. Everyone went to the airport. In my case, most of the Jewish community comes to see me off. My mother and father, Alex, Betty and Ellen, are all there. And Fleur is there, too, standing over on the far side of the terminal building. She's within sight, but we're not communicating. Then somebody notices her, and says to my father, "Look who's here." So, my father looks over at Fleur and promptly passes out on the floor in the middle of the terminal building!

(Scene 3) Pandemonium! My father is lying on the floor, passed out, dead to the world. Everyone who isn't trying to revive him is in shock or is looking at me as if I had just shot him. My brother is speechless. My sisters are hysterical.

Somebody is yelling, "Get a doctor!"

Suddenly, the boarding announcement for my flight blares out of the PA system, followed by silence...in the middle of which my mother looks straight at me and says in a clear, even voice that everyone can hear: "You will not be happy until you kill him."

I turn slowly, walk out to the plane and board it. I don't look back.

(Fade out)

That was the scene I left behind and the burden I carried with me when I left Barbados to start my new life in Canada. I thought the Fellini movie was over, but it wasn't — not quite yet....

One of the first things I did when I arrived in Montreal was to sit down and write a letter to my parents. I apologized for the scene at the airport, and for the two years of havoc I had caused. In fact, I apologized for everything I could think of that might have distressed them and finished by saying, "But now it's over so I hope we can all move on." I got a nice letter back from my father saying, "Thank you for your letter. I'm glad to hear it's all over." I also wrote to Fleur. The gist of my letter to her was, "We both knew it was coming to this. You saw the scene at the airport. I've already caused a lot of hurt and I don't want to cause any more. God bless you. Goodbye."

Fleur attended the same school as my two sisters. Ellen was only six years old at the time and was pretty much an appendage to Betty — always holding onto her skirt as if she were attached. Soon after I sent my letter to Fleur, she met Betty at school and told her that she had received a letter from me.

Ellen overheard this conversation, and that evening she asked my parents, "Did you get a letter from Maxie?"

"No." they replied

"Oh," she said, "...because Fleur got one."

My father was devastated all over again! He wrote to me immediately, telling me I had always been untrustworthy, that my word meant nothing, that he never ever wanted to see or hear from me again, that I shouldn't try to contact anyone else in the family, and that I should change my name so I wouldn't disgrace them any longer.

So, there I was, eighteen years old, inexperienced, having just arrived in a new world, and having to deal with, "You are a disgrace! Don't ever contact us again." and "Change your name." Even my brother, Alex, for the first time in his life, decided to get involved and he wrote me a zinger, too. His message was, "When are you going to stop being the destruction of this family?" and "How much more pain do you want to cause? I am worried that Daddy may try to kill himself."

I kept writing to my father but he wouldn't open my letters. He stopped eating, he lost weight and wouldn't shave. He wouldn't even go to the store. He just 'checked out'. Weeks went by. I kept writing and he kept refusing to open my letters. After about three months of this, one of my dad's friends, Joe Krindler, visited Montreal and he came to see me. He was very polite, but he was also very firm with me.

"Max," he asked, "what are you doing? You are destroying your family. At this rate your father is going to die."

So I told him my story. I told him that I had done the proper thing. I had to write that letter to Fleur; it was a goodbye letter. I also told him that I had had no contact with her since and that there wouldn't be any further contact because the relationship was over — finished!

Mr. Krindler went back to Barbados and somehow managed to get my father's ear. A short while later, my father came to Montreal to see me to patch things up. It was a very special visit. We were both hurting and needed to put the entire episode behind us. His visit was especially memorable because, for me, it was a clear acknowledgement that I was important to him and I saw it as a sign of affection and love. I certainly needed some of both at the time.

And so the Fellini movie ended.

3

WELCOME TO CANADA

SENDING ME TO MONTREAL HAD ITS CHALLENGES for my father as well as for me. He had to borrow the money to cover my airfare, plus he gave me $300 so I would have some money to start my new life. As for me, I had just turned eighteen, and had never before left the Island of Barbados. I had been exposed to very little of the outside world. I was inexperienced, lacking in self-confidence, and had very little self-esteem. And that's how I started my new life in Canada.

There was no direct flight to Montreal from Barbados in 1953, so I took a twelve-hour flight to New York, via Puerto Rico, and from New York I took a train to Montreal. My uncle John picked me up at Central Station and took me out for lunch, then he drove me to Hillel House to get some help finding a place to live. Hillel House is a support center for Jewish students on the McGill University campus. There I was given a list of names and addresses of Jewish people who had rooms for rent. I rented a room at the first place on the list, which happened to be the home of a very orthodox Jewish family.

Before he left me, uncle John introduced me to the Yellow Pages, showed me how to use them, and then he said, "Here's my phone number. Call me if you need me."

And that was the extent of the support I got from my uncle John when I arrived in Montreal.

SETTLING IN

WHEN I ARRIVED I HAD NOT YET RECEIVED my O-level (matriculation) results from Barbados and without them I could not be accepted in the day school program at McGill for the fall term. However, I could enroll in the night school program and work for a CA firm. In the second year, provided the results from my first year of night school were satisfactory and my O-level results met the requirements, I could choose to transfer to the day school program. So I enrolled in the night school CA program.

Even in retrospect, it is difficult for me to reflect on that time. I had lived a totally sheltered life in Barbados in a completely different culture, and now, suddenly, I was virtually alone in a big city. I had very little self-confidence and I needed a job. I got hold of the Yellow Pages and looked up Chartered Accountants. The first listing was a firm called Benjamin, Small and Company.

The morning of my second day in Montreal I got up early and, with the help of a street map, I walked the three miles to their offices. I walked because I was still uncertain as to how I was going to survive financially in Montreal and I did not want to spend the ten cents it would have cost to take a streetcar. I went into the Benjamin, Small office and asked the receptionist if I could speak to somebody about a job. She took me in to see Mr. Benjamin. I told him I was new in Montreal, that I had just enrolled in the night school CA program at McGill and that I needed a job.

He said, "I'm sorry, but we filled all our positions for new students back in June and July, so we have no openings. You may have a problem because most of the other accounting firms have filled their positions, too."

I said, "Oh, OK. Thank you very much."

As I was about to leave his office, he observed, "You have a heavy accent. Where are you from?"

"I'm from Barbados."

"When did you arrive in Montreal?"

"Yesterday."

"And you're here already looking for a job?"

"Yes."

"You're hired!"

I worked for Benjamin Small for four years. It was practically the only "job" I ever had.

The next day, my third in Montreal and my first at Benjamin, Small and Company, I met Irving Haznof and Marty Payne, two young men who worked for the firm. They were to become two of my closest, life-long friends.

The YPA

I am convinced that my meeting Irving Haznof was another one of my guardian angel's interventions. Irving belonged to a social club, The Young People's Association of the Spanish and Portuguese Synagogue (YPA). He took me to the club, and he introduced me to a group of young Jewish people with whom I had more in common than the very religious people I had met in the neigbourhood in which I was living. Besides their social activities, the members of the YPA were actively involved in fundraising. I was very impressed by their knowledge and understanding of how to conduct their business affairs effectively. They had a president, a secretary and a treasurer, they held formal meetings and they kept minutes of their meetings.

All of this was beyond my experience at the time and I truly admired those young people. I thought they were all very sophisticated and worldly. In fact, I was in awe of them. I joined the YPA and became actively involved in the club's activities. We met weekly to socialize and to plan social functions and fundraising events. Often, a group of us went out together, dancing and bowling and that sort of thing. So, after only a few weeks in Montreal I had a nice group of friends.

I really got involved and participated, working on all of the club's events. One of them was a big fund-raiser dance, the 'Spring

Fling'. We raised money by selling advertising in the program booklet to various companies. I took it upon myself to get as many ads as I could. I went to banks, business offices, and all sorts of other places. I sold a lot of advertising space, raised a lot of money for the event, and received a lot of personal acknowledgement for what I had accomplished. Meanwhile, my living arrangement in the house of the orthodox family wasn't working out for me. I was very uncomfortable there, so after about three months I moved closer to the neighbourhood where my new friends lived.

As time went by I became more connected with the members of the YPA and more involved in the life of the club. The Executive Committee continued to run their remarkable business meetings, and I learned a lot about how to manage the club's affairs. Another year went by and it was time for the members to elect a new slate of officers. The incumbent president, a very impressive guy who was doing a great job, announced that he was going to run for another term. When the chairman asked the floor if there were any other nominations, someone put up their hand and said, "I nominate Max for president." And someone else said, "I second that." I was shocked! Frankly, I thought they were out of their minds. There were nominations for other positions, too, and a girl named Shirley Mauer was nominated for secretary.

I really didn't know what to do about all this nomination and election stuff but, fortunately, those who nominated me guided me through the campaign and election process. To my amazement I was elected president! Shirley Mauer was elected secretary. Although I found it difficult to understand how anybody could think of making me, Max Konigsberg, president of the club, I was delighted and that experience had a huge impact on my self-esteem. It was like getting a massive injection of self-confidence and it made me realize that there might be more to me than I thought there was!

Being elected president was the first of two experiences that started the process of building my confidence and self-esteem. The second occurred shortly after I started my second year at McGill.

The CICA Episode

I was attending a class in economics one evening when a gentleman entered and asked the professor if he could speak to the students. I remember the classroom well because it was built in the style of an old amphitheatre, with a central stage (dais) and curved tiers of benches and desk-fronts rising from below. The professor gave his lecture from a lectern on that stage.

The visitor announced that he was from the Canadian Institute of Chartered Accountants (CICA) and went on to explain that the CICA Board always invited a second-year accounting student to attend and participate in the Board meetings. He asked for a nomination from our class. In an instant, someone said, "I nominate Max Konigsberg." and another student said, "I second that nomination." The next thing I knew I was attending and participating in the CICA Board meetings! And the Board members all seemed genuinely interested in what I had to say. It was a very exhilarating and empowering experience!

Those two experiences were my first tastes of personal empowerment and, unquestionably, they gave me a new and very different perspective on who I was. They put me on the path of getting rid of my terrible self-image and low self-esteem. It was truly heady stuff. Once again, my guardian angel was guiding me and manipulating events in my favour.

After my first year at McGill, I was supposed to stop working and transfer from the night school CA program to the day program. However, at the end of my first year, my dad came to Montreal and we had a talk about finances. He told me that my brother Alex would soon be ready for McGill but that he could not support both of us, so a decision had to be made as to which one of us would go to university full time. I got the impression that he was asking me to make that decision. I knew what he wanted: he thought Alex would put a university education to much better use than I would. For me, it was no contest. The obvious decision was that Alex would go to school full time and that I would continue in night school.

So, Alex came to Montreal and enrolled at McGill to study law and I stayed on in the CA program at night school and continued working at Benjamin, Small for the next three years. I was disappointed at the time, but I understood that my father could not afford to support both of us. As everything turned out, it was a good decision because both my brother and I went on to become very successful in our chosen fields: my brother as a lawyer and I as an entrepreneur in business.

SHIRLEY MAUER

MY INVOLVEMENT WITH THE YPA had a much more profound effect on my life than just boosting my self-confidence and self-esteem. As president I had to work closely with Shirley Mauer who, as I mentioned earlier, was elected secretary at the same time. I had a girlfriend at the time who was 16 and in her last year of high school.

Shirley was the same age as me and, initially, I never thought of her as anything more than a friend. As far as I was concerned, she was out of my league. My 16-year-old girlfriend was more my speed. Occasionally, Shirley and I worked together at the synagogue — just the two of us. We would do some work together then I would leave her alone to do the typing and I would go to visit my girlfriend. I thought highly of Shirley, but that was the extent of our relationship. One evening, after a club meeting, a friend and I were walking Shirley and one of her girl friends home. We were behind the two girls and I said to my friend, "The guy who gets that girl" (pointing to Shirley) "is going to be a very lucky guy."

One Sunday afternoon not long after that, a group of us from the club went bowling. Everyone was having a good time and, for me, something happened that day that is indelibly imprinted on my memory. Shirley was wearing a somewhat revealing, off-white, scoop-neck sweater and the sight of her bowling stirred in me a new kind of interest and I began to see her in a new light. I thought, "What a beautiful woman. And what a figure! Look at how she carries herself, how poised she is, so self-assured."

A week or so later, Shirley showed up at the regular club meeting limping and with a bandage on her ankle. She had twisted it earlier in the week and it was still quite sore. I should mention that my girlfriend at the time was not a member of the club. Most of the club members were older, and were either working or attending university. Anyway, after the meeting there was, as usual, dancing to the juke box. We had been dancing after our Wednesday evening meetings for more than two years, but I had never asked Shirley to dance. However, that evening for the first time, I asked her to dance, promising to be very careful so as not to hurt her ankle. We danced together for the entire evening.

When it was time for refreshments, we needed a bottle opener and Shirley volunteered to go to the caretaker's office to find one. I went along with her. On the way we had to walk up some stairs and on the second step I just stopped, looked at her, pulled her towards me and kissed her. At that moment, I was totally smitten and absolutely infatuated. Of course, before we parted that evening, I asked her for a date for the following Saturday night. From then on, my every waking thought was about Shirley.

The next day I received a letter from my father telling me he was coming to Montreal on a business trip and that he would be arriving the following weekend. He knew I had a girlfriend and he suggested that I bring her along for dinner on Saturday night with him and my uncle John. He knew my girlfriend's name, and he knew it was not Shirley! Suddenly I had a problem. My father expected to meet the girlfriend he knew about. I called Shirley and told her my father was coming into town, that I had to go to dinner with him so I had to reschedule our Saturday night date. I then invited my about-to-be-ex-girlfriend to join me, my dad and my uncle John for dinner on Saturday night.

The following week, uncle John invited me to go to Ottawa with him on the Sunday of the May 24th weekend to visit his son, my cousin, Gordon Spergel, his wife Laura and their family. Uncle

John suggested that I invite my girlfriend to join us. I told him that she was very busy studying for her final exams and that I would bring another friend instead. I then called Shirley and she agreed to come along. We went out together on Saturday night and to Ottawa on Sunday.

From the moment I picked up Shirley on that Sunday morning, and the way we looked at each other, it was obvious that something was going on between us. The drive to Ottawa was a sort of blur because I was so happy just to be sitting beside her. We spent some time with my cousin and his family, and then Shirley and I went to see the Parliament buildings. I remember the tulips on Parliament Hill being in full bloom. Shirley's ankle was still bothering her and, with walking and all, she decided to sit down on the grass in front of the Parliament buildings.

I looked at her sitting there, surrounded by tulips, and all of a sudden it struck me like a thunderbolt. I knew I was truly in love — not just infatuated!

As I was looking at her, I suddenly heard myself saying, "Would you marry me?" I was almost as shocked as she was!

To my amazement, she said "Yes."

Given where we were, we couldn't be very demonstrative about how we felt. However, after I got over the shock, I sat down on the grass beside her and we started to fantasize about what our future life together could be. I was dizzy with excitement; it was hard to believe this was really happening to me.

We came back to Montreal from Ottawa starry-eyed. I also came back with a problem. I had a girlfriend, and I had to break off my relationship with her. My way of dealing with the problem was to avoid it. When she called to ask me when I was coming over, I told her I was busy, that I had things to do, etc. That kind of answer was uncharacteristic of me and I'm sure she knew it was just an excuse to avoid seeing her face-to-face. Finally, she put her foot down. She called and said, "I want you over here! Get on a street-car, regardless of what you're doing, and come — now!"

So, I went, and she said to me, "OK, tell me what's going on."

"You know, I've been thinking." I said, "We're really both very young. We're getting too serious, and I don't really trust myself being involved in such a committed relationship. I think we should cool it a bit and start seeing other people."

She said nothing for a long time, then asked, "Is it Shirley?"

"Shirley? What Shirley?" I replied, "What makes you think that Shirley has anything to do with this?" (Obviously, I was handling this whole thing very well.)

"Don't think I'm a dummy," she said. "Every time we have been together with Shirley, you always seem to gravitate to her."

"Interesting", I said, "I never knew that." But it was the truth.

Then I admitted, "Yes, it's Shirley," and that ended that relationship!

For the next few weeks Shirley and I had a great time together. We were in love and totally committed to each other — or so I thought. Then I started to have doubts. I was nineteen years old, earning $18 a week, with no idea of what my future might be. Shirley was clearly not a girl to be toyed with and we were on track to get married. I became very nervous. All sorts of uncertainties went through my head and I began to feel overwhelmed.

One evening I went to see Shirley and said, "I think we're moving too fast. We should slow it down. Let's continue seeing each other, but we should also start dating other people for awhile."

She gave me a long look, then said, "OK."

Before we parted, I said, "We'll talk. We'll remain close. We'll talk soon."

On my way home I began to realize what I had just done and for the next few days my life was in absolute turmoil. I was torn by feelings of indecision, uncertainty, love and a terrible sense of loneliness. Then things went from bad to worse.

I called Shirley on the Friday evening and her mother told me she had just left and would be out of town for the weekend. I said,

Mister Cool, in Montreal, 1954
▲

▼
*With Uncle John at
Plattsburg Beach, NY, 1955*

▼
The day I proposed — May 24th, 1955.

"What do you mean, out of town? Where did she go?" And her mother told me Shirley had gone up to the Laurentians with her girlfriend. Now, on top of everything else, I felt angry, jealous and betrayed. I resented terribly the thought that she could dismiss "us" so easily. Suddenly, *I* was the injured party!

On Monday morning my guardian angel showed up through a friend, Michael Goldenberg, with whom I was working on an audit. Michael asked, "Max, how come I saw Shirley up at the Vermont Hotel in the Laurentians last Saturday night dancing cheek-to-cheek with another guy?"

"What?" I exclaimed. I immediately got on the phone to Shirley and said, "We're meeting for lunch."

At lunch I asked, "What did you do?"

She said, "I went away for the weekend. I was so hurt that you could say what you did that I just had to get out of town. I was not going to spend the weekend at home being upset. So I called my friend and we went up to the Laurentians."

I had had enough of that and I had had my wake-up call. I said to her, "OK, forget what I said the other night. I'm sorry. I don't know what came over me. All I want is for us to be together and to go ahead with our plans."

And that was that. I never, ever again had second thoughts about us. Thank you, thank you, my guardian angel!

NUPTIALS

WHEN I PROPOSED TO SHIRLEY on that May 24th weekend I was, as I said, 19 years old, earning $18 a week, and I still had three years ahead of me at McGill. We decided we would get engaged in August, and wait for three years until I finished school to get married. I wrote to my parents with the good news. I told them I had met a wonderful girl and that we were planning to become engaged in August. I enclosed a photograph of Shirley at the beach wearing a bathing suit.

My poor parents! Keep in mind that just a few weeks earlier my father had been in Montreal and had had dinner with me and my

▼

The picture of Shirley I sent to my father
when I told him I was getting married.
(Legs like a gazelle!)

▼

Shirley and me posing at
the Haznof's wedding

▼

My father and me during his visit
to Montreal in 1955

40

(then) girlfriend. Now I was announcing that I was planning to marry someone he had never heard of! (And I expected my father to think I was stable?)

My dad wrote back with, "Are you out of your mind? Where is your head? How can you even think of getting married? I see from the photograph that your new girlfriend is beautiful, she has legs like a gazelle. But what's wrong with her — why would she want you? What's your rush? Wait! You have lots of time to get engaged." I wrote back to him and told him I understood his concerns, but that Shirley and I were in love and that we had already made a commitment to each other. I told him she was the very best thing that could possibly happen to me, we were going to get engaged and things would work out.

I could say now, as I might have then, "There goes my dad, putting me down again." But as I think about it, this entire episode does sound off the wall. I was not yet 20 years old, I was in a new country, still in school, and earning barely enough to support myself. A month earlier, there was someone else in my life and my parents didn't know this "new" woman even existed. Now I was telling them I'd met the love of my life and I was going to spend the rest of my life with her. Who could blame them for thinking I was out of my mind?

Weeks went by. Letters went back and forth — my dad trying to get me to listen to (his) reason and me not listening. Then Shirley took the initiative and wrote to my parents. Her letter obviously made an impression, because whatever she said brought my father around, from being absolutely opposed, to supporting the marriage fully. (He may also have been influenced by the thought that marriage might have a stabilizing effect on me.) But the timing of our engagement was still a problem.

"Wait until December," he suggested, "and your mother and I will come to Canada for your engagement."

"Agreed! ", I wrote back.

So, my parents came to Montreal in December and Shirley and I became "officially" engaged.

▼

Celebrating our engagement
My parents behind Shirley; her parents behind me

▼

On our honeymoon in Barbados

We were supposed to wait for another two-and-a-half years to get married, but by the following spring that time period seemed like an eternity. Shirley was working as a bookkeeper earning $50 a week. I was making $35 a week. (I had been given a very generous increase of $17 a week when I got engaged.) We figured we could do just fine on our combined income, so we revised our original plan and set our wedding date for the following summer. And, with family blessings on both sides, Shirley and I were married on August 7, 1956. We were both twenty-one.

My dad came to the wedding; my mother did not. They decided that instead of incurring the expense of having my mother come to Montreal, they would cover the cost of our going to Barbados for our honeymoon and have a wedding reception for us there with all of my extended Barbadian family. It was a great occasion! Everyone fell in love with Shirley and she fell in love with the Island.

When I told the story of my water polo "career" before I left Barbados, I ended by saying, "That was not, however, my last encounter with Lorenzo Best." I also said that the last game I played before going to Montreal was the one where Best was taken out of the water and my team, Harrisons College, won the cup.

Three years later, when Shirley and I went to Barbados for our honeymoon, a reporter for the *Barbados Advocate*, the Island newspaper, took a picture of us at the airport when we arrived. The next day that picture was run in the newspaper with the caption "Konigsberg Returns to Barbados with his Bride. As it happened, a water polo team, the Bonitos, was scheduled to play against the Water Police team. The Bonitos captain saw the picture in the newspaper and, remembering my success at marking Best, invited me to join the team for that game. I was flattered to be asked, and vain enough to want my bride to see me play, so I accepted.

I showed up for the game, donned my swimsuit and put on the little cap water polo players wear. I had kept a low profile before the game and, when the whistle blew, I went into the water to play defense. Best had no idea that I was there. When the game started,

I swam to my position slightly behind him and began marking him. We were both facing in the same direction, so he did not see my face — and even if he had, with my cap on we all looked pretty much the same.

After a few plays, Best started to sense something familiar. He turned around and looked straight at me. His jaw must have dropped a full two inches. When he recovered, he asked, "Where the hell did you come from? There's no way I'm playing against you!" He took off his cap, threw it into the water, went up onto the bridge and disappeared. I was out of condition because I had not played in more than three years. After another 15 minutes or so, at which point I was totally exhausted, I had to leave the water. That was my final encounter with Lorenzo Best.

As far as I know, Best is still in Barbados. I have fond memories of our encounters, and I wish him all good things.

MARRIED LIFE

FROM THE BEGINNING, Shirley and I had what can only be described as a turbulent relationship. Of course, we were passionately in love with each other, but there were other dynamics that challenged us. For example, I grew up in a home environment where my father was the dominant figure. My mother adored him and was in awe of him. For her, whatever he said was as if God had said it.

On the other hand, Shirley was brought up in a household where her parents' relationship was exactly the opposite. Her father allowed his wife to be the dominant one. So, I came into our relationship subconsciously expecting that my wife would behave pretty much as my mother and that I would be the dominant figure. Shirley came into the relationship subconsciously expecting me to behave like her father and that she would play the dominant role. From the very beginning, the stage was set for a lot of friction. We also had strong differences with respect to politics, health matters and raising children, all of which created fertile ground for disagreement.

Our Wedding Photo
August 7, 1956

Politically, coming from a small Jewish community in Barbados, we all felt somewhat isolated and we therefore had a strong affinity for Israel. In fact, we were all very strong Zionists. On the other hand, Shirley was for Canada first and Israel second. It was not that she was anti-Zionist, she simply had a different perspective, and that, too, provided lots of opportunity for disagreement and argument.

On the health side, in my family there was no sympathy for not feeling well or being tired. Giving in to pain and fatigue was considered a sign of weakness. However, Shirley's background was very different. Shirley's mother was the only survivor of eight children, all of whom had died of various illnesses when they were young, so Shirley was taught to be very careful about her health, to protect herself and to guard against illness. In her family, everyone was very concerned about health matters and she expected the same from me. Because of my background, however, I was unsympathetic and I did not give her the support she needed. Eventually, this led to a serious breakdown in confidence. Shirley felt she could not rely on me to be there when she needed me, and that I was not committed to her well-being. In self-defense she decided that inasmuch as I would not be there for her, she would have to take care of herself. This became a major issue between us and lasted for a very long time.

When we had children we had different approaches to raising and nurturing them. Understandably, Shirley was very protective of the children, especially about health issues. On the other hand, I encouraged them to be hardy and strong. Also, I thought she was very strict and controlling. Considering my background with my father, who was so overpowering and strict with us, I was very permissive and non-confrontational. I said "no" to my children only when I considered it to be absolutely necessary. It seemed to me that Shirley said "no" all the time. Shirley thought I was lax and because of that she felt it was up to her to discipline the children. These differences in our approaches to the raising of our children introduced more conflict and added further strain to our relationship. Despite our different approaches to our children, I must say that the three of them turned out well and we are very, very proud of them.

All of the tension and discord between us hardly contributed to domestic bliss. Fortunately, in 1979 (after we had been married for 23 years) we attended a weekend program called "Marriage Encounter." The program was designed to help couples take a look at themselves and their relationships and give them an opportunity to explore and tell the truth about how they relate to each other. It was the first time we ever examined our relationship seriously.

Taking an in-depth look at what was going on between us was not easy. We always knew we were very much in love and passionate about each other, but it was only then that we discovered we were not friends. We learned that we were non-supportive and competitive, and that we were quick to blame or find fault with each other. This revelation led us to embark on a journey to learn more about ourselves and what drives us.

Having raised the issue of our turbulent personal relationship, I must point out that it did not spill over into our business relationship. Paradoxically, we worked amazingly well together. We respected and were totally supportive of each other. In fact, we loved working together!

Marriage Encounter was the first of many courses, seminars and programs we took over the years that helped us transform our relationship. I often wonder how our marriage would have survived without all of the work we did. Out of that journey, over time, we became supportive and nurturing, we got rid of the baggage we were carrying and our love and passion were able to blossom and grow. And that's where we are today.

4

NEW DIRECTIONS

S O THERE I WAS, MARRIED, working at Benjamin, Small, and in my fourth year of the CA program at McGill. At the end of that year, I failed an auditing exam. At first, it seemed like a serious setback. After all, I had spent four years focused on and committed to becoming an accountant. However, it did make me take a hard look at my future.

After much thought I again came face-to-face with the fact that school had never been easy for me and that university studies were especially difficult. (It would be many years before I learned that I had always struggled with a learning disability.) Besides, I had never really been happy in accounting. I was not stimulated by my work and I wasn't satisfied. I read my failing the exam as a very clear message: a career in accounting is not for me! And so I decided to get out of accounting.

I discussed my decision with Shirley and she gave me her full support. I credit my guardian angel for having me fail that exam and redirecting me to another career that would prove much more suitable for me. Had I been able to do better and pass that exam, I probably would have kept struggling and plugging away, and eventually I would have become a Chartered Accountant. I know I didn't have the temperament or personality to be a good accountant, and if I had stayed in accounting I would never have felt fulfilled. I made the decision to leave accounting with no idea of what I would do next.

I wrote to my father and told him that I was leaving accounting. He was understandably disappointed and wrote back immediately saying, "Don't quit! Rewrite the exam and stay with it." I told him, "This is not about quitting! Accounting is just not for me! I have gained a lot of experience in the last four years and I will find something else — something that is more appropriate for me." And so I gave my notice to Benjamin, Small & Co. and left McGill.

At Benjamin, Small, I had been part of the auditing team for a lingerie manufacturing company, and when I left the firm I was offered and accepted a job as Controller of that company. After a couple of months in my new job, it became clear that I was totally out of my league and, eventually, I had to leave. I don't remember if I quit or if I was fired, but in any case, thankfully, I was not successful in that job. Again, had I been more able and succeeded in that position, I would have wasted another four years or maybe even been stuck in that job forever, and I would never have had the opportunity to reach my full potential.

Once again, my guardian angel was looking out for me, directing me away from a dead end and toward exploring new possibilities.

"SHIRLEY,...I WOULD LIKE TO OPEN A STORE"

I WAS UNEMPLOYED FOR THREE MONTHS after I left that company. I had a few job interviews, but nothing materialized from them. I didn't know what to do with myself. After three months of frustration, wandering around, doing nothing, I went with Shirley into a ladies' wear store called May's in the Norgate Shopping Centre. While I waited for Shirley to try something on, I talked with the owner of the store, Ernie Sakaranski, and somehow our conversation triggered an idea.

When we left the store I said, "You know what, Shirley, I think that's what I would like to do. I would like to open a store." Over the next few days we explored that possibility at length and the more we talked about it, the more the idea appealed to us. It is ironic that my father was a storekeeper in Barbados and my uncle John was a store keeper in Montreal, but my becoming a storekeeper had never occurred to me until my visit to May's that day.

There was a new strip of retail stores under construction on Van Horne Avenue near Victoria Avenue, three blocks from where we lived. I decided to explore the possibility of renting one of those stores. I went over to the site and spoke to the owner, Mr. Dubrovsky. Our conversation went something like this:

"Mr. Dubrovsky, I would like to rent one of your stores."

"What kind of store are you planning to open?"

"I don't know."

"I can't rent you a store until I know what kind of store you intend to open."

"Oh. OK, so I'll open a toy store."

"I'm afraid we already have a toy store."

"OK, then I'll open a children's wear store."

"Sorry, we already have a children's wear store."

"So, what don't you have?"

"We don't have ladies' wear."

"So, I'll open a ladies' wear store."

"All right. Now, how many square feet do you need?"

"I don't know. How many square feet would be appropriate for a ladies' wear store?"

"Well, I have a space of 1,500 square feet available."

"OK, I'd like to lease it."

"Fine, but first, I need to know who you are and what assets you have."

"I have $2,500 in savings* and I would like to go into business."

"I'm sorry. I can't give you a lease because you don't have enough assets to guarantee the lease, but I'll rent you a store for $250 a month and, as long as you pay the rent, you can have it.

"OK. I'll take it!

(Very sophisticated negotiating and decision-making!)

Given our toy store/children's wear/ladies' wear conversation, I'm sure Mr. Dubrovsky didn't expect me to be in business for very

---

*$1,000 had been left to Shirley by her grandparents, and the remaining $1,500 was from wedding gifts.

long. I went back and told Shirley what had happened and that evening we met and shook hands on the deal with Mr. Dubrovsky. We named the store Sher-lee's Teens to Maternity. A few years later we changed the name to Shirley K Fashions.

A couple of days after we agreed to rent the store, I received a job offer from a leading manufacturer of ladies coats and sportswear, which seemed like a good opportunity for me. I told Shirley about it when she came home from work and asked what she thought I should do. Without hesitation she answered, "You decided to go into business. I think you should stick with your decision." So the matter was settled. And that was that! I was 22 years old, starry-eyed, full of hope, and I was going into business — inexperienced, with very little money, and totally ignorant of the pitfalls ahead of me!

A condition of the agreement with Mr. Dubrovsky was that the store would be ready in a month and that I would start paying rent then. So reality set in. What do I do now? Then I remembered my conversation with Ernie Sakaranski. I went to see him and told him I had rented premises for a ladies' wear store in another neighbourhood, that I had to move in and open in a month's time and that I didn't know what to do next. I asked for his help.

"You have to fixture and furnish the store", he said, "and you should put an ad in the paper and hire somebody to help and work with you — somebody who has some experience in ladies' wear."

He gave me the name of Mr. Siklos, a store-fixture contractor. I met with Mr. Siklos the following day and told him that I needed fixtures for a new ladies' wear store I was opening in a month's time. Our conversation went something like:

"All right, Mr. Konigsberg, what kind of clothing are you going to carry in your store?"

"I don't know."

"But I can't fixture the store until I know what kind of merchandise you'll be selling. Do you need shelving, storage units, racks for hanging garments, etc? I have to know what kind of merchandise you'll be carrying."

"I don't know."

He then took a different tack.

"Do you think you'll be carrying dresses?"

"Yes, I guess so."

"Will you be carrying sweaters?"

"I guess so."

"Do you think you'll be carrying slacks?"

"I guess so."

Every time he asked me a question, my answer was "I guess so." Anyway, after a few minutes of this he made some assumptions about what I might need and he went away and priced out the job at $2,500. He had been in business for several years, so I'm sure it was obvious to him that I didn't know what I was doing. He could have stopped me in my tracks right there, but he didn't. Instead, he took a chance on me. He did the job and he offered me terms I could handle — two years of monthly payments.

At that point I was *really* committed. I had a store, rent to pay, and obligations to a contractor. Meanwhile, nobody had answered my ads for help. Back to Ernie! I told him what I had done about fixturing the store and that nobody had answered my ads.

"What do I do now?" I asked.

He said, "Well, this is a market week and all the ladies' wear manufacturers are showing their new lines at the Mount Royal Hotel. Why don't you go and buy?"

"What do you mean, 'go and buy'? I don't know what to buy."

And Ernie said, "So go down to the Mount Royal, visit the showrooms, ask the sales people to help you and buy the merchandise you think you would like to sell in your store."

When Shirley came home from work that evening, I said to her, "You have to come buying with me. I can't buy ladies' clothing by myself."

She said, "OK, but I have a job, so I can only go with you at night."

So we went buying in the evening.

Learning the Business

WE KNEW NOTHING ABOUT BUSINESS in general and even less about ladies' wear retailing. Anyway, Shirley and I went to the Mount Royal Hotel in the evening to "buy."

The first supplier we saw was Title Dress from Toronto. They made expensive cocktail dresses. We asked their sales rep if we could see their line. He didn't know who we were, but he was very polite and asked us to sit down. He then started parading beautiful models in front of us wearing the new line of Title dresses. I had looked at women before but, until that moment, I never really looked at what they wore.

I will always remember the first model; she came out in a beautiful strapless bustier dress with a royal blue velvet top and a big peau de soie skirt with crinolines. She was gorgeous and so was the dress. I looked at everything the models wore with my eyes popping out of my head. Shirley was sitting beside me and she, too, was very taken with the garments. We were then given an order pad and asked to pick out the styles we wanted to order.

We picked the styles we wanted, and we saw that each style came in five sizes and three colours so we wrote 15 of each style. The salesman looked at our order and asked how many stores we had.

"Just one, which is opening in a few weeks," I replied

"Do you have any experience in ladies' wear retailing?" he asked.

"No." I answered.

Then he said, "Well, this is not the way to buy expensive dresses. What you should do is take a size 5 in one colour, skip a size and take a size 9 in another colour and a 13 in the third colour. That way, with three dresses you can show all three colours and have a range of sizes for your customers to try on. Then you take special orders. That's how you buy these dresses."

So, we ordered three each of, perhaps, seven styles. We thanked him for the lesson, left him with the order. (For the record, three years later all three of that first style, the blue velvet bustier, ended up on a "$5 sales" rack. We did not sell even one of them!) We then went across the hall to a company called Michael London.

Mr. Miller, the owner of Michael London made blouses that sold for $2.98. He showed us his new line. Now, after our Title Dress lesson, we thought we knew how to order. So, when he gave us an order pad we picked out the styles we liked and we wrote pink in size 5, blue in size 9 and green in size 13, and other styles in alternate sizes. As we were writing our order, Mr. Miller asked,

"Do you have any experience in this business?"

"Well, we just left an order with Title Dress next door and he told us this is how we should write our orders." was our reply.

Then, in a very patronizing way Mr. Miller said, "That's the way you buy Title dresses, but it's not the way you buy $2.98 blouses. For these blouses, you need to buy a dozen of a style."

So that's what we did. We wrote a dozen per style. While we were doing this, Shirley looked up at him and saw him smirking.

"You're not going to ship us this order, are you?" she asked. "You see that we don't know what we're doing. Instead of sitting there smirking at us and then tearing up our order after we leave, you could help us and maybe we could become a good customer."

He was clearly taken aback and, after a brief silence, said, "Forget writing an order, I'll send you the blouses you should have." Which he did. We developed a rapport with Mr. Miller and over the years we did a lot of business together. That evening was the beginning of our business education: two young kids with so much to learn.

When the time came to open the store, I had not received even one response to my ads for sales help. In the meantime, I was working all day receiving merchandise and getting the store ready. At night, Shirley and I worked together, ticketing and steaming the merchandise and generally getting everything ready for the opening. We had no staff, no help. This went on for a few days, then I said to Shirley, "I guess you're going to have to quit your job and come and work in the store." She agreed and gave her employer notice the next day. But she couldn't just walk away. She was the office manager and she had to train someone to take over her job.

We actually opened the store on October 21, 1957; we were very proud and excited. Shirley worked in the store during the day and for her previous employer at night while she trained a replacement for her old job.

We were such novices. We didn't know the first thing about running a retail business. We knew nothing about budgeting or how much to buy. We had no plan, we just bought.What little bit of knowledge I thought I had gained from my accounting experience proved to be more misleading than helpful. For example, I did a quick reckoning when I knew my rent was going to be $250 a month, $3,000 a year. I estimated total annual expenses at $12,000. From my experience as an auditor, I knew that other fashion retailers worked on a gross profit margin of around 33 per cent of sales at that time, so I figured I needed $36,000 a year in sales to cover the $12,000 expenses and that one-third of all sales over $36,000 would be profit. I reckoned that if we had sales of $60,000 a year we could expect to make an annual net profit of around $8,000, which would be a good start and a reasonable living for us.

However, this was all pie in the sky because most of my assumptions were wrong and I did not allow for any of the unknowns of the ladies' wear business. I did not take into consideration that it was a seasonal business, and that there are four seasons in a year. I did not understand that, whether I sold one piece of merchandise or not, in order to have a proper selection, I would have to put approximately $30,000 worth of merchandise into the store four times a year — which meant $120,000 worth of merchandise at retail every year! So, even if we did have sales of $60,000 a year we would be out of business in no time. We needed sales of at least $100,000 a year just to pay for the merchandise!

That is just one of many examples of how inexperienced we were. There was so much we didn't know. In the first twelve months we were in business, our sales were only $36,000 and we started digging ourselves into a deep hole of debt.

Statistics show that only seven per cent of new start-up businesses survive beyond the first two years. Put another way, 93 per cent of all new start-ups fail within the first two years. Considering who we were and our lack of experience, I am still amazed that we turned out to be one of the seven per cent.

Looking back, there were a couple of factors that really helped us. First, most of our customers fell in love with Shirley and they kept coming back to see her. And we were able to hire some staff that our customers related to, so sales kept increasing after our first year. Second, after our initial buying experiences with Title Dress and Michael London, our approach to our suppliers when we were buying was, "We're twenty-two years old, we have this store, we've put everything we have into the business and we're going to work very hard. We know nothing about this business and we need your help, please." We asked for help and we got help. This became our *modus operandi* — we allowed people to contribute to us — and I am proud to say that with that approach, in all the 46 years we were in business, no one ever tried to take advantage of us. In fact, people were amazingly generous to us. The following are a few examples that I still remember very clearly.

The manufacturers' salesmen, for instance, were very supportive. They always came to visit, to check things out, to see how we were doing, and to bring us information about what was happening at other stores. They would tell us what was selling and what was not. It seemed that every one of them somehow adopted us.

Mr. Jacob Stein, the owner of a company called Jacob Dress was a great supporter. We had bought some dresses from him and one Friday evening not long after we opened the store, he came over to see us. He looked around for awhile and then he said to me, "Max, my dresses are wrong for you. They're not young enough for the clientele you're obviously trying to attract. I'm going to drive my car up to the back door. I'll take back the dresses and send you a credit." Mr. Stein did not have to do that. I had bought his dresses and, at that stage, they were my responsibility — but he did not want to see us get hurt.

There was also Mr. Phillips from Vanity Frocks. We were one of his customers, but I stopped buying from him because I owed him around $900 that was six months overdue and I didn't have the money to pay him. It so happened that at that time Vanity Frocks had a very hot selling dress. So I went to Mr. Phillips with a cheque for $300 and told him I realized my account was overdue, but I needed five of his dresses. He gave me the five dresses but then he said to me, "Max, you've owed me $900 for over six months. Obviously you must be tight for money and there must be other suppliers who are giving you a hard time. So, take back your cheque and take the dresses. Pay me when you have the money." I took the dresses and my cheque and went back to the store.

These are only a few of many examples of people who went above and beyond to help us. Our suppliers gave us credit, shipped to us, and we paid them whenever we could. However, the reality was that we were buying goods but were not selling enough to pay for them and cover our costs. As a result, we were getting ourselves deeper and deeper into debt.

5

FAMILY DYNAMICS

I LEFT MY PARENTS' HOME IN BARBADOS IN 1953 to move to Montreal. Two years later my brother Alex followed, and my sister Betty a year after that. After we moved away, my parents felt they could not live without their children. So, in 1959 my father liquidated all his assets in Barbados and he, my mother and my youngest sister, Ellen, followed us to Montreal.

It was not possible to take money out of Barbados, so my dad had to practically give everything away. He sold his store, which was a valuable asset, for only a small fraction of its worth, and he got next to nothing for his home and furniture. As a result, he came to Montreal with considerably less than what he had been worth. Making the decision to leave Barbados to move to Canada was very difficult and costly for my parents. Right up until 1953 when I left the Island, it had been a struggle for them to make a living. However, in the mid-fifties tourism to the Island started to become active, the economy improved and for about three years my parents' business did reasonably well. Now, in order for the family to be together, they had to start all over again with little money in a new country. That was the price they had to pay. But there was an even higher price to be paid.

My father suffered a nervous breakdown soon after coming to Canada. He was 48 years old. Having to give up everything and make such a drastic move proved to be too much for him. I mentioned earlier that my dad was penniless when he started out in Barbados. When he arrived in Canada he saw himself as being a poor man again. He felt that he was alone in a huge country without the support of his community. He had lived in a caring environment in Barbados and had been an influential person on the Island. He had been one of the leaders of the Jewish community, in Barbados, and now he felt he was a stranger and alone.

There was also something else that I know plagued him. He was haunted by what had happened to his family in Europe during the War. Except for one sister, all had perished in the Holocaust. He could never forgive himself for the fact that he had survived and they had not. I remember how devastated he was when he learned how his family had died. That was the terrible past he lived with and I am certain this also contributed to his breakdown. But he wasn't alone in his loss. My mother lost her entire family in the Holocaust, too. Between them they carried an enormous burden of loss.

Considering his background and all of these dynamics, it was not surprising that my father became depressed and eventually had a complete breakdown. As part of his therapy, he was given thirty-five shock treatments, which was a very radical procedure. Those treatments reduced him to a shadow of his former self. During the time he was undergoing treatment he knew me and my mother, but he did not recognize my brother or the other members of the family. Eventually he recovered, but he was never again the man he was before he became ill.

Because of my dad's illness, there was a major change in my relationship with him until he eventually recovered: our roles reversed. It was as if I had become the father and he had become the son. I was the caregiver. I had to take over — both for him and from him — because he was unable to cope.

All the years my parents lived in Barbados my mother had been a businesswoman running their store. When they moved to Montreal, Shirley and I had our one store and we decided that my parents should come into the business with us. My father invested some money and became a partner, and both my parents started working with us in the store.

Three months after my parents arrived in Montreal, but before my father was hospitalized, my sister Betty married Jack Feinberg, an American from New York City. After the wedding in Montreal, the couple packed their car and left for New York, stopping over at the Neville Country Club in the Catskills for their honeymoon.

I watched my father's face as Betty got into the car to leave. It was already clear to me at the time that he was not well, but now he was in agony. He had just recently given up his entire life in Barbados in order to come to Montreal to be with his children, and now, within weeks of his arrival, his eldest daughter was moving away.

Two days later I drove to the Neville Country Club with my brother Alex as support to talk with our sister and new brother-in-law.

The gist of our conversation was: "Look, you can't do this. If you leave, it will kill Dad. You have to come back to Montreal." So, I made them an offer. "Go to New York for a year," I said, "Save some money and come back to Montreal. Put the money into the business and Jack will become a partner. We will open another store that Jack can manage; Betty can always find work in Montreal."

They agreed, then Alex and I drove back and told my dad that I had offered Jack a partnership in the business and that Betty and Jack would be coming back to Montreal within the year. Although it did not change the fact that he was ill, it did ease some of the pain he felt as a result of Betty's leaving.

THE MATERNITY BUSINESS

ONE NIGHT, WHILE OUR FIRST STORE WAS BEING BUILT, I woke up around 3 a.m. worrying about a simple question: "What possible reason could anyone have to shop in my store?" Although I wasn't aware of the concept of differentiation at the time, I was actually having a discussion with myself about how I was going to differentiate my business from others. It occurred to me that women were getting pregnant all the time, but I didn't see any maternity stores around.

I woke Shirley and said, "I think we should put a maternity department in the store. At least that would give some ladies one good reason to come to us." Shirley agreed and we put a small department of maternity clothes in the store.

At that time, there was only one major manufacturer of maternity clothing in Canada, Jack Margolis Maternity. Shirley and I went to see Mr. Margolis and persuaded him to supply us with maternity merchandise and to give us credit. However, we were not successful with his products. Customers came in to look at the maternity clothes, they would try them on, but they did not buy. One day I asked some customers why they were not buying.

The conversation went:

"Don't you like the merchandise?"

"Oh, yes, it's beautiful."

" So why aren't you buying?"

"We'll come back."

"No, no! Tell me, really, why aren't you buying?"

At that point, one of them finally said,

"Well, this is all Jack Margolis merchandise. We can go to the factory and buy direct at half the price."

Clearly, I could not compete with Jack Margolis, so I went to see him, told him what I had learned and that I couldn't do business with his merchandise. He was very sympathetic and said, "Max, I understand, but I cannot change the way I do business. It is successful for me. Send back the merchandise and I'll give you a credit for it. However, if you really want to be in the maternity business, you should carry something different from what I have. Let me give you the names of some American manufacturers. Go visit them and buy some styles that are different from mine. That will give customers a reason to buy from you." We took Mr. Margolis's advice and bought our maternity clothes from several American manufacturers, and they sold.

This is just one more example of how people in the business took care of us. Mr. Margolis did not have to do what he did for us. He was very generous in his willingness to help us, especially because it represented a real cost to him. He was creating a competitor for himself by giving his own customers an alternative to his merchandise.

Meanwhile, it did not take long for Shirley and me to see that having my mother work with us in the store was not a good idea. We were constantly stepping on each other's toes. My mother was accustomed to being in control and working in a different culture and environment. To solve the problem, we decided to open a small maternity store on Queen Mary Road for my mother to run. She ran that store for more than twenty years.

When Betty and Jack were ready to return to Montreal, I opened a third store in the Wilderton Shopping Centre, also on Van Horne Avenue. Jack looked after the Wilderton store, Shirley took care of our first store, and my mother was in charge of the maternity store. Once he recovered, my father, looked after banking and record-keeping. He also acted as a "float" between stores, overseeing operations and managing the cash flow. I was responsible for buying and over-all management.

The Wilderton store was in the same trading area as our first Van Horne store. As it turned out, opening that store was not a very smart move. In fact, it was a big mistake. By investing in a second store in the same trading area we were competing with ourselves for the same customers. Not only did the Wilderton store *not* do the business we needed, it also cannibalized our first store and sales in that store declined. Thus began the first of several downward spirals we would experience over the next 40 years. And it was another example of our naïvety, lack of experience, lack of understanding of such things as customer base, market share, cannibalization, demographics, and our inability to read and understand the marketplace.

Actually, we had one fundamental problem. We were not doing enough business. We were building up debt and I did not even realize it. I had no idea of how much stock we had or how much we needed to sell. Inventory was continuing to pile up, but I was completely oblivious to it!

Enter Mr. Kolodny!

Mr. Kolodny owned a ladies-wear store in another part of Montreal, but he happened to live close to our Wilderton store. He developed a fatherly interest in us and used to drop in to see us from time to time. One day, he came in, looked around, and asked, "What are you doing? What are you going to do with all this merchandise? Have you any idea how much inventory you have here? This is seasonal merchandise and it is more than you can sell in three years." Mr. Kolodny made me aware of stock levels and perishable merchandise inventory; he made me see that I had far too much inventory and that my payables were piling up. It was then I knew I was in trouble.

A few days after Mr. Kolodny's visit, Larry Shapiro, a salesman for one of our suppliers, dropped into the store. From the time we started in business, Larry had become a true friend. I shared with him my new revelation that I had more inventory than I could possibly sell. I said, "I'm not sure what I'm going to do with all this merchandise." Larry thought for a bit, then said,

"There's a store in the Lucerne Shopping Centre that just went bankrupt. The owner, Margot, signed the lease personally and is responsible for the monthly rent payments. I believe she would be interested in making a deal. If you were to put some of your merchandise into that store to clear at reduced prices, pay the rent, and pay her a small salary to run the store, it would be a good deal for both of you. You would turn some of this merchandise into cash and her debt to the landlord would be covered."

So he brokered a deal and suddenly we had a fourth store. Opening that store seemed like a good idea at the time, but it really didn't work. We just added costs for very little return, and an even bigger problem was beginning to develop.

When Shirley and I got married we knew we couldn't afford, nor did we want, to have children right away. But after two-and-a-half years of marriage we decided we were ready. Our first daughter, Esther, was born in 1959. Three years later, we were blessed with our son, Philip, and eight years after that, with our youngest child, Rachelle. When Esther was born, Shirley could only work part time. *She* was the connection that most of our customers had with the Van Horne store and when they came in they always asked for her. When they were told, "She's not here," they left. The fact is that when Shirley began working part-time, sales nose-dived. To add to this, the Wilderton store hadn't taken off, at the Lucerne store we practically gave away the merchandise, and my mother's maternity store was barely covering expenses. We were on the brink of bankruptcy but, luckily for me, I didn't know it. If I had known, I guess I would have thrown in the towel. Instead, in my ignorance, I just kept plugging along, surviving one day at a time.

Shirley's father, Harry Mauer, was a craftsman furrier who had worked for the same company for many years. The fur business was undergoing major changes in the fifties, and he did not have enough work, so he decided to try to open a small business of his own. One Saturday he went out with a real estate agent looking to buy a coffee stand in an office building. Shirley's dad was very proud of the business Shirley and I had built so, not surprisingly, he asked the agent to come to our Van Horne store and meet his children. The agent came into the store, looked around, and asked, "Would you like to sell this store?" I said, "Oh no, this store is not for sale." He then said, "Are you sure, because I have a buyer who particularly wants to be in this area."

I certainly hadn't entertained the thought of selling the store. In fact, I didn't even think it was saleable! Now I gave it some serious consideration. Our business was in trouble. I reckoned that if I closed the Van Horne store we would pick up sales at the Wilderton location and have at least one good store rather than

Our first-born,
Esther, 1959
▲

▼
Mr. Berstein, the pioneer, with
Shirley in Montreal, 1959

Rachelle, dining with me,
1970
▲

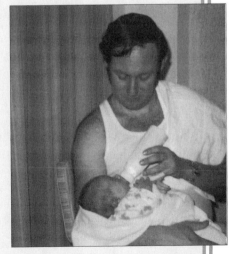

▼
Philip, with me at the beach
1962

two duds. Also, the money from the sale would surely help pay off some of our debts. By Monday morning, we had agreed on the price and I sold the store. Part of the deal was that I would give up the store in three weeks' time.

Selling the Van Horne store and the timing of the sale was an enormous stroke of good fortune and turned things around for us. Back then, in the early sixties, Montreal did not have the number of stores it has today. There were very few stores for the population, and running a sale or a promotion brought people flocking from all over the city. For the next three weeks we ran a "Going out of Business" sale at the Van Horne location. Our two fashion stores had recently received full selections of new summer merchandise. The sale was right at the beginning of the summer season, the weather had turned hot and we were selling new, fresh, summer merchandise at discount prices. People came from far and wide. We sold off the goods, new and old, and emptied the fashion stores. With that money, and the money we received from the sale of the store, we were able to pay off our suppliers and credit was no longer a problem.

After we closed the Van Horne store, as I had hoped, customers from that store gravitated to our Wilderton location, which then became very profitable. Also, as a result of selling off all our excess merchandise, it was possible to dispose of the Lucerne store. Once again, we ended up with two stores, both of which were profitable.

Thank you, guardian angel, for manipulating circumstances in our favour.

At the end of this whirlwind of events, business started to pick up and we were able to breathe more easily, but only for a little while.

A Close Call

In the mid-sixties a spectacular new office and retail development — Place Ville Marie (PVM) — was being built in the downtown core of Montreal. It was the first major high-rise complex of its kind and had a completely new component, an underground shopping plaza, the first in Canada, When rental agents first started to lease stores in the complex, they did not have an easy time getting tenants, so they were offering very good deals to prospective retailers. I was approached with a great offer, which I discussed with my father and Jack. However, we all agreed that the developers were making a big mistake in building a shopping center underground. Who in heaven's name would want to go underground to shop? So, in our great wisdom we turned them down. However, when Place Ville Marie opened, and for decades afterward, it was acknowledged as the number one retail real-estate property in Canada — maybe even North America. Everyone who opened in PVM did very well and their success there helped many of them expand their businesses into national chains, but we missed the boat!

A couple of years later, there was another major development in downtown Montreal, Place Victoria, also with an underground shopping plaza. That complex was in the banking district in the lower downtown area, not in the central core, and was being touted as another PVM. I was very keen to get a store in the new complex. I didn't want to miss the opportunity a second time, but we didn't have the money to open another store, so I decided to try to get some outside help.

At the time ALGO Fashions, owned by two brothers, Joe and Ben Schafer, was the largest ladies' fashion manufacturer in Canada. I had heard that they had backed some small retailers to help them start up or expand their businesses, so I went to see Ben Schafer and told him my story about missing the opportunity in PVM and that I didn't want to miss the opportunity again in Place Victoria, but we didn't have enough money to open a new store. I asked him for a loan to help me open that store. Ben told me he would speak to his brother, Joe, and get back to me. I met with Joe and Ben a few days later and they told me they had decided not to give me the loan because they did not believe in the Place Victoria complex. They didn't want to support me in making what they thought was a bad business move.

They then went on to tell me that if I were determined to open a store anyway, they would extend us credit for whatever merchandise we wanted to buy from them. In essence, they were telling me that they were willing to help by extending credit, but they were unwilling to go beyond that. I had no other source, and without the money I simply could not go ahead. So, to my great disappointment at the time, we were unable to take a store in Place Victoria.

As it turned out, Place Victoria wasn't even remotely in the same league as PVM. If the Schafers had lent me the money to open that store, they would have contributed to the demise of our business — absolutely! Thank you Joe and Ben Schafer; thank you guardian angel!

Meanwhile, there was no shortage of difficulties back at the ranch. Even though much of the pressure was off, we were not what anyone would call effective retailers. I hadn't yet learned what is and is not important in running a business. I still knew nothing about budgeting and merchandise management. My father and I were arguing about everything. He understood levels of inventory; I did not. He understood needing cash to pay bills; I was just flying high.

We were three families — my parents, Betty and Jack, and Shirley and me — all having to survive from the income of two stores. We had one car among the three families and although our two stores were doing better, there was barely enough to sustain us all. I guess this forced us to come up with some interesting and original ideas for managing our business and personal lives so that they complimented each other.

The Atlantic City Adventure

In the summer of 1968, we were just surviving. There wasn't much money and there wasn't much opportunity to take time off work. However, by that time our children, Esther and Philip, were nine and six years old, and we wanted a family vacation. We decided that we would like to go to Atlantic City, but we had no money to spend on a vacation, so I came up with a plan.

At that time, we used to buy our maternity merchandise from the United States, and we were paying transportation and brokerage costs to bring the merchandise into Canada. I figured that if we could bring the merchandise in without paying the cartage and the brokerage fees, the money we saved would pay for our vacation. I called our suppliers in New York City and asked them not to ship to us for the next few weeks — we would come to pick up the merchandise ourselves. So Shirley and I packed up the car and our two children and drove down to Atlantic City, where we spent ten wonderful days.

When we had finished our vacation, my brother-in-law, Jack, took a bus from Montreal to New York City and we drove in from Atlantic City to meet him. The plan was that Shirley and the children would go home by bus and Jack and I would load the car with all the boxes our suppliers were holding for us, and drive back to Montreal. We put our car into a parking lot near the bus terminal and Shirley and the children stood guard all day while Jack and I went back and forth to our suppliers picking up boxes — one here, two there, three from somewhere else, and so on. We carried the boxes on our shoulders to the parking lot and stacked them beside the car. We did this all day — back and forth, back and forth — and eventually we had a huge pile of boxes sitting next to the car.

Then it was time to pack up the car, but no matter how we struggled, there was no way all of those boxes would fit into the vehicle. We had no roof rack, so we got some rope and loaded as many boxes as we could directly onto the roof and tied them down to the door handles. This meant we couldn't open the car doors, so we had to crawl into the car through the windows. Even after that, there were still a few boxes that we couldn't fit in. So we unpacked everything and took the back seat out of the car. That gave us the room we needed to get the last few boxes into the car, which was now completely filled, including boxes tied on the roof.

When Shirley and the children were ready to go to the bus station we had a small problem with some "extra" baggage — the car seat. So we took it to the bus station and put it with the other baggage to be loaded onto the bus. Eventually, the driver came along and started throwing all the baggage into the luggage compartment. When he saw the car seat, he asked, "What the hell is this?" And Shirley said, "That's all that's left of our car." He looked at her in amazement and shook his head, but he didn't say a word. He just took the car seat and threw it into the baggage compartment and away they all went back to Montreal.

Jack and I drove all night because we couldn't leave the car parked unattended, and we arrived at the border around five a.m., too early to clear Customs. So we lay on the grass next to the car and slept until the Customs office opened at eight.

What we saved on shipping and brokerage more than paid for our vacation and bus fares!

6

GROWING PAINS

In the mid-1960s, developers began building shopping malls across Canada. In Montreal, Cadillac-Fairview was building Fairview Mall in Pointe Claire. I went to see them about getting a ladies' fashion store in their new mall. "Give us your financials, and we'll see," they said. I gave them our financials and they said:

"Sorry, we can't rent you a store."

"Why not?" I asked.

"Because the way we get our mortgage is by renting to tenants who are financially triple-A. You do not meet that standard, therefore we cannot take your covenant as a guarantee on a lease." So I didn't get a store in Pointe Claire.

A year later Cadillac-Fairview began construction of another new mall in Montreal, Les Galleries d'Anjou. I went back to them to rent a store and, again, I was told, "Sorry, we can't rent you a store."

Once again, my guardian angel came to my aid and precipitated a change in direction. The agent asked, "Don't you have a maternity store on Queen Mary Road?"

"Yes." I said. So he offered to rent me a small space for a maternity store, saying that they would make an exception to their triple-A rule because they didn't have a maternity store in the mall and it would complement their mix.

Out of my vast knowledge and great wisdom I said, "No. Maternity is a small business. It cannot survive in the suburbs. The customer base is too small. A maternity store has to be in a central location so people can come from all over the city."

"Well, I'm sorry." he replied

Seeing that I wouldn't get a fashion store in the new mall, I suggested an alternative. I said, "I'll open a maternity store if you agree that if, in one year, I don't do x dollars in sales, you'll allow me to convert it into a regular sportswear store."

He thought about it for a moment, and agreed. I figured I'd got the better of him because I was certain that the maternity store wouldn't work and that I was going to get my foot in the door with Cadillac-Fairview for a regular fashion store. I assumed that once I was operating effectively in one of their centres, that would open the door for me for future stores. So I opened a maternity store in Galleries d'Anjou in the fall of 1968.

That store shot down my theory about the maternity business. What can I say? To my amazement, we did very well in that store, far better than the Queen Mary store, and that encouraged me to open another maternity store on St. Hubert Street in Montreal. Now we were back with four stores, three of them in maternity wear, and off again in a new direction.

That was another example of my guardian angel manipulating events and pointing me in a new direction, the maternity business. Had I been given a regular fashion store as I wanted, we would never have expanded our maternity business which, to a large extent, was ultimately responsible for our success. Operating in that niche market allowed us to be exclusive and special. It would have been much more difficult for us in the mass ladies' wear market.

Forced Expansion

I WENT TO NEW YORK REGULARLY on buying trips and, over the years, became good friends with a buyer, Steven Bennett, who worked for a large maternity chain, Maternally Yours, that had about 80 stores across the United States. One day Steven called me and said,

"The president of our company would like to talk to you. Next time you're in New York, please come to see us."

On my next visit to New York, I went to see the president and he said, "I hear you're doing nicely in Montreal in the maternity business. We've decided to expand our business into Canada, and we'd like to buy your maternity business and have you work for us."

I said, "Good of you to think of me. Thank you. I'll consider it."

I went back to Montreal and talked to my father and Jack, and we agreed that we were not interested in selling. A day or two later I called the president of the New York company and said, "Thank you for considering me, but I'm happy in my own little business, and I'd like to keep it that way."

My friend, Steven, called me later and said, "Max, you're making a terrible mistake. We are coming into Canada and will be opening up a lot of stores all across the country. You can't possibly compete. We'll put you out of business and you'll lose everything. You will be much better off taking this deal and being part of a large organization. This is a good opportunity for you, especially because you would be running the Canadian operation for us."

I said, "OK, go back and tell your boss that I'm reconsidering his offer, but that I need a few weeks to sort things out."

It was 1969, and my father and I decided we would take a trip across Canada to get a feel for what was happening in retail in other parts of the country. So off we went.

Developers were in the process of putting up shopping centres in all the major cities in Canada at the time. Good rental space was available and during that trip we rented nine stores in major malls in seven different cities — Toronto, Winnipeg, Calgary, Edmonton, Vancouver, Quebec City and Halifax. We signed the leases with exclusive clauses for maternity in each of the malls. When we returned to Montreal, I called the gentleman in New York and thanked him for his interest in the company, then told him I had decided to stick with my original decision and not sell. (We figured that with exclusive leases in all the available malls, where could he go?) As things turned out, Maternally Yours never came to Canada.

Once again, my guardian angel showed up to direct me. Had that U.S. company not approached me, I would not have thought of going across the country with such a bold expansion plan. Our decision to expand at that time proved to be pivotal to Shirmax's ultimate destiny, even though the road ahead would be very bumpy.

After signing the leases on our nine maternity stores, we decided to close out the regular fashion stores altogether and to concentrate on the maternity business. Again, we were off in a new direction, starting a national maternity chain. And now the roller coaster ride really started. We had leased space for nine new stores and we did not have the money to build and stock them, nor did we have the infrastructure we needed to manage them. We went to our bank manager and sold him on the idea of our becoming a national chain, and he promised to support us.

A Rough Patch

A couple of months later, CATASTROPHE! I was in Edmonton doing the groundwork for a new store opening there, when my father called and said, "Max, you'd better come back to Montreal. I'm afraid the bank is foreclosing on us." It turned out that our bank manager had not told his head-office about our expansion plans and when they got our financial statements, saw the plan for our expansion program and the amount of money we were putting into capital expenditures, the vice-president called my father with the foreclosure news.

I returned to Montreal immediately and we went to the bank's head office where we met with the V.P. who was quick to tell us we were out of our minds and that he wouldn't support us. He lectured us on the facts of life *vis-à-vis* birth control, and informed us that the pill, which had just come onto the market, would reduce the number of pregnancies significantly. He predicted that maternity was a dying business and that we were doomed. He finished his lecture by saying, "Besides, you don't have the financial wherewithal for such an expansion." Then he told us we had thirty days to come up with the money we then owed the bank or he would close us down.

We were in big trouble. We had no money, no support from our bank, and I was committed to opening nine new stores. We had no alternative but to stop paying our suppliers and to use all the money that came in to pay off the bank. Somehow we survived from day to day.

Once again, we were on the brink of bankruptcy. Thankfully, none of our suppliers wanted to see us go down and they continued to support us. When we opened those nine new stores it was the beginning of Shirley K Maternity, becoming a national chain.

As things turned out, the bank manager was right about the birth rate going down, but he was dead wrong in predicting that maternity wear was a dying business. In fact, it turned out that when people were able to manage the size of their families, they could afford to buy maternity clothes, whereas when they were having lots of children, they couldn't. So, as the birth rate went down, maternity sales actually went up! Who could have predicted that? I'm afraid that our first years of ups and downs, good times and bad, set the pattern for my entire business career.

We had no infrastructure and no support staff, so I had to open all nine of the new stores by myself. I was flying back and forth across the country looking after all the openings. We had three stores, Quebec City, Toronto and Edmonton, all being built and all scheduled to open around the same time. I was stretched beyond belief.

A Diamond in the Rough

I put an ad in the Edmonton paper for a store manager and sales staff, indicating that I would be interviewing at the Holiday Inn on a specific date. I left Quebec City, where I was overseeing the construction of that store, and flew to Edmonton to hire staff there. Only one lady showed up for an interview. Her name was Sally Simmons. She told me she had been a housewife and a mother for the past 25 years, that she now wanted to do something else, and that she was interested in part-time sales. I thanked her and promised to call her later that afternoon.

Time ran out and nobody else showed up. I had only one name, and I had to catch a plane back to Quebec City for another set of interviews there. The Edmonton store was opening in two weeks time, I had met only one person and she was interested only in part-time work. She had left me her address and phone number. I called before I left for the airport but there was no answer, so I decided to stop off at her apartment on my way to the airport. I rang the doorbell and her son answered the door.

"Is Sally at home?"

"No."

"Do you know when she will be back?"

"She just left for Vancouver."

"I saw her for an interview earlier today and I promised to call her back. How could she have gone to Vancouver?"

"Well, a friend who has his own plane called and told her he was flying to Vancouver and asked her if she would like to come along, and she went."

"I'm going to be in Quebec City tomorrow, this is my phone number there. Please try to get hold of her and ask her to call me. Please tell her it's urgent!"

Sally called me in Quebec City the next day and I asked, "What happened? I told you I would call you in the afternoon."

"I was sure you weren't going to hire me and I got this opportunity to go to Vancouver to visit my daughter, so I took it."

"Well, you're hired, and you're going to manage the store."

"Are you kidding? I told you all I want is a part time job. I can't manage a store. I know nothing about store management. Besides, I'm not interested."

"OK, I'll give you a part-time job, but please do me a favour. When you get back to Edmonton, please put an ad in the paper with your phone number so you can hire some staff. I'll send you the wording."

"I'm not hiring anybody...!"

Eventually I persuaded Sally to help me out and try to hire some staff. I finished my business in Quebec City, went to

Toronto for the store opening there, then back to Quebec City where I opened that store, then I returned to Edmonton. Meanwhile, Sally had put an ad in the Edmonton paper as I had asked, but no one had responded, so the two of us worked together to open the store.

We worked for two long days and on the third day, we worked around the clock, cleaning up all the construction debris the builders had left, ironing all the new merchandise, and setting everything up for the opening on Friday morning — and we made the opening! In the meantime, given that I had no other options, I was hoping that Sally would agree to manage the store, at least until we found a manager. I was booked to go home to Montreal on the red-eye on Saturday evening.

After we closed the store at 6 o'clock on Saturday, I started to show Sally how to handle the bank deposit for the day's receipts. I was explaining everything to her, but she was not paying attention, and then she started to cry.

She was completely exhausted, and she said, "Look, I don't want this job, it's not for me, I can't do it, I don't have a clue how to do cash, I don't understand what you're talking about. I quit."

I sat down on a chair and it was my turn to cry. *I really cried!* I asked, "How can you quit? I've been away from home for three weeks, opening these three stores. I've got my ticket for the last flight tonight, and I have to go home."

She said, "That's your problem."

And I said, "Yes, it's my problem, but please, you have to help me out. Forget the cash. Put the money in a shoebox. Just open the store on Monday and Tuesday, serve the customers, and add whatever you take in to the shoebox. I have to go home now, but I'll be back on Wednesday and I'll take over the store from you then." I left her there with the store, and I went home to Montreal.

On Tuesday, I called and told her I'd just booked my flight and was coming out the following day to take over from her.

She asked, "Why are you coming?"

"To take over from you."

"No, you don't have to do that, everything is OK."

"What do you mean?"

"The money is deposited and I'm in charge. I will hire staff and I will handle everything. Don't worry about it."

I did not see Sally again for nine months. In fact, she did not see anybody from head office for nine months. She was really on her own.

This is a prime example of how inept we were as an organization and the conditions under which we started to build a national chain. Sally turned out to be an absolute gem and worked with us until she retired twenty-two years later. She moved on from managing that Edmonton store to become one of our first area supervisors, responsible for all of Western Canada. When we later developed our Plus-Size division, she moved to Vancouver to take on the new challenge of developing that business on the West Coast.

Going High-Tech

Looking back, I laugh at this story; but I have to admit I didn't think it was funny at the time.

When we were up to about eighteen stores, it became pretty clear that we needed to strengthen our management capabilities and resources. We hired a controller whose name was Paul Shobert. As it turned out, Paul did not have the qualifications to be a controller. He had worked for Honeywell, so his expertise was more computer-related. Within no time, Paul persuaded us to buy a computer (from Honeywell, of course), then he hired a programmer and they set up our operations on the computer.

Paul was a very nice guy who knew a little bit about a lot of things but, truly, he was competent at nothing. He was meddlesome and he stuck his nose into everything, causing confusion everywhere. But worst of all, he was undisciplined; there was no documentation for the computer systems he built, so the installation was a mystery to everyone except Paul and, if any-thing went wrong, he was the only one who could fix it. It was a recipe for disaster.

After about two years of continuous pressure to fire him from all the staff, especially from my father and our outside accountants, I decided to let Paul go. So I had our office manager strike a severance cheque for Paul, and I called him into my office. I told him things weren't working out and that I was letting him go, then I handed him the cheque.

His response was, "Max, I can't leave you now. Your business is all on computer and I'm the only one who knows how to operate the system and how to find anything. This business will collapse if I leave."

Without even looking at the cheque, he tore it into four pieces, handed them to me and walked out of my office, leaving me with my mouth wide open. Paul remained with us for another five years, during which time we never spoke of that incident.

Over time, we managed to work around Paul and get both the systems and the documentation we needed so that when he finally left us the transition was relatively painless.

7

DATOU

IN THE EARLY DAYS WHEN WE WERE still small, we had a warm family atmosphere in the company and all of us, staff and management, had some special relationships. Occasionally, they were *very* special.

When we started to expand the maternity business across Canada, I hired a buyer, Helene Oppenheimer. Helene was single and lived with her parents. They owned two pedigree miniature Schnauzers and before she came to work with us she had taken a year off to breed a litter of dogs. They eventually sold all the pups except one, which Helene kept for herself. His name was Datou.

Helene had been with us for about three months when she went into the hospital for a surgical procedure. I went to visit her when she went home after the operation.

When I arrived at her parents' home she was crying, her eyes were all red and she was on the verge of hysterics. I asked her what was wrong and she said, "Well, you know I have this dog, Datou, which I love dearly. When I went into the hospital for my surgery, my mother came and spent the day there with me. That was the first time Datou had ever been left at home alone, and he literally destroyed the house. He tore up the furniture and ripped curtains off the windows. My mother was very upset and now says that I can't keep the dog at home any more — that I have to get rid of him."

We had tea and cookies and I listened while Helene and her Mother explored the possible options available to them. Then Helene had an idea and asked me, "Why don't you take Datou? At least, if you have him, I could see him every now and again and I wouldn't feel as badly as if I had to give him up to a stranger."

80

I replied, "Helene, you have to be kidding. You really don't know Shirley. She is fastidious about her house. My kids have been begging for a dog for a long time, but there's no way Shirley will let a dog in the house, especially one that has already destroyed one house. You're barking up the wrong tree."

And that was that. I ended my visit and went home.

That night at the supper table I told Shirley and the kids about going to visit Helene and the story about the dog. I ended by saying, "Helene had the audacity to suggest that we take the dog!"

At this point I have to say, *my wife is an enigma*. I have never been able to figure her out from one day to the next, and as soon as I think I've got her pegged, she surprises me. So, Shirley looked at me and said, "So maybe we should take the dog."

"Are you out of your mind?" I asked. "This is a dog that ate all their furniture."

"Yeah," she replied, "but the dog was left alone. Rachelle is still a baby and I'm home with her all the time, so there's no reason why the dog would be left alone. Maybe we should take the dog."

The kids were delighted. They went wild, screaming and yelling, "We're going to have a dog, We're getting a dog!"

So I called Helene and said, "Listen, I'm more surprised than you can imagine, but Shirley says that she'll take the dog."

Helene said, "Great, I'm so relieved and so happy. You're a lifesaver. Give me $300 and you can have the dog!"

"What?" I said, "Listen, if I wanted a dog, I would go to the SPCA and get a real dog for no money. I am not paying you any $300 for this dog."

"But Max, that's what it has cost me for vet bills, with shots and all the rest. I just want to get some of my money back."

"God bless you," I said, "and good luck to you, but I am not paying any money for the dog so forget about it."

And, again, that was that, or so I thought.

A couple of weeks went by and it was time for Helene to come back to work. The first day back she brought Datou with her. Cute little dog. Needless to say, no work got done that day. Everybody made a fuss and played with the dog the whole day.

So, my father went to her and said, "Helene, Datou is a lovely dog, and for today it's OK, but you cannot bring him to work again." She said,

"But Mr. K. I don't know what else to do with him."

And my dad replied, "Helene, I cannot help you there. Datou cannot come to work with you. You cannot keep a dog at work."

However, the next day she came to work with the dog again, and my father went to her and said, "Listen, Helene, I sympathize with you, but I'm sorry, you cannot bring Datou back."

The third day she came to work with the dog again. Finally, my dad got through to her — and I supported him.

At that time, we had a young man working with us in the warehouse whose name was André. Helene made a quick decision and made a deal with him. She decided that she would move out of her parent's home and get her own apartment so she would be able to keep her dog. But this was January and she couldn't get an apartment until May, because that's when all leases expire in Montreal. Her agreement with André was that he would keep the dog for her from January until May, and that she would take her dog back when she moved into her new apartment.

I think Helene and André made their arrangement on a Wednesday or a Thursday. In any case, on the Friday of the following week, she said to André, "Are you coming to work tomorrow (Saturday)?" He said "Yes." And she said, "I'll come in too. I want to see Datou. Bring him in tomorrow. Mr. K. won't be in the office on Saturday so he won't know."

On Saturday, however, André came to work without the dog. Helene asked him "Where's my dog?"

André said, "You know, I forgot to bring him."

"What do you mean, you forgot him? So bring him in on Monday."

"But Mr. K. is..."

"Never mind Mr. K. I want to see my dog. Bring him in on Monday."

On Monday André came in without the dog again. And Helene asked, "Where's my dog?"

André said, "Helene, I'm afraid I have bad news. The very first weekend after you gave me the dog, I went up north to visit some friends at their country house. I took the dog with me, but when I got there he ran away and I lost him."

Well, Helene went absolutely ballistic. The screaming and the wailing that went on in that office was unlike anything any of us had ever heard. It was worse than if somebody had died. I had never owned a pet, so I couldn't understand her extreme behaviour over a dog. (It was only after I became a pet owner myself that I could empathize with the way she carried on.)

My father was very upset too, because he felt responsible for the chain of events that resulted in having Helene give André the dog. Anyhow, while all of this commotion was going on, I had to leave for the airport on a week-long business trip across the country to visit our stores. So I watched this scene with Helene and her hysterics for about an hour, then I left the office and went to the airport.

I had a very busy week: running from store to store, working all day, catching late night flights, arriving even later in another city and getting up early in the morning to start the cycle all over again. I was very preoccupied, so I actually forgot about Helene and her dog. I spoke to Shirley every day, but she didn't say anything — not a word — nothing even remotely related to the dog. When I got home at the end of the week, what did I see when I walked in the door?

Datou's in my home!

"What is this dog doing here?" I asked. And Shirley answered, "Well, Helene found the dog, but she couldn't leave him with André any more because she doesn't trust him, so I agreed to keep Datou for her until May."

To which I responded, "Are you out of your mind? You're going to keep a dog here from January to May? Our kids are going to get attached to him and then you're going to give him back?"

But it was too late. Shirley had made a commitment and Datou was staying.

I should explain at this point that soon after I left to go to the airport, Helene called a friend and the two of them went up north to cottage country, where André told her he had lost the dog. They went to the police station, and learned that someone had reported finding a dog. The police directed her to the house where she found Datou! But she was faced with another problem. Shirley had kept in touch with Helene and when she heard about it she told Helene that she would keep Datou for her. That's how we got the dog!

As I expected, Shirley and the children became very attached and fell in love with Datou. In fact, Datou became Shirley's dog and was her constant companion. As for me, I knew that I would be giving the dog back in May, so I didn't allow myself to get attached. I kept my distance.

Shirley's Dad, who wasn't well at the time, used to come to visit us and, along with Shirley and the kids, he became very attached to Datou too. He especially enjoyed taking him for walks. However, in April he became very ill and just about t the last thing he said to Shirley before he died was, "Don't give the dog back. You can't do that."

When May came around, Helene got an apartment and said to me, "I've moved into my apartment and now it's time for me to get Datou back. Please bring him to work with you tomorrow."

That was on a Thursday, and she wanted to take him home Friday night. On Friday morning I came to work without the dog and I said to Helen:

"I did not bring Datou. I'm sorry, but I cannot give him back. My kids are attached to him and he's attached to our family. I cannot do that to my kids; I'm sorry, but I cannot give you back the dog."

"You can't do that to me. I went to all the effort and expense to get my own apartment so I could have Datou with me. Your kids will get over it. You all have each other. I am alone. You've got to give me back my dog!"

She made such a case, I could not argue with her, so I agreed to take the dog to her that evening. Shirley and I picked up the children and Datou, and we went to Helene's apartment. She made a big to-do about Datou, and then it came time for us to leave, and the kids started to carry on.

"Datou! We can't leave Datou!" they wailed.

It was heartbreaking...but we left Datou with Helene and we all went to a movie. (We saw *The Ten Commandments*. I will always remember that because of the circumstances of our going to see it.) For the entire weekend, everyone was in mourning for Datou. It was all very sad.

On Monday morning I went to work, and Helene was there with Datou. "What happened?" I asked. You know you can't bring the dog to work."

"I've decided to give Datou back to you. It's not fair to Datou because he has never been alone. He has always been in a house with people , but with me he's going to live all day in the house by himself and it's just not fair to him. I got a price for another Schnauzer puppy on the weekend; it will cost me $500."

Like a shot, I said, "OK, you've got the $500."

I was so excited; at that moment I realized that, despite our beginning, I, too, had come to love Datou.

That evening I took Datou home to everybody's delight. He lived with us for eleven years until he died. He was a fabulous dog, the giver and the recipient of much love and affection.

I've told this story not only because Datou was an important member of our family for eleven years, but also because it illustrates the kind of relationships we had within our company. Like Helene, when people joined us they became like family almost right away.

8

FURTHER EXPANSION

As time passed, we continued to expand our maternity business across the country until we had about 55 stores. By the mid-seventies we were living with a major problem; none of the three principals of the company — my father, Jack, nor I — had the competence we needed to run and manage a retail fashion chain spread out across Canada. So we decided to bring in some new management and began to build an infrastructure.

Of course, more people and more infrastructure involved more cost, and 55 small maternity stores could not support the additional cost. We needed to grow our business; if we did not grow, we would not have the synergies and the economies of scale we needed to be financially viable.

Given the demographics of Canada, it was becoming difficult to continue expanding our maternity business simply because further expansion would eventually lead to our cannibalizing our existing stores. That was a serious problem for us because the maternity business was the only business we were in. So, we began to explore other avenues for growth, and information came our way that once again set us off in a new direction.

The Plus-Size Business

At that time, maternity garments were made large and oversize to hide pregnancy. That meant that many maternity garments could accommodate plus-size customers. Our maternity stores were the only stores where plus-size ladies could find younger, fashionable clothes to fit them. So many of them came to our maternity stores to shop and we realized that there was a need in the marketplace for younger, stylish, plus-size fashions.

At the same time, plus-size women in the United States were also demanding younger, more fashionable styles. The U.S. maternity manufacturers were the first to respond to this demand. They started to produce some of their maternity styles in plus-sizes and they were very successful. Several of them encouraged me to start a retail division for plus-size clothing in Canada. So, the combination of knowing from our own experience that there was a growing demand for plus sizes, having access to reliable sources from the U.S. and knowing that we would soon max out our maternity business, led us to start a new retail division for younger, fashionable plus sizes — Addition-Elle.

In May, 1979, I hired Louise Tanguay as the buyer for the new Addition-Elle division, and we set out to re-invent the plus-size business for Canada. I say re-invent because there was already a well established plus-size business, Penningtons, but it catered primarily to mature women. Louise and I worked well together and in the fall of 1979 we opened our first Addition-Elle store in Montreal in the St. Bruno Shopping Centre. Although it got off to a slow start, over time, as we learned more about our customers, our assortments became more focused and we started to do well. By the late '80s, we had expanded the division across the country to about 85 stores and were the dominant retailer for the younger, fashion conscious plus-size customer in Canada.

In the spring of 1993 we started another plus-size division featuring casual sports clothing for even younger customers, A.E. Sport & Co. And in 1997, after we had about 30 A.E. Sport stores, we started a third plus-size division called Lingerie by Addition-Elle. The three separate divisions were combined into one large store with three doors under three separate banners. By the time we sold the business in 2002 we actually had more than 200 plus-size stores under those three banners in 85 locations.

As that business grew, I backed off from the day-to-day buying and merchandising and became more involved in management, organizational development and strategy. As I backed off, Louise Tanguay took on more and more responsibility. As Vice-President of Merchandise for the plus-size division. Louise was, unquestionably, responsible for the success of that business!

More Family Dynamics

IN THE MEANTIME, WE HAD TO DEAL with some challenging family matters. I mentioned that our early years were an enormous struggle. We went through several years on the verge of bankruptcy and were under constant financial pressure. Given my father's background, those years were very hard on him. He was terribly afraid that he and his family would not make a living and that all of us would be out on the street. He wanted us to be very conservative and to avoid taking risks. On the other hand, I was determined to build the business. (I was like Lord Nelson; I put my hand over my good eye and said, "I do not see the enemy.") I just kept plodding along — building and expanding. So my dad and I found ourselves pulling in opposite directions and this created a lot of friction between the two of us.

When my younger sister, Ellen, married Peter Shapiro, Peter had not yet established himself in a career and, as we were already a "family" business, we invited him to come in as a partner. However, because Peter had almost no business experience, we immediately became not just three incompetents driving the business, we were four, and that added more tension. As I added more staff to our management team, my father and Jack felt more and more isolated, and this, too, added tension. Unfortunately, the strain of our business relationships spilled over into our private lives and affected everyone in the family. Sadly, we lived with those dynamics for almost eight years — until my father died.

So much for a "family" business!

A Chicken Farm?

At one point in the early years, when we were having financial difficulties and my father was afraid that we wouldn't make it, he went to visit a cousin in Connecticut who had a successful chicken farm. While he was there, he inquired into the possibility of our entire family moving to Connecticut and opening up another chicken farm. His cousin thought that was a good idea and my dad came home very excited by the prospect and suggested that we close down the business, where all of us were working very hard and accomplishing very little, and all move to Connecticut and start a chicken farm.

He told us, "I don't see us being successful in the retail fashion business. It is a very difficult business, and I'm sure we could do much better in the chicken business."

When Shirley heard this, she stood up, put her hands on her hips and said, "I am not moving from Montreal, and I am not going to Connecticut to live in chicken shit! Besides, I have faith that we will make it in the fashion business and we don't need to run away."

And that was that. If she wasn't going, I wasn't going...so none of us went.

The story of Sally Simmons in Edmonton was not an isolated case. It showed how inept we were as an organization at the time. As we continued our expansion nationally, we needed more help, so I decided to search for an Executive Vice-President to help us manage the company.

I contacted Allan Etkovitch, an industrial psychologist who specialized in executive placement, and asked him to do a search for an Executive Vice-President. He agreed, but he told me that in order to find someone who would complement me, he would have to get to know me better. He asked me to come in for two days of intensive aptitude testing, which I did. A couple of days later I met with him to review the test results. He opened our discussion with:

"Max, according to the test results and my interviews with you, it is my opinion that you do not have the temperament or ability to manage a medium- to large-sized company. If you persist and expand your business beyond where it is, you will fail. You are not a businessman, you are best suited to be a social worker."

Considering what was to happen over the next thirty years, one cannot argue that he was completely wrong. In fact, he was actually quite accurate. The person he was describing was really who I was at the time. I accepted Etkovitch's evaluation as being the truth. However, I refused to accept that I could not change that truth, and I started to explore what it would take to become an effective leader of an organization.

As things turned out, I did not follow through with Mr. Etkovitch's mandate to hire an Executive Vice President because I had an opportunity to hire someone I knew.

In 1978, MIA Fashions, a fashion retailer in Montreal, went bankrupt and I was able to persuade Laurie Lewin, the Executive-Vice President of that company, to join our organization. Laurie had been trained as a professional manager in the UK before coming to Canada, and he brought with him a whole set of management skills, abilities and experience that we hadn't had up until then. He was a valuable asset to our business and a great complement to me personally.

A couple of years later, in 1980, I further strengthened our management team when I invited James Landry to join us. James was a CA and had been a partner with our accounting firm. He joined us as a V-P Finance and over time became Executive Vice President, the number two person in the company and my closest confidant. James remained with the company in that capacity until Shirmax was sold in 2002. I will have more to say about both Laurie and James later.

In 1978 when my son, Philip, was fifteen, he spent a year at a school on a kibbutz in Israel. Not long after Laurie joined us,

Shirley and I went to Israel to visit Philip. Coincidentally, my parents were in Israel on holiday at the same time. While there, Shirley and I spent four very special days with my mother and father in Jerusalem. The business pressures and conflicts between my father and me were left in Montreal and we enjoyed a marvelous time together. My father knew everything about the history and geography of Israel, and he took charge. He was our tour guide and he gave us an incredible lesson on that country. It was a wonderful experience.

When Shirley and I returned home, we left Philip in school, and my parents to finish their holiday in Israel. From our time together there, I saw how different my father was away from the business and how happy he could be. That experience made me aware of the sacrifices we were making by having my father in the business with me. I decided the time had come for him to retire.

Peace with my Father

My parents returned from Israel the day before I was scheduled to leave on a buying trip to Europe. That evening, I said to my dad, "I'm leaving for Europe on a buying trip tomorrow but before I go, I want to tell you that I think it's time for you to leave the business. The strain of the business and our family relationships is taking its toll on you, and it's costing us all dearly.

"When I come back from Europe, I would like us to go to Florida and I will help you buy an apartment for you and mom. You can spend winters there, and the summers here. Dad, we've got to do this. It is time for you to leave the business."

I tormented myself before I approached my dad with this proposition. I was sure he would be devastated and would absolutely refuse. I was prepared for a battle, but to my surprise, he agreed. And so, I left for Europe the next day.

On the plane trip over, I began to feel very uneasy. The way my dad gave in was totally out of character for him and I wondered if he was becoming depressed again. Unfortunately, it was much worse than that.

Two weeks later, when I returned to Montreal, Shirley met me at the airport with the news that my dad was in hospital with lung cancer and, a brain tumor. He was dying. I was devastated — as were we all. My dad had been a chain smoker since he was fourteen and I guess it caught up with him. I went to the hospital and did not leave his bedside, day and night; I shaved him and washed him and I took care of him until he died seven weeks later.

Ironically, he did not die as a result of his cancer. The doctors had actually projected an additional year for him. He died forty-eight hours after his first chemotherapy treatment, which knocked out his immune system.

Although our grief was almost beyond our ability to endure, those seven weeks were truly amazing. My father was dying, but he quickly came to terms with it and he actually seemed to embrace it. He had spent his entire life in a huge struggle. He worried about everything and worried for everyone and, most of all, he lived with huge guilt of having survived the Holocaust. For the first time in his 66 years he gave up struggling and was at peace. His only concern was for our mother and her well-being after he was gone.

He had always kept his affairs in order, so there was very little to do in that respect. He spent his last days empowering all of us. He called us together and spoke to us as a group, and then to each of us separately. He gave us each a lecture, his advice on how we should live our lives, and he gave us his blessing. Before he died he told me in front of everyone that, as his eldest son, he expected me to take care of the family. I was honoured that he expressed that kind of confidence in me.

Those seven weeks were a blessing for all of us. Although there was a lot of sadness, there was also a huge amount of love and inspiration. The fact that our father was dying became a catalyst for us to put aside whatever family difficulties we were having. From that time on we have all been a wonderful supportive family for each other.

I mentioned earlier that my dad was a *khazan*. I loved to go to

I mentioned earlier that my dad was a *khazan*. I loved to go to services when he was officiating. He had a beautiful voice and put an incredible amount of heart into chanting the services. I was so proud of him. In the last weeks before he died, although he was weakening continuously, he recorded many of the songs and chants from various services. He wanted that to be part of his legacy to his family. We all have copies of those tapes and we cherish them dearly.

Soon after my father passed away, Jack decided that it was time for him to leave the business. He had raised the subject with me on several occasions in the past, but I had always been able to talk him out of it. Jack was my best friend and we worked very well together. But I knew he was not happy so I agreed. I arranged to buy him out, and at the same time I also bought Peter out. Thus each of us went our separate way in business. Eliminating the tensions in our business relationships allowed us to appreciate each other and to become the family we are now.

9

PERSONAL DEVELOPMENT

WHEN I HIRED LAURIE LEWIN as our Executive-Vice President in 1978, we had about fifty-five maternity stores and had not yet started the Addition-Elle division. Within days of his joining us, I left on my two-week trip to Israel and left Laurie in charge. A week after I returned from Israel I again left for a two-week buying trip to Europe. When I returned from that trip, I spent seven weeks with my father in the hospital, and a week sitting *shiva* (mourning) after his death. So I had been away from the office for thirteen weeks.

I knew that Laurie had made some staff changes during my absence, but it was only when I came back that I became aware of the extent of those changes. Laurie had replaced most of our senior people with people who had been part of his team at MIA Fashions. Laurie was a very strong and assertive executive and, given that he had many of his people strategically placed in most key positions, he was effectively in control.

In no time Laurie and I began to butt heads. Not only did he take charge of what I had hired him to do — help me run the company — he took over completely. I felt shut out and like a stranger in my own company. As each month passed, I felt more and more displaced and inept. I kept backing off and the weaker I showed myself to be, the stronger Laurie became. It was clear to everyone who was in charge. Finally, I decided that I had lost control and that there was no way I could get it back. The best thing I could do was try to sell the company and salvage whatever I could. So I went to the managing partner of our accounting firm and asked him to help me find a buyer. After making that decision, I took a week's holiday with Shirley at a Club Med in Haiti.

One afternoon I was sitting on the beach chatting with Ellie Stahl, a women we had met at the Club, and she asked me what I did for a living. I told her about losing control of the company and my decision to sell. I said I did not know what I would do next.

After listening to my story, Ellie said, "It seems to me that you are making a very serious decision and I wonder if you have really thought it through? I recently attended a two-weekend course called "The *est* Training", which I found very enlightening. I think that course would help you clarify what you are doing and why you are doing it. I really urge you to consider it. There is an evening introductory session you can attend and then decide if you would like to take the course."

I told Shirley about my conversation with Ellie and, in light of our positive experience with Marriage Encounter, we both decided to attend the introductory evening session. We also invited our 18-year-old son, Philip, to join us. The three of us registered for the course. A couple of weeks later, along with approximately 300 other participants, we attended the two-weekend program.

At that time The Training was offered by the *est* organization, which was headquartered in California. Several years later, *est* became Landmark Education, and the course was replaced by the Landmark Forum. Landmark Education today offers personal development programs in 26 countries and is considered to be the largest off-campus educational institution in the world.

Of all the times my guardian angel has directed me, none was more significant than her arranging for that chance encounter with Ellie Stahl, because The Training turned out to be the single most important and powerful experience of my life. For me the experience was transformational and, I can say unequivocally, it was a turning point in my life. I now look at my life as "before" and "after" The Training.

THE *est* Training/THE FORUM

THE *est* TRAINING WAS DESIGNED TO HELP participants achieve a new level of self-awareness and live a "life that works." It teaches you to expand your awareness moment by moment, and empowers you to become an observer in you own life. It is as if you become two people: one the "actor" or the "doer"; the other the "observer." When you can actually observe yourself in play in your life, you can identify those behaviours that are not contributing to you and change them. The ability to be an observer in your life gives you the power to create and live a "life that works."

The Training started me on a journey of exploration and self-discovery. I became intrigued with the sources of personal power, both in the context of one's own life and in the context of large organizations. That program inspired me to take many more advanced Landmark courses over the next ten years, and it was through them that I came to understand more about who I was, what was driving me and how I behaved, reacted and responded to life's events. From all that work I became empowered to such an extent that, over time, it was as if I had become a new person.

The Training gave me new insights into how we live as human beings and *how we can live* with much more control and power. Now, let me explain, using "responsibility" as an example.

Before taking The Training, my idea of the meaning of responsibility was to embrace, take care of and handle my obligations; I had to do the right thing. I had to look after my family, earn a living, obey the law, etc. In short, I was like most people — a responsible citizen. However, the Training gave me new meanings — new *distinctions* — for "responsibility." I expanded my understanding and embraced responsibility in a much more powerful way. I began to see myself as *the cause* of everything that affects my life. I understood that I am not responsible for events and circumstances that I do not create and over which I have no control. However, I came to understand that:

I am the creator of, and responsible, for the interpretations and meanings I apply to those events and circumstances.

The weather is a good example. If I look out the window on a rainy day I can say, "Woe is me. Another miserable, rainy, dismal day!" That's one interpretation I can apply *or* I can take responsibility for my well-being and apply another interpretation. I can say, "Thank God for the rain. It's going to make everything green and lush. I love this time of year."

The first interpretation does not make me feel good and does not contribute to my well-being. On the other hand, the second interpretation does. Put another way, although I have no control over the weather, I can take responsibility and control how I allow the weather to affect me. So...

My quality of life is affected more by the interpretations and meanings I apply to events and circumstances than by the events and circumstances themselves. And if the interpretations and meanings I apply to events and circumstances do not contribute to my well-being, inasmuch as they are my creations and I had the power to create them in the first place, then I also have the power to change them; I can create them another way so they do contribute to my well-being.

In summary, my new *distinctions* for, and my broadened understanding of *responsibility* gave me both power and some control over my quality of life. My eyes were opened to the fact that I had not taken responsibility and that I had not *managed* that in the past; I had lived my life as a victim of events and circumstances.

Closure

A case in point was my troubled relationship with my father. I had taken no responsibility for the breakdown in our relationship. Indeed, I blamed him and held him responsible for everything that had gone wrong between us. I felt that he had been unfair to me and had judged me wrongly over several important family issues.

I was deeply hurt and very angry. I loved my dad dearly. I had enormous respect for him and I always had sought his approval, but it seemed to me that I could never get it.

When my father died, I remember standing over his grave as they lowered his coffin into the ground and, in my grief, I mumbled under my breath, "How could you have done this to us? With all your wisdom, how could you have been so blind?"

I carried that blame and anger with me for another three years until I took The Training. Around 2 a.m. on the third day of The Training I had a breakthrough. I was sitting in the course room, very tired and not consciously listening. My defenses were down. A man who had been sitting a couple of rows behind me stood up, took the microphone, and began "sharing."

"I have been sitting here thinking about my relationship with my father," he said, "and I see that I have not been a good son. I have never allowed myself to see or understand my father's point of view. I have taken no responsibility for our relationship and have been blaming him for all that is wrong between us."

Those words caught my attention, burned into my foggy mind, and I thought, "Oh my God, that's exactly how I have been with my own Dad!" I realized I, too, had not considered his point of view, his needs, his fears, or whatever was driving him. I had been totally blind to my responsibility in the breakdown and I had not taken responsibility for the relationship. I saw that as much as anything else, it was my interpretation of what my dad said and did that had contributed to the breakdown.

At that moment I took responsibility for our relationship and it was transformed forever.

A few days later I went to the cemetery, stood over my dad's grave and said, "Rest in peace, my dear father." The anger and hurt were gone. Even though I could not talk it out with him in person, I took responsibility for my part in the matter, and what is left now is only love and understanding. I now have a great relationship with my father, and I attribute that result entirely to my new distinction for responsibility.

TAKING BACK THE COMPANY

BEFORE I TOOK THE TRAINING, I was having an ongoing argument with Laurie Lewin over a project that he wanted to put into place but which I felt was inappropriate. However, he just kept moving ahead with his plan.

On the Monday after I had completed The Training, Laurie and I attended our regular Monday afternoon management meeting with about twenty managers from different departments to review the previous week's sales, discuss strategies and make decisions on appropriate actions. The meeting was in Laurie's office, which happened to be a large corner office overlooking the parking lot. He was chairing the meeting and I was one of the attendees. The first order of business was to put his plan (with which I did not agree) on the table for final polishing.

When he introduced the topic for discussion, I said, "Laurie, we're not going forward with this plan." Our exchange then went something like this:

"What are you talking about? We've put weeks of work into this and we're ready to move ahead."

"I know, and I'm sorry about that, but you know I've never agreed with this plan. It is a wrong strategy, I don't believe in it and I cannot allow it to go ahead."

" I don't have to put up with this! We agreed on this and we're going ahead."

"No, we are not. And you're right, you don't have to put up with this. That's your decision. But we are not going ahead with this plan."

Everyone in the room was dumbstruck! They had never seen me go up against Laurie before. He said "OK," then he got up, put his briefcase on his desk, stuffed it with a bunch of papers, put on his jacket, picked up his briefcase and walked out. He had to pass his office windows to get to his car, which was parked right outside his office. There was absolute silence in the room while everyone watched him take out his key and put it in the car door. He stood there for a few seconds, then he pulled out the key, turned around and came back into his office. He put his briefcase down on his desk and said, "Well, I guess we're not going ahead with that project! "

At that moment, I had my company back.

Before taking The Training I had been intimidated by Laurie and, as the CEO, I was not living up to my responsibilities to lead the company. Out of The Training, I became empowered and I was no longer intimidated, and I assumed my proper role as leader.

In retrospect, it is clear that I had not yet developed many management skills. I should not have confronted Laurie as I did in front of the entire team that included people who reported to him; I should have handled the matter with him one-on-one before the meeting.

It was very lucky for me that he turned around and came back because Laurie was a great asset at Shirmax. After that, we worked fabulously well together for the next several years. Then one day Laurie received an offer from a company in the U.K. which he felt he could not pass up — and he left Shirmax. We kept in touch while he was in England. Eventually, he returned to Canada and has had a very successful career as the President and CEO of La Senza Corp. I have enormous respect for Laurie and what he has accomplished.

The episode with Laurie and my revelation about my relationship with my father are only two examples of how my life changed and how I became empowered as a result of taking The Training. My whole way of thinking changed. The way I look at the world and how I allow events and circumstances to affect me, changed. The way I interpret events and circumstances changed. The judgements that I brought to events and circumstances changed. The fundamental change was that I no longer lived my life as a disempowered victim. I began to operate from strength and with personal power.

10

FURTHER EDUCATION

After the training i took many other courses and seminars offered by the *est* organization, and I continued to broaden my vision for what was possible in both my business and my personal life. All of them contributed to my education and to my seeing the possibilities of building an extraordinary organization, and living an extraordinary life.

The Body Seminar and the Marathon

The Body Seminar was an associated course I took right after The Training. It was the catalyst for another significant change in my life from being relatively sedentary to becoming very physically active.

I enrolled in The Body Seminar in April, 1981, when I was 46 years old. The course itself focused on self-improvement and was designed to help participants experience all aspects of their body. We were encouraged to make a commitment to fix what we didn't like about our bodies if it was fixable, and if it was not fixable, to "make friends with *and like* what we have." For me, that particular seminar led to an experience that hearkened back to the traumatic race I ran in Barbados when I was 17 years old. To explain:

When I started the seminar I had a bit of a belly, and I was not prepared to "make friends with it." I was too vain. So I decided to try to lose weight, and the belly. I had been doing the dieting-and-weight dance for many years; five pounds up, five pounds down, and I knew that if it was going to be different this time, I had to make a long-term commitment to lose weight and keep it off. Now, it just so happened that I had watched the running of the Marathon at the Olympics on television a year earlier. That race really impressed me. Because I had had a little experience as a runner when I was 17, I was in awe of the people who could run a Marathon, a 42 km race. Until then, I had never thought of running a Marathon. But at the Body Seminar, running a Marathon seemed like a good way to shed some weight and lose the belly, so I stood up and declared to the room, "I will run the Montreal Marathon in September." And I started training.

Five months of training for a 42-km race is a very short training period, especially if you have not been exercising regularly and you are out of shape. Nonetheless, I watched my food intake, trained vigorously, and ran and ran and ran. I lost 40 pounds, suffered various injuries, had many cortisone shots, visits to chiropractors, etc. The training also intruded on my family life. When my family was having supper, I was out running. When Shirley wanted to socialize in the evening, I was out running. My whole life at that time became focused on training and running.

Eventually, Shirley put her foot down. I needed her support, and I got it, but only on the condition that I would do only *one* Marathon. During the training period, I also received a lot of support from Rubin Reisler, whom I met at the Body Seminar. He became a life-long friend as well as my running buddy.

On the day of the Marathon, I took the subway to St. Helene's Island where the run was to begin. On the way I was surrounded by dozens of young men and women. They made me very aware of my age and I asked myself, "Max, are you nuts? What are you doing here?" I took my position on the bridge, with about 8,000 other runners, and waited for the race to begin. I was intimidated by the whole situation. There were two young black men standing next to me who were obviously in great physical shape. They were hopping up and down, warming up like two magnificent race horses, anxious to start running. Now *that* was intimidation.

Again, I asked myself, "Max, what are you doing here?"

The starter's gun went off and the race began! The two black runners took off and quickly disappeared. My training partner, Rubin, had agreed to meet me at a pre-determined spot and run the last 16 km with me as support. When he joined me I was already struggling, but I had had the support of family and friends along the way to cheer me on and every time I saw a familiar face it gave me renewed energy and I kept going.

At about 34 kilometres, I "hit the wall." Now, anyone who has never had the experience is unlikely to understand what that means. *You just run out of steam*; you become completely depleted and you have nothing left. Every step is agony and is executed with a groan; you are sure you cannot take another ten steps.

With the finish line still seven kilometres away, I said to Rubin, "It's all over, I have nothing left and I can't go any further."

He tried to encourage me and I managed a few more steps, then I saw the two black guys lying by the side of the road, finished! That sight, brought back the vision of my race in Barbados when I had been intimidated because the runner ahead of me was black and I "didn't even try." But seeing those two black guys lying on the side of the road gave me a surge of energy that enabled me to finish the race.

I ran that Marathon in 4 hours and 10 minutes. At the finish line I couldn't wait to find Shirley to say, "I'm sorry, but I've got to do another one. I didn't do this Marathon; it did me." My training time had been too short, I had lost too much weight, and I had not been adequately conditioned. I was not strong enough.

A year later I ran the New York Marathon with two good friends, Marvin Helfenbaum of Montreal and Joel Schwartz of New York City. It was their first Marathon. Our plan was to run together. Marvin knew I had hit the wall in my first marathon and he was determined that none of us would hit the wall in New York. He was very disciplined and developed a running strategy for us. He had set times for every five kilometres to ensure that we ran more slowly at the beginning so that we had enough energy left to finish the race.

Reuben Reisler and me,
Montreal Marathon,
1985 ◀

Marvin Helfenbaum
▶ *and me, Montreal*
Marathon, 1985

I was better trained and in much better condition for New York than I had been for Montreal. I had also put back some weight and I was much stronger. At about 25 kilometres I said to Marvin and Joel, "I'm sorry, but I can't hold back anymore" and I took off and left them behind. I ran much faster for the balance of the race and finished in 3:44, feeling very strong and not at all depleted. But even though I had had a great Marathon, I was not satisfied. I felt sure I could have run a much better time had I had not held back in the first half. So I ran another Marathon in Montreal a year later. Then my wife's patience ran out!

Although I stopped running Marathons, I remained a serious runner for another eight years until I switched to power walking and biking. I have never given up my commitment to staying physically fit. My thanks to the Body Seminar.

Training for and running a Marathon requires a major commitment and an enormous amount of effort. In fact, it often requires more effort than you feel you can give. I have enormous respect for anyone who can make that kind of commitment and actually complete a Marathon.

The lesson I learned from my Marathon experience is that one of the criteria for success is *doing whatever it takes.* If anyone were to ask me today, "What do the people who have built successful businesses and sustained them over time have in common?" I would answer, "It is doing whatever it takes. No 'yes but', 'it's too difficult' or 'I can't do it', you simply do whatever it takes." My Marathon days instilled that in me. Doing whatever it takes became part of my way of being and I believe that attitude has contributed substantially to whatever success I have had.

THE SIX-DAY COURSE

BY FAR THE MOST POWERFUL COURSE I took with *est* was the Six-Day Course, which was given at a location in the Catskill mountains.

The course focused on the study of five principles:
Responsibility
Commitment
Integrity
Impeccability
Support (Giving and Receiving)

From studying these principles, participants learned new distinctions for them. New distinctions meaning: new understandings, new insights, new perspectives and new meanings for those principles. For five consecutive days we spent eighteen hours a day studying each principle. On the sixth day we had an activity-based event called the "ropes" course, where we applied the new distinctions we had learned for these principles.

The ropes course was a one-day event involving several intimidating and challenging physical tests that included rappelling oneself backwards down a rock face, traversing a gorge by pulling oneself across a span of ropes strung between two mountain peaks, and a number of other equally challenging feats. Let me describe the circumstances under which I acquired my new distinctions.

Before participants were allowed to enroll in the Six-Day Course, we were required to make a commitment to two conditions. The first was that we would do exactly what we were told and the second was that we would participate fully in the ropes course. Anyone who would not, or could not commit to these two conditions would not be accepted. I agreed to the conditions and I enrolled.

There were about 130 of us in the course. The course room, where we spent 18 hours a day, was set up theatre-style, with an elevated platform at the front where the course leader sat. We slept approximately two to four hours a day, we had one hour for dinner and two short rest breaks.

On the first day the course leader introduced himself and talked a bit about what we could expect over the next six days. He also reminded us of our two commitments: to do as we were told, and to complete the ropes course. He then asked us to turn around and to look toward a far corner of the room where there was a huge pile of what looked like junk — bundles of tangled up rope, wheels, mallets, pegs, pulleys and more.

He then said, "You see that pile of stuff over there? That's your ropes course. We have a ropes course leader on staff who knows how to set up all this equipment. The day before your ropes course, a group of volunteers will come here, take instructions from the ropes course leader, and *those volunteers are going to set up your course.* You will be putting your lives on the ropes that they set up for you."

Everyone was horrified! Volunteers will be setting up the ropes course? Nobody told me about this before I enrolled! This is outrageous! I've been deceived. It isn't right. I am going to die on that ropes course! etc., etc. *I'm going to die on the ropes course* became the foundation on which we went on to study the five principles, with the spectre of death constantly in the background.

A good example of how our fear of dying was used to reinforce what we were learning occurred on the day we explored the principle of commitment. We had spent the entire day defining, discussing, debating and dissecting everything anyone could possibly imagine about commitment.

About two in the morning, when everyone was very tired, the course leader asked us,

"Would everybody please stand up."

So we all stood up.

Then he said, "Thank you. Now sit down."

Everyone sat down.

"Please stand up."

We stood up. "Now sit down."

We sat down.

He continued having us stand up and sit down. By the 10th time, half the room remained seated. By the 20th time, no one stood up.

After a long silence, our course leader asked, "What's going on here? I asked you to stand up. Why aren't you standing up? I thought that when you enrolled in this course you made a commitment to do as you are told."...then the answers poured forth:

"Yes, but this doesn't make any sense."

"It's two o'clock in the morning; we're tired, and you're asking us to stand up and sit down for no good reason."

"There's no purpose to this."

"This is childish."

"I'm not a robot."

"I'm not going to do what you say if it doesn't make sense." And so on.

The course leader then asked a second time, "But didn't you make a commitment that you would do as you are told?"

And the answers came again:

"Yes, but this doesn't make any sense. It's stupid. I'm not just going to stand here and have you take advantage of me." And on and on.

"But you made a commitment that you would do as you were told. Now, if whatever I ask you to do is not comfortable or does not make sense to you, you're not going to do it? So what does that say about what commitment means to you? Apparently, the way you live with commitment is that you're committed only for as long as it's comfortable or convenient, or as long as it makes sense to you, but the moment you're not comfortable or the commitment doesn't suit you, you're not committed any more.

"Now, let's just think about that. If the volunteers who are coming here to set up your ropes course are committed the way all of you are committed, that is, as long as everything is comfortable, convenient, and makes sense to them, then someone is going to die on that ropes course. If the ropes course leader says, 'I want you to hammer this peg into that rock 100 times to make sure the sucker never moves', and a volunteer thinks that he knows better than the course leader and decides that 30 times is enough and it is stupid to do more, someone will die on that course.

"Don't think you are unique. Most people live their lives with exactly the same kind of commitment all of you have just shown. Now, every one of you has to come to terms with what commitment really means to you. If you are committed only for as long as it's comfortable or it suits you, then you are not keeping your word. That's not commitment. And that's not what we've spent the last 18 hours talking about."

So, from a background of someone dying on the ropes course, everyone in the room embraced a powerful new distinction for commitment! And from that same background we went on to study and learn powerful new distinctions for responsibility, integrity, impeccability, and support. We also learned that even though the volunteers had never set up a ropes course before, all of them had already taken the Six-Day course and so they were living out of those same distinctions and applying those distinctions to setting up the course. Nothing would be left to chance; we were safe.

Discovering a Truth

On day four of the course, we studied "Integrity." Late that evening I had an experience that highlighted for me how much my organization did not work and it focused me on what was missing in the company in a way that nothing ever had before. That experience created a new beginning for Shirmax.

Outside the course room the participants were divided into small groups of eight, which functioned as "support groups." Maria Moutsov, a woman from Montreal, was one of the members of my support group and at one point during a late break she came over to me and asked, "Max, what's the matter? You look like you're upset and having a hard time." I told her everything was fine and that I was not upset. But she kept pressing me and I realized that, truly, I was not myself. I was very impressed with the organization that ran the Six-Day Course and how effective they were. By comparison, my own organization was grossly ineffective. None of the principles we were studying (responsibility, commitment, integrity, impeccability and support), especially in the light of my new distinctions for them, existed in my organization.

After I had shared all this with Maria, she said something to the effect of:

"Max, aren't you being a little hard on yourself? Maybe you're focusing too much on the negative and not appreciating all the positive aspects of your organization. I am familiar with your company, and I think you should be proud of it. It's not just a money-making enterprise. You are making a difference in your community. You are dressing pregnant women and helping them feel good about themselves. Have you any idea how important your contribution is to them?

"And, as if that wasn't enough, you found another huge void in the marketplace: "plus" sizes. You are giving plus-size women the opportunity to dress well and feel good about themselves, too.

"Also, I run a placement service and from time to time I try to steal people from your company. I can't get them to move. So, you can't tell me that you're not doing a lot of things right. I don't think you're justified in feeling the way you do.

"Tell me, Max, *on a scale of one to ten, how would you rate your organization?*"

I thought for a moment and in the light of what Maria had just said to me, I replied, "About seven out of ten."

And Maria said, "So there you are. Sure, you have some fixing to do, but I don't see that it warrants your being depressed about it."

I felt much better when we resumed our session.

I went to bed about 4:30 a.m. and even though I was sleep-deprived and dead tired, I could not fall asleep. As I said earlier, we had studied integrity, telling the truth, that day and, lying there, visualizing my company at work, it became clear to me that I had not told Maria or myself the truth when I rated the company seven out of ten. With my new distinctions as a back-drop, I saw that our management group was not operating as a team with a common objective. They were not supporting each other and pulling in the same direction. No one was taking responsibility. Rather than supporting each other, everyone was being defensive, undermining and blaming everyone else. There was lots of complaining and frustration. Commitment, Integrity and Impeccability were not part of our culture. Everyone was vying for my attention and I was caught in the middle. All of the responsibility for everything was on my shoulders. It was clear to me that by any definition of an "organization that works" my organization did not work. In the morning I went straight to Maria at breakfast, and I said to her, "Maria, I am out of integrity with you. Last night I told you that on a scale of one to ten I would rate my company as seven. That is not the truth. The truth is that two out of ten would be generous! "

That moment was one of the most important "ah-hahs" of my business life. I saw that I had not been telling myself the truth about the state of affairs in the company, and how much not telling the truth costs. I also began to understand how difficult it would be for me to transform the company into an effectively-run organization.

After experiencing my new distinctions at work in the ropes course, I saw that if I could live my life out of these five principles, I would have the makings of an extraordinary life. And if I could bring those same principles into my business, it would create incredible workability, so I made a commitment to bring these principles into both my life and the organization. My enthusiasm to make that happen was truly boundless and I put a lot of pressure on all senior management to take The Training. That upset a lot of people and they refused because they felt I was push-ing them beyond the scope of business and intruding into their personal lives. But that did not dampen my commitment to bring those principles into the company. I just had to find another way.

Harvey Horowitz

After the Six-Day Course, Shirley and I enrolled in a Communications Workshop, which was also given by *est*. Harvey Horowitz was the course leader of that workshop; he was a great teacher. From my experience with him in that workshop and other subsequent seminars, it was clear to me that he knew and understood all the principles and distinctions that I wanted to bring into the company, and that he lived his life according to those principles. Harvey was interested in doing some outside consulting, so I invited him to join our company. His mandate was to help me bring those principles and distinctions to the organization. On a day-to-day basis Harvey also became my coach, helping me develop my communication and management skills.

Harvey designed a number of work shops especially for us and presented them to all management. Within a short time, however, those programs were perceived as a covert way to expose them to The Training. After about a year, there was a virtual revolt and I received a delegation from the management group with an ultimatum to cease and desist from promoting anything that was even remotely associated with The Training, or they would resign *en masse!*

I was shocked by that development because I truly did not realize how zealous I had become and what effect my zeal was having on the people around me. Of course I acceded to their demand; I had no choice. I agreed not to promote or even talk about anything related to The Training at Shirmax.

Harvey and I worked well together and we developed a great relationship. However, under the circumstances, Harvey decided to leave Shirmax, but he did not leave me. Our relationship has continued until today and, even though I am no longer in business, I still consider him to be a mentor and dear friend.

Despite my promise, a promise that I kept absolutely, my determination to create the kind of organization I envisioned did not wane for a moment. I simply stopped sharing The Training with the people at Shirmax and started living my life out of the principles I had learned. I shared and promoted those principles as if they were my own. That was accepted by everyone and, over time, I was able to shape and mold the Shirmax culture to embody those principles. But it was not an easy task and it certainly did not happen overnight. Along the way I continued to take other Landmark courses in an effort to further my education and improve my management skills.

MASTERY OF EMPOWERMENT

THIS COURSES WAS GIVEN OVER SEVERAL DAYS at a location in the mountains of upstate New York. As the title clearly states, the course was about empowerment: learning how to empower others to be as good as they can be. Two incidents occurred during that course that made deep impressions on me.

There were about 75 people in the course. We were given an assignment by the course leaders to work together as a group to set up and operate a model business, a hypothetical organization and operation. The course leaders left us to our own devices, but remained in the background as observers.

It did not take long for the entire exercise to disintegrate into chaos. There was no leadership, people were not working together and everyone had his or her own agenda. There was no "team"; everyone was trying to outdo everyone else and no one was listening. Eventually, my patience ran out and I saw that it was necessary for someone to take charge, so I stepped in and imposed myself as the leader.

The group was a mixed bag of people from many walks of life including professionals and presidents of large corporations. I set out to try to bring everybody into line and create some order out of the chaos. That proved to be difficult, and when the going got really rough, my true colours emerged — my true colours at that time, that is! My management style was very heavy-handed, based on threats and orders to "do it my way." Eventually, the course leaders stepped in to analyze what was going on in the room in terms of "empowerment." The objective of the exercise, after all, was to get us in touch with the concept of empowerment and observe our ability to empower others. Because I had drawn attention to myself by trying to take charge, they used me: focusing on my behaviour and my management style as an example of what not to do and what was inappropriate. They used me as a scapegoat and were very hard on me.

It was clear to everyone from this exercise that I was a disaster as a leader. This was a "mastery of empowerment" course and it was obvious that I didn't have any understanding at all of the meaning of empowerment. The experience was both confronting and humiliating. I came face-to-face with who I was as a leader, and it was one of the catalysts that triggered a process of change in my management style.

I will always treasure the second incident. For the duration of the course, all the participants were assigned to teams. Each eight-member team functioned as a "support group." Team members had the opportunity to observe each other and, on the final day, each team was asked to meet together and each of the members took a turn in critiquing the other seven members, not as criticism but out of support. The objective was for each member of the group to contribute to the other members and make them aware of aspects of their lives that could be improved. There were no holds barred and the sessions were very confronting but they were also valuable opportunities to learn, in a supportive environment, how we were seen by others.

One of the members of our group was an astronaut who had been a fighter pilot in the Korean War. He was the last to give his critique, so by the time he got to me, I had already been "critiqued" by six others, and I must admit I had taken quite a beating. When his turn came, he said, "Max, no matter what anybody else says, I would have you as my wing man any day." I never forgot that. I consider it the finest compliment anyone ever paid to me. He was saying that he would put his life in my hands. For me, that was very, very empowering.

So, Harvey was no longer with Shirmax, and I had made a commitment to stop my crusade. However, my problems had not gone away and I still blamed my executive team for all that was wrong with the company. I felt they were inept and ineffective and that they could not help me take the company where I wanted it to go. I had pretty well decided that I had to replace most of them, but, fortunately, before I could take any action, my guardian angel intervened by sending me David Melnik, who prevented me from making that terrible mistake.

The AMA President's Course

MARTIN RICHTER WAS ONE OF THE OWNERS of a major ladies' fashion-buying office in New York. He was also one of my first mentors. I was on a buying trip to the Orient with Martin and, one Sunday afternoon, after a busy week, we were resting by the pool at our hotel in Taiwan and I shared my frustrations with him about how inept I felt we were as a company.

Martin couldn't advise me as to strategies, but he recommended that I attend the President's Course offered by the American Management Association (AMA). He told me that the AMA teaches a management model that is used by most mid- to large-sized organizations around the world. He suggested that if I took the President's Course I would learn that management model and the processes fundamental to managing an organization effectively. I followed his recommendation and enrolled in the course.

The course I attended was given at Pebble Beach Golf Resort in California. It was a very difficult and intimidating experience for me. There were approximately 60 people, all of whom were accomplished executives and business leaders, and then there was me. I felt that, by comparison, I was inadequate and that I had none of the abilities or business acumen the others had. They were professional managers and I was a "babe in the woods." From the course I learned a structured approach to managing and I was given a management model to follow and implement.

David Melnik

David was one of the participants in my course. He was a lawyer and CEO of a trust company in Toronto. I guess that, because I felt so intimidated by the others, and maybe because David resembled my father, I gravitated toward him. From his interactions and contributions in the course, it was clear that David had some very special abilities. He is a very knowledgeable and experienced business executive, skilled in the principles of business organization and management. He is also a genuine people-person who is focused on empowerment. At the time, David was planning to resign from the trust company, and his future plans were still vague. I asked him if he would consider coming to Montreal on a part-time basis to help me with the management of my company.

David came to Montreal and spent several days with us in a series of management meetings. At the end of those sessions, he came to me and said:

"Max, I think you want something from me that I cannot give you. You are asking me to help you run your business. I cannot do that. I am not a retailer. You are much better at your business than I can possibly be, but I see that you need help with your management and leadership skills.

"Your people are not the problem — you are! You are the source of most of the problems here and you are out of your depth trying to manage this group of executives. You need help. You need coaching on empowering your people. You act out of frustration; you are a yeller and a screamer, and you intimidate people. It is amazing that they stay here and work with you.

"If you would like, I will undertake a mandate to be your coach; to help you improve your communication skills, teach you how to behave as a senior executive, and teach you how to empower your people, and to be an effective leader. I can also help you bring structure and organization to your company."

116

I said, "Thank you very much, David, but that's not what I need. You want to fix me, but that is not my priority. I need help running this company and I was hoping you would help me with that. If you can, fine; if not, thank you."

He said, "I'm sorry Max, I cannot help you." And he left and went back to Toronto.

Over the next couple of weeks I was able to absorb all that David had said to me and, fortunately, I realized that everything he had said was true. I went to Toronto, met with David and said, "OK, I accept. We will do it your way."

David worked with me as my coach for two-and-a-half years. Just as he was candid in his evaluation of me, he was equally frank in his ongoing coaching, teaching and training. He watched me with a very critical eye, he didn't mince words and told me "like it was." In many respects my relationship with David mirrored the relationship I had had with my father. As with my father, it seemed I could do nothing right, but I welcomed his critiques and input because I knew what was at stake. I took it all, I absorbed it all. I was like a sponge. It was David who made me see, understand, that I had been the source of the problems we were having. Luckily, I never got around to a wholesale replacement of my executive team. Instead, over time, I learned to work with and empower them to be successful.

After two-and-a-half years of David's intense coaching, I felt I had had enough. I said , "David, it's time for me to fly on my own," and that part of our relationship was over. However, he did stay on as one of my Board of Advisors, which became the Shirmax Board of Directors when we went public in 1986. He remained on our board until the day we sold the company. David had a profound influence on me and to whatever extent I improved over the years, much of the credit certainly goes to him. David and I remain very close friends.

My reference to going public in 1986 brings to mind an incident that occurred several months later and which had its origins, albeit obliquely, in my early school days.

Some time after we went public, I was in a meeting with our auditor, Justin Frye, a senior partner of Coopers & Lybrand, our accounting firm at the time. Justin happened to mention that he was going to Bridgetown, Barbados for a few days to meet with the Managing Partner of Coopers & Lybrand in Barbados, a gentleman by the name of Trehane.

"Trehane?" I asked. "There are many Trehanes in Barbados, what's his first name?"

"Harold," Justin replied.

"Harold Trehane? That's impossible." I said. "Harold Trehane was a boyhood friend of mine. We were both at the bottom of the class when we were in high school and I know he quit school before graduating. I lost touch with him when I left Barbados."

"Interesting" said Justin. "You wouldn't know then that a few years after leaving high school, Harold took a correspondence course in accounting and became a Chartered Accountant. Harold is now a very successful CA and has been the Managing Partner of our firm in Barbados for many years.

"Well, I'll be damned." I said, "Please give him my very best regards when you see him."

So when Justin Frye went to the Island and met with Trehane, he started his conversation with, "One of our clients in Montreal, who is the CEO of a major public fashion retail company, asked me to pass along his best regards to you. His name is Konigsberg."

"Konigsberg? Which Konigsberg?"

"Max Konigsberg."

"That's impossible. Max and I went to school together and we were both very poor students."

"Well," Justin said, "For two students from the bottom of the class, you've both done very well for yourselves."

"Well I'll be damned," Harold said.

And so it was that Harold Trehane came back into my life, and I am happy to say that we have maintained contact ever since. I feel just as happy for his achievements and success as I'm sure he feels about mine.

I tell this story here partly because of the co-incidence of our re-establishing contact but also because when we were boyhood friends, neither of us expected to become very much of anything — let alone "successful."

11

HARVARD

AS PART OF MY CONTINUING EDUCATION, and David Melnik's strategy to shape me into an effective CEO, David recommended that I attend the Owners and Presidents' Management Course (OPM) at Harvard. The OPM course is essentially a high-level, accelerated management program, offered primarily to accomplished business owners and presidents. It is given in three one-month semesters over a three-year period, and requires one month in residence at Harvard for each of the three years.

There were about 140 students in the class. Everyone was virtually hand picked because enrolment is limited to only a few executives from each business and professional category. There were two or three lawyers, two or three accountants, a couple from each of the different manufacturing, financial, investment and retail sectors. As I recall, I was the only person from the retail fashion and manufacturing industry. The class was a very well-rounded community of senior business leaders.

As with the AMA President's Course, most of the participants were experienced business executives. There was a lot of accumulated knowledge in the class. Again, this was another intimidating experience for me. I felt out of my depth and overwhelmed by my classmates. However, I looked on the course as a serious investment both in money and in time. I was there to learn as much as I possibly could and I intended to get my money's worth and maximize my return for the time I was spending away from my home and business.

Much of the course was based on the case method and each day we studied a number of business cases. I kept wondering if I was getting anything out of it. There was so much to read and learn, I felt I could not absorb it all, and that some of it was beyond me. However, after each semester, when I returned to my business and my life at home, I was both surprised and gratified to discover how much I had learned and retained, and was able to apply to my business. There was one particular episode that was especially exciting and memorable.

The Business Game

Toward the end of the second semester, we began to hear occasional references to a business game, a four-day competition at the end of the third and final semester. As I understood it, the purpose of the game was to test our abilities to apply virtually everything we had learned over our three semesters. The game itself was a computerized business model using a complicated business-simulation program involving in-depth analysis and interpretation of massive amounts of information along with extensive background reading. Based on their analyses, teams of four would adopt strategies, make business decisions and input data in the computer for a specific time-frame. All the teams were competing with each other in the same market.

I was totally intimidated by the prospect of having to play the "game" from the first moment I heard of it. My strengths are in buying and selling ladies' clothing. I am a fashion retailer; I am not a mathematical person nor am I a strong reader. Also, I had never even touched a computer! The thought of spending my last four days at Harvard involved in a competitive computer game that was beyond me was terrifying. I was convinced I would not be able to participate effectively in the game and I saw it as a humiliating way for me to end my days at Harvard. I lived through the last one-and-a-half semesters haunted by that spectre and my sense of dread increased exponentially as game day approached.

When competition day came, the class was divided into 35 teams of four. Each team was selected randomly by computer and

In class at Harvard, 1989

was identified by a number only. The names of the participants on each team were not identified so each player knew only what team he/she was on and his/her three teammates but they did not know who was on any of the other teams. I was on team number seven.

I was intimidated, and that was my state of mind when team seven first got together as a group. It was also the state of mind from which I judged myself and my teammates. I knew I was incompetent and I was hoping I would be able to ride inconspicuously on my teammates' coattails. I knew the other members on my team only by having seen them in class and, from what I had observed, it was clear that this was not going to happen.

One team member was a headhunter who I thought looked and spoke like a football player. I saw nothing about him that made me feel confident he would make any contribution, so I wrote him off. Another member was an engineer with a speech impediment and a perpetually disheveled look about him. I could not understand anything he said and, because of the image he presented, I did not want to hear anything he had to say. Another write-off! Our fourth teammate was a mystery man who, as far as I could tell, had paid his tuition just so he could say he had gone to Harvard. He rarely attended class, he stayed out most of the night, and he barely participated in class when he was there. Total write off! And then there was me! We were in trouble right from the get go.

The first thing we had to do as a team was to choose a leader. I wanted to hide out. The last thing I wanted was to be leader of any team, especially this team, in a game that I thought was beyond me. But they chose me as leader anyway, and there I was... .

The game was played using the model of mid-sized companies in the business of manufacturing and selling widgets. All the teams were competing in the same market, and were all given the same information every quarter. That information included all the data such a company would need to plan strategies and make and execute effective decisions. It also included such things as economic trends and projections, size of market, manufacturing costs, labour availability and costs, time frames to manufacture, availability and cost of financing, and much more.

There were also numerous penalties for inefficiencies, such as manufacturing more inventory than could be sold and for excess financing, etc. The business simulation covered a four-year period, (sixteen quarters) with each of our days counting as one year. So, each day we played four quarters.. At the beginning of each quarter we were given our own operating results for the last quarter, the operating results of all the other teams by number, and the updated economic data for the next quarter.

At the beginning of each quarter, based on our operating results to date, the operating results of all the other teams and our projections for the future, we entered our strategies for the next quarter into the computer. Those strategies were then evaluated by the computer and the associated results were generated and published so we all knew how every team was doing at the end of each quarter. We were competing in three categories: highest profit, largest market share, and highest return on equity. And so the game began.

Our team started the first quarter like a performance of The Three Stooges, and I say "three" because our fourth teammate, the mystery man, was not there to participate. I was the leader and I didn't have a clue where to begin. I was not able to get through reading all the information we had to cover, and even at that I did not understand much of the data I did cover. The "football player" started the computer and began typing and talking a blue streak. I was so overwhelmed I could not internalize what he was saying. Meanwhile, our disheveled engineer was talking about some of the background material we had been given, but I couldn't make sense of what he was talking about. We were getting nowhere and time for entering our moves for the first quarter was running out. We had to put something into the computer, so my two teammates collaborated and just entered some moves without any input from me.

Shortly after the deadline for data input, the operating results of the first quarter were posted. Some teams had made as much as $500,000. Others made less, a few broke even, and some lost money. Team seven, my team, lost $500,000 and stood 35th out of 35 teams! The three of us were depressed and visibly upset. We had nothing to say to each other. What could we say? We were looking at a disaster and it seemed there was nothing we could do to make things better.

The second quarter emulated the first and we lost another $350,000. At lunchtime I couldn't stand being with my teammates any longer, so I went to lunch with some friends from the class and complained to them about the situation I was in and that I did not know how I was going to survive another three-and-a-half days of this torture. On my way out of the cafeteria I met my professor and complained to him about our inability to participate in the game. He just dismissed me with, "Max, you'll do OK," and he turned and walked away.

I decided I had had enough and I went back to my room, intending to stay there and hide out all afternoon. In fact, I had decided to stay there for the next three days! I could not continue to subject myself to that much humiliation. While I was in my room I absentmindedly picked up the binder that had been given to all of us when we first arrived, containing profiles of all the people registered in the course. I casually opened it and, as my guardian angel would have it, flipped to the page with the picture and profile of my "football player" teammate. I read his profile and was amazed to learn that as a hobby he developed computer software. So obviously he was some kind of a computer whiz. I then looked at my other teammates' profiles and learned that our disheveled engineer was a distinguished scientist and mathematician with a list of degrees as long as my arm.

I immediately went back to our meeting room and confronted my two teammates with their profiles. I asked the "football player" why he hadn't told me about his abilities with the computer. He said that he had tried to talk to me, but that I wasn't listening. Then I asked our engineer why he hadn't told me of his experience and background. He, too, said he had tried, but that I wouldn't listen.

I was quiet for a while, then I said, "Well, I'm listening now."

I then asked the "football player", "Do you understand how to play this game on the computer?"

"Absolutely."

I then asked the engineer, "Can you absorb and analyze all the information and interpret it for me?"

"For sure."

Then I said, "I don't know how to use the computer and I can't read all the background stuff, but the business of projecting, planning, manufacturing and selling widgets is right up my alley. I've been making decisions like these for years. It's my area of expertise. If you (the engineer) can interpret the data for me, I will call the moves, and if you (the football player) put the moves into the computer, we may be able to turn this thing around."

And suddenly, *we were a team!*

We started our third quarter $850,000 in the red, while some other teams were already over a million dollars in the black. We had also used up much of our strategizing time between the second and third quarters getting our act together, so we had to make some hasty decisions for the third quarter and we were only able to break even in that quarter. For the fourth quarter our engineer was fabulous; he pulled out his slide rule and not only did he interpret the information for me, he also gave me "what if" scenarios so I could understand the implications and dollar potential of our moves. Capitalizing on this support, I developed the strategies and recommended all future moves. In the fourth quarter, we made money. We made even more in the fifth, sixth and seventh quarters, and picked up some ground on the other teams. We continued moving ahead steadily, but by the time we reached the twelfth quarter, we were still far behind the leaders.

On the morning of the last day, I approached my teammates and said to them, "Coming third, or even second, really means nothing. The object of this game is to win. You either come first or you lose. I would like to try to win this game." So, the three of us sat down and worked out what we thought would be a winning strategy.

I knew that in order to close the gap we had to make some very aggressive moves. We could see that the leading teams were being cautious. The economic projections for the next four quarters were very strong and demand could be high, but no one appeared to be building inventory. I believed that the key to achieving maximum results was to *build* inventory and I thought our competitors were going to run out of stock. If I was right, we had to gear up, bring on more staff, buy the necessary raw materials and do it immediately. There was a risk involved, but I knew that without sufficient product we could not achieve the sales levels and returns we needed, so I planned our inventory aggressively to meet the anticipated increased demand.

In the last two quarters, the economy was good, demand was high, we had inventory and our competitors did not. We made our moves, then the game was over. Results were issued for the 14th quarter, but not for the last two quarters. By the end of the day we had no idea what the final result of the game would be.

The next morning the class met in the assembly hall to hear the results of the game. The professors who had designed the game and were responsible for adjudicating the results came into the hall with three bottles of champagne, one for the winning team in each of the three categories. One of the professors announced that, more often than not, a different team won in each category. On rare occasions one team had won in two categories. However, having one team win in all three categories was unprecedented. Then he announced that team number seven had won in all three categories!

No one knew who the players were on team seven, so when the four of us came forward and took all three bottles of champagne, there was silence at first, then there was an explosion of applause and cheers. Later, some of my classmates accused me of setting them up, given my whining and complaining on day one. At dinner that evening we opened all three bottles of champagne and shared it with everyone. We were heroes.

As it turned out, this game was right up my alley. Planning, projecting, manufacturing and selling was what I did, and I had exactly the kind of support I needed for what I could not do.

Given my scholastic background, it was a tremendous accomplishment for me to attend and be a graduate of the Harvard Business School. It was even more meaningful to me to have been part of the team that won that prestigious business game. It was a terrific high for me, and a wonderful way to end my Harvard experience.

I learned some very important things about myself by participating in that business game. I learned that I was inclined to make unwarranted snap assumptions about people. I was too quick to judge. I jumped to conclusions about people without having adequate information and I wrote them off. Also, when I was frustrated, I was not a good listener and I was not approachable. Understanding this forced me to acknowledge that I had to make some fundamental changes in my behaviour and, over time, I was able to change my behaviours and interactions with people, and better able to work with and empower them. I became an effective leader. Most important, I learned the power of "team." Except for our mystery man, every one of us on that team brought something different to the table, and when we put what we had together and all pulled together in the same direction, we were unbeatable. That experience contributed to my becoming passionate about and totally committed to team as being the number one "key success factor" in our organization.

12

CHALLENGING
THE GIANT

In the mid '80s, the Canadian market was virtually saturated for many Canadian retailers. Everyone, including our own company, was under pressure to expand and continue growing. Expanding to the United States seemed to be an obvious option. Although this was also true for other retail sectors in Canada, for the purpose of this discussion I am speaking here only about the retail fashion industry.

Many of us in the industry surmised that the United States represented a large, lucrative market, and we believed we could take the U.S. by storm. So a number of top Canadian fashion retailers, including Shirmax, ventured south. Almost without exception, all of us were terribly beaten up. In one way or another, most of us managed to extricate ourselves from our U.S. adventures after taking a financial bath, and we limped home to our safe Canadian retail environment to hide from the retail sharks south of the border.

In our case we had been studying our would-be American competitors in the maternity business for a long time and, in our arrogance, we were convinced that we were better than they were. So in 1986 we put together an ambitious expansion plan for our maternity division into the U.S. We started with eight stores all at the same time; one in Paramus, NJ, three in the Washington/ Georgetown area, one in Chicago, one in Buffalo, one in Richmond, VA, and one in Boston. We felt we needed to establish a "presence" in the U.S. as quickly as possible and to that end we took pretty well what we could get in terms of store locations.

Because we were from outside the country, the landlords insisted on special guarantees and ten-year leases. Consequently, moving into the U.S. involved a substantial long-term commitment.

We opened our first store in Paramus in June and our second store in Tyson's Corners in Washington in August, two of the top retail malls in the U.S. From the outset we did not know what hit us. It seemed as though we had scored a home run; July, August and September were great months and those two stores immediately became the top two stores in our entire chain! However, in November, December and January, the bottom fell out. Customers flocked to our stores in the first three months but after that it was as if we had become invisible. We never recovered. We could not figure out what had happened; why did we do so well in those two stores in the beginning and why did the bottom fall out after three months?

In the meantime, we opened the other six stores in centres that were not as good as those in Paramus and Tyson's Corners, and none of them ever really took off. Instead of generating profits, the U.S. Division recorded losses. We kept operating there for about three years and that small division became a significant drain on our finances and other resources. So there we were, with an albatross around our neck, expensive leases for another seven or eight years with the prospect of it being a continuous drain for that period. We were looking into a black hole.

Enter my guardian angel!

In 1990, Mike Kershaw, who was president of Shirmax at the time and was touring our U.S. stores, walked into one of our main competitors' stores, a maternity operation called Mothers' Works. By co-incidence, one of their senior executives was visiting that store at the same time. Mike introduced himself and, in the course of the conversation that followed, Mike suggested that they consider buying our U.S. operation. I would not have had the nerve to ask anyone to do that. In fact, I would have been thrilled to pay just to get rid of them, especially in light of our long-term leases. But Mike had more *chutzpah* than I did and before we knew it we had sold our U.S. stores for something in the neighbourhood of $1.5 million. Not only did this stop the hemorrhaging, we recovered some of our accumulated losses and we bowed out gracefully. Thank you guardian angel.

Almost all of the other Canadian fashion retailers who ventured south met with the same fate. Of course, there were questions around our industry. What happened? Why couldn't we compete? What was missing? After my own adventure, I spent a lot of time trying to figure out just what caused this result. Why could we not compete? Eventually, I came up with what I believe is the answer.

The fundamental reason was that we Canadian retailers were what I call "hope" retailers. By that I mean we put beautiful merchandise into beautiful stores and "hoped" it would sell. However, the American retailers, our competitors, were and are what I call "push" retailers. They put beautiful merchandise into beautiful stores and then they push the hell out of it — promotion after promotion after promotion — until they push it out of their stores. The key to their strategy is that their promotions are not just about clearing out merchandise. They plan and buy into their promotions. They buy with the appropriate margins to be able to promote and still be profitable. On the other hand, we put beautiful merchandise into beautiful stores and presented it beautifully, and we did very well at the beginning of the season. But when the American retailers started promoting, we did not promote. We maintained the integrity of our merchandise and our stores. Meanwhile, the customers were being attracted elsewhere by promotions.

The fact is we were not nearly as good retailers as we thought we were, and the U.S. retailers were far better than we gave them credit for. They were accustomed to dealing with intense competition and they knew how to survive and prosper in a retail jungle. Also, they had the experience of two and three generations of retailing, and the size and the economies of scale that made it no contest. We were much smaller and we had no comparable experience.

In comparison, we were like babes in the woods. We had been successful in our own "safe" Canadian retail environment, but we could not compete in the U.S. market, and we came back to Canada to hide. However, as things turned out there was nowhere to hide, because the U.S. retailers followed us home.

In the 1990s there was a huge influx of U.S. retailers into the Canadian retail market, but they did not meet the same fate as we did going into their market. Instead, they brought their strategies to Canada and they now dominate the Canadian retail landscape. Canadian retailers no longer have a place to hide.

In the last decade there has been a bloodbath among Canadian retailers. Canadian retail giants such as Woodwards, Eaton's, Simpson's, Dylex (with all its divisions), the original Dalmy's, Penningtons, and Pascal Hardware, to name just a few, are all gone. Those who survived had to learn, and learn fast, how to compete with the retail sharks from south of the border and had to raise dramatically their level of retailing savvy and sophistication.

As a result, the disparity between U.S. and Canadian retailers no longer exists to the same extent. Most Canadian retailers that survived and went on to prosper are now acknowledged as outstanding retailers. But I still wonder about their ability to compete successfully in the United States.

Only time will tell.

13

FROM SUCCESS
TO FAILURE

THE YEARS FROM 1981 TO 1986 WERE GOOD YEARS for Shirmax. The economy was doing well and we were learning more and more about the art of merchandising and retailing. We were doing a better job at managing our affairs, we were expanding, building the company's infrastructure and getting a handle on logistics. We were profitable and achieving a certain amount of success. The prospects for the future looked very good. We were feeling cocky and very sure of ourselves. My friend and mentor, David Melnik, taught me that "Nothing too good or too bad lasts for too long." In reality, this turned out to be a bitter truth for Shirmax.

There is a maxim:

Failure often leads to success, but success always leads to failure.

Success leads to failure because success leads to arrogance. With success, we start to believe we can do no wrong, we believe our own press, and we do not take action to make things better. On the grounds that "if it ain't broke, don't fix it", we are content to leave well enough alone. Change is one of the main criteria for success in business, but when we are blinded by success and cannot see the need for change, that is a recipe for failure. Therefore, "success always leads to failure."

The following is a preamble to what was to become the biggest downward spiral in Shirmax's history. When the Quebec Stock Savings Plan (QSSP) was introduced in 1984, because we had had a few successful years and had been profitable, we had the opportunity to take the company public. Under the plan, anyone who invested in a QSSP company was eligible for a tax credit. Investors were paying handsomely for shares in QSSP companies, and the companies that went public under the QSSP enjoyed a very high price-to-earnings ratio.

We decided to take advantage of the opportunity to go public and inject funds into the company. Our plan was for the company to issue two million shares to the public at $5 a share with a total value of $10 million, and eight million shares to me, personally, with a value of $40 million.

Comark, is a division of a large multinational organization that owned a number of retail operations in Canada. They heard that we were considering going public and they approached me directly to ask if, instead of going public, I would consider selling the company to them. Comark put forward a hypothetical number of $40 million, together with a management contract for me to run the Canadian operation for them. This meant I would have $40 million, but I would no longer own the company.

For me, that was a watershed moment. It was a great opportunity, especially considering that I would have had the money with no more risk. I wrestled with Comark's proposal for only 24 hours, then I called them and said, "Thank you very much for your interest, but no thank you." I made the decision not to sell because I loved what I was doing. There was still much I wanted to do. I still had mountains to climb. Besides, I was not captivated by the money. Shirley and I live modestly, and we had enough. We had no desire to cash out and change our lifestyle, and that was the end of that!

Little did I know at the time that we would be heading into very rough waters and I would have to wait for more than twenty years to see Shirmax at that level of value again. But, regardless of what we went through in the following years, I never regretted that decision. Instead of accepting Comark's offer, we went public and raised $10 million for the express purpose of expansion.

So, we were doing well and the future looked rosy, but we did not understand that retailing was in for a huge change and that our business concepts were not keeping pace but were growing stale. We did not understand that what had worked successfully in the '70s and '80s would not work in the more difficult economy of the '90s and the realities of the coming millennium. We could not see what was coming because we were blindsided by our past success.

We made our decision to go public and expand rapidly when the economy was at its peak, just before Canada fell into the worst recession since the Great Depression. The failing economy, coupled with our tired business concepts, started the company on a downward spiral. It was in this business environment that I had an eye-opening experience with two young people in the organization. That experience taught me a profound lesson that led to a major change in the Shirmax culture and supported our future growth and development.

King of Maternity

By 1985 we had built a very solid business called Shirley K Maternity. We had about 75 stores: we were doing well, the business was profitable and was producing an excellent cash flow. At the time, Shirley K was the cash cow that provided us with the wherewithal to start the new business in plus sizes.

Now, I must provide some background here.

The maternity business is inherently a small business. Only one per cent of the female population is pregnant at any one time, so there is a finite customer base. Individual Mom-and-Pop maternity stores have been around for generations, but the people who ran them barely made a living. Until the '70s, no one had ever built a successful maternity chain anywhere in the world. Then we came along and built a national chain in Canada that performed very well and generated high dollar revenues per square foot.

Unquestionably, we were the premier retailer of maternity clothing in the world at that time. I styled the garments, put together the lines and manufactured them. In fact, I was the expert in how to design and fit a maternity garment. I knew what would sell and what would not and I created the retail organization to sell them. No one else in the world had as comprehensive a background and understanding of the maternity fashion business. I was the guru; I was the king of maternity. Then, in the late '80s, our business began to falter.

After considering every reason we could think of as to why we were not doing well, and not being able to justify any of them, I took our buying team to the United States and Europe on a special research mission to try to figure out why we were failing. We thought we found the answers and so we developed a new plan to revive our maternity operation. Our plan was to build on our established foundation. We felt sure that our styling and fit were appropriate for the maternity customer, so we thought all we had to do was improve on what we already had. We built bigger stores, offering more customer services as well as personal comforts to our clientele, and created better and more attractive presentations of the merchandise.

Our approach was to add value and inject a new excitement, but our formula was essentially more of the same, only bigger and better. We had addressed everything we could think of but it did not make any difference. The business continued to decline and I was at a loss as to why or what to do about it. After awhile, I found myself justifying "big time"; I blamed the economy, a shrinking customer base, and changing customer values. I even blamed the weather. I had all sorts of excuses to try to justify why my business was faltering. I could not see the truth, but my son and nephew could.

Thyme Maternity

My son Philip graduated from high school when he was 17 and came to work at Shirmax for a couple of years before he went off to study at the New York Fashion Institute. He came back to the company three years later. Meanwhile, my nephew, Howard Feinberg, had gone to the Business School at the University of Western Ontario. When he graduated, he came back to Montreal and he, too, came to work with us. Philip and Howard were more than cousins and close friends; they were like brothers. They were born only six weeks apart, they grew up together, went to school together, and went to camp together. They even celebrated their Bar Mitzvahs together. They were inseparable friends and were very supportive of each other.

When Philip and Howard began working together at Shirmax, they started to give me a hard time about our maternity business. They saw that it was eroding and they began telling me what was wrong with the business. How dare these two know-it-all smart alecs, only 22 years old and with no experience, tell me, The King of Maternity, what was wrong with my business! After putting up with their "abuse" for awhile, I decided to teach them a lesson. Since they were my son and nephew, I figured it was worth the investment to put a lid on their arrogance. I told them I would allocate sufficient funds for them to open five new maternity stores and compete with me. I promised not to interfere.

I provided them with office space, gave them access to the company's infrastructure as well as whatever resources and support they needed. Howard was responsible for creating product, marketing and sales; Philip was responsible for the mechanics of the operation, planning, distribution, allocation, etc. They took two other young people from inside the company to join their team. After a short brainstorming period, they came up with their vision, and a plan, for a new maternity chain. I did not agree with the name they chose, (Thyme Maternity), the store design, the fit and style of the clothing or, in fact, anything they did. But I did not interfere. I knew they were on the wrong track and I was convinced that my experiment was going to be a very brief affair.

Howard and Philip opened their first store in the Place Vertu Shopping Mall in Montreal, which was not a top-of-the-line mall.

Howard and Philip
The two Caballeros, 1960

Philip and Howard , again
at their joint Bar Mitzvahs, 1973

Within a couple of weeks of their opening, word got around and customers from all over the city flocked to that store. With every new store, the same thing happened. Customers flocked to them and business in the five Shirley K Maternity stores in Montreal began to nose-dive. The rest is history. The new Thyme stores went on to be very successful and produced among the highest revenue per square foot of all fashion retailers in the shopping centres.

The Thyme Maternity fashion concept was entirely new and was fundamentally different from the Shirley K fashion concept, and therein lay my problem. At Shirley K, the strategy was to hide the pregnancy, and therefore Shirley K clothes were large and loose, designed to camouflage the pregnancy. On the other hand, Thyme's strategy was to celebrate pregnancy; their concept was to show off the pregnancy. They made clothes with a totally different fit, clothes that molded the body and showed the belly. Also, because of Shirley K's success over the years, its merchandise kept moving up into higher price brackets and we eventually found ourselves at the top end of the market, both in terms of price and age of the customer. Shirley K was targeting women in their late twenties and early thirties whereas Thyme came right down into the middle of the market both in age and price, catering to younger customers. It was no contest. Thyme caught on like wildfire.

My approach to dealing with the declining business was out of step with the times. On the other hand, the Thyme concept was exactly what the customers wanted. Eventually, I had to concede that Howard and Philip were right and that I, the King, was wrong. I intended to teach them a lesson, but instead they taught me one. The King was dethroned! Together, we decided to close the Shirley K division and simply move all of our maternity business over to Thyme. Howard took charge of that operation and continued with Shirmax as Vice-President in charge of the Thyme Division. Philip moved on to develop both an Internet business and an international licensing business for the maternity line. They both remained with Shirmax until the company was sold in 2002.

Considering how everything worked out in the end, it was a stroke of luck that I did not shut the door on Howard and Philip. Fortunately, I gave them the opportunity to prove me wrong.

My approach to dealing with the declining business was out of step with the times. On the other hand, the Thyme concept was exactly what the customers wanted. Eventually, I had to concede that Howard and Philip were right and that I, the King, was wrong. I intended to teach them a lesson, but instead they taught me one. The King was dethroned! Together, we decided to close the Shirley K division and simply move all of our maternity business over to Thyme. Howard took charge of that operation and continued with Shirmax as Vice-President in charge of the Thyme Division. Philip moved on to develop both an Internet business and an international licensing business for the maternity line. They both remained with Shirmax until the company was sold in 2002.

Considering how everything worked out in the end, it was a stroke of luck that I did not shut the door on Howard and Philip. Fortunately, I gave them the opportunity to prove me wrong.

I learned several lessons from that experience.

I learned what it can cost a company when one's mind is closed; it can cost you everything.

I learned that when you do not allow your people to blossom, the lost-opportunity cost can be enormous.

I learned that young people — in fact, most people — have a tremendous amount to offer and it is essential that they be given the room and the opportunity to run with their ideas.

I learned that focusing on "bigger, more and better" is not always the answer. In fact, it can be a very dangerous trap!

And I learned to listen and to try to hear what people were saying to me.

All of the lessons I learned from this and other similar experiences were the catalyst for the programs I developed and delivered in the company.

STORM WARNINGS

IN THE LATE '80S, AT THE TOP OF THE ECONOMIC CYCLE and the peak of the rental market, we leased 40 new stores as part of our expansion program. Accordingly, we paid top rental rates. We did not see a recession coming; or, rather, we did not see it coming soon enough. So, the recession had started by the time we opened those 40 stores. Up to that time all regional malls in this country had opened with at least 90 per cent occupancy.

When the recession hit, retailers put a halt to their expansion. But we were early birds and had already committed to leases, so we opened most of our new stores in malls that were only partially leased. The malls for which we had paid top dollar turned out to be inferior, and the stores never got off the ground. And, because of the ever-deepening recession, consumers disappeared, our profitability declined, and we started losing money — more and more, year after year — for the next five years.

By 1991, I began to see that the businesses that would survive through the recession would be those that presented new and fresh concepts, that captured the imaginations of newly aware, demanding and value-conscious consumers. Our old, tired retail concepts did not meet those criteria. So we started the process of reinventing our two businesses. By the summer of 1993 we had developed and opened new prototype stores for both the maternity and plus-size divisions. These prototype stores would have to be rolled out across the country to replace our existing small, old and outdated stores. Tremendous capital was required to do this; capital that, given our accumulated losses, we did not have.

Shirmax as a Manufacturer

Another major challenge we had to deal with was our manufacturing division. When we started to expand the maternity business in the early '70s, we had a vision of the type of merchandise it would take to create an outstanding maternity chain. Until then, all our product was coming from the U.S. and was expensive, very "middle America," and not very fashionable. And it was inconsistent with my vision. So we began to experiment with some manufacturing in the back of one of our stores. We started with one man cutting a few pairs of maternity pants that we then gave to contractors to be sewn. We put those pants into a couple of our stores...and they sold. Then we brought in a few machines, hired some ladies to sew, and started making some tops. I watched what regular fashion leaders were doing and I converted those styles into maternity garments. Compared to the U.S. product, our prices were better, our styling was better, and whatever we put into the stores sold. We kept making more and more of our own merchandise and it was not long before we needed more space and we expanded into new premises.

I knew nothing about manufacturing, so I hired a friend, Nat Cohen, to develop Shirmax as a manufacturer. Nat had owned his own manufacturing company so he brought a great deal of experience when he joined us. Before that, we were just a Mickey Mouse operation. It was Nat who built our first real factory and who set us up as a manufacturer. Once we had our own facility, we stopped buying in the U.S. and started designing and making all of our own maternity clothes. Nat was with us for a couple of years and then things kind of grew beyond him because, even though he had been a manufacturer, his interest was in product development, not in machines and production. So he left us and went back into business for himself. We were very lucky with our next hire, Frank Solerno, who was a true nuts-and-bolts manufacturer. He knew how to run an effective shop and how to manufacture the product from beginning to end. He knew his business, he ran a very tight ship and he did a great job for us.

In the meantime, we had expanded beyond the maternity business and had started our Addition-Elle division. Again, we could not find the product we really wanted for this new division from outside suppliers. At the time everything made for plus-size women was called half-sizes, and was styled for older customers. As with our maternity division, our vision was for more youthful looking and much more fashionable designs for plus-size women, so we started styling and manufacturing our own merchandise for the Addition-Elle division as well.

The manufacturing arm of the company grew to become a very substantial part of our business and, as I said earlier, having no background in manufacturing, I relied heavily on Frank Salerno, our Vice-President of Manufacturing, who ran the division.

As our business grew, so did the manufacturing arm. We were operating in three different locations and we needed more space to streamline and improve our operations. At the same time, our head office and warehouse had both become much too small. It was time for more space.

The Shirmax Building

In 1985 we bought a parcel of land on Jarry Street in Montreal and designed and built a 180,000-square-foot facility — the Shirmax building — at a cost of $12 million.

It was never our intention to have the company own the Shirmax building and have it saddled with that kind of debt, so we built it with the intention of selling it and leasing it back. At one stage, I wanted to own the building personally and lease it back to Shirmax. I was enamored with the beautiful piece of real estate and thought it would be an annuity for me personally since I would have a guaranteed tenant. However, I had a major battle over this issue with my brother, Alex. As a member of the Shirmax Board, Alex was vehemently opposed to my owning the building because he saw it as a conflict of interest, especially as we were a public company. Alex won out and we sold the building to a third party.

Once again, my guardian angel was looking out for me because, had I owned that building when we filed for protection in

1993, I would not be writing this book now. We would never have survived because the additional debt we would have been carrying on the building would have pulled us down.

In addition to his responsibility for the manufacturing division, Frank Salerno took on the responsibility of overseeing the construction and set-up of the new facility, which included a beautiful head office, a state-of-the-art distribution center, and a leading-edge manufacturing operation. Frank did a great job. He was an outstanding member of our executive team and he made a major contribution to the growth of the company. Frank and I developed a special bond, and we had a great relationship.

Having our own manufacturing facility gave Shirmax a huge strategic advantage. It helped us build our businesses when the kind of product we needed was not available to us in any other way, and it continued to be a strategic advantage for a number of years. Then, in the late '80s, it became a strategic disadvantage.

The manufacturing plant was set up to cater to all of our needs as a retailer, making slacks and jeans, skirts, blouses, T-shirts, dresses, jackets, etc. It was a multi-purpose plant. However, a multi-purpose plant cannot be as cost-effective as a plant that is set up specifically to manufacture hundreds of thousands, or even millions of a specific commodity each year. When we were smaller we could not buy from outside suppliers because it did not pay them to make small quantities. But as we grew, the numbers of units per style that we needed were large enough to make it viable for us to purchase from outside suppliers. So as time passed, we found we were able to buy better and cheaper from outside suppliers than from our own plant.

The objective of any manufacturing plant is be as efficient as possible. The plant must be fed so it maximizes its capacity, otherwise costs will become prohibitive. In order to feed our plant, we were forced to order what the plant could make rather than what we needed for our stores. As a result, we ended up paying more attention to the needs of the plant than the needs of our customers, and that began to hurt our retail operations. Also, when we were buying everything from our own plant we were the only source of styling and creativity. However, by sourcing from a wide range of suppliers, we were able to tap into their creativity and styling, which made our offerings to our customers much more diverse and appealing. Once we became large enough to outsource, our manufacturing facility was no longer competitive or viable, and it became a liability.

All of these issues around our manufacturing operation contributed to the downward spiral that we began to experience in our business. When there were signs that Shirmax was getting into serious financial difficulties, we started downsizing and restructuring. One of the first things we did was to close the manufacturing operation in the spring of 1993.

The Truth

There is a concept very dear to my heart, which has to do with telling the truth. I deal with "the truth" in detail in Part Two, but it is worth mentioning here because it is relevant to our manufacturing experience.

I assert that it is often difficult for all of us to be objective and to see and tell ourselves the truth about those things nearest and dearest to our hearts. We have no difficulty seeing the truth about how well something is or is not working when someone else has created it or is responsible for it. However, we often have great difficulty seeing and telling ourselves the truth about those things that *we* have created, are *responsible* for, in love with, committed to, or passionate about. I also assert that the implications and costs of *not* telling ourselves the truth can be enormous.

We had invested a lot of effort and money into developing the manufacturing division. It was a "class act" and I was very proud of it. However, at a point, it started to become obsolete for our purposes. But, just as with the faltering Shirley K division, I could not bring myself to acknowledge the truth about our precious manufacturing division, and we kept struggling to make the plant more efficient. To make matters worse, we forced our buyers to buy from our own plant rather than from other sources where they could have acquired better or equal products at better prices. That simply compounded our problems.

We could not acknowledge the truth about what was happening to our manufacturing division. Continuing to support that division had a serious effect on our retail operations and this, too, contributed to our downward spiral. The truth was right in front of our noses, but we could not see it. We suffered for nearly four years before we finally saw and acknowledged the truth. At that point, we finally shut down the manufacturing division, took our losses and moved on. But it was all too little, too late!

THE NIGHTMARE

IN OCTOBER 1993, AFTER FIVE YEARS OF LOSSES, our financial viability was questioned by one of our biggest creditors, a factoring company that financed many of our suppliers' accounts receivable. That company put a "stop credit" on Shirmax, which started a domino effect with other suppliers and, overnight, our credit evaporated. Then our bank withdrew its support and the unthinkable happened — we were forced to file for bankruptcy protection. Here began the worst and most unbelievable nightmare of my entire career.

In hindsight, it should have come as no surprise that we got into financial difficulty. As I mentioned earlier, when we raised $10 million for expansion in 1986, we used that money to bring 40 new stores on line at the top of the economic cycle. That proved to be an enormous drain. The timing also coincided with our retail concepts becoming obsolete and our manufacturing operation becoming a liability. All of these factors contributed to our losing money.

In the early spring of 1993 alarm bells began to go off, and James Landry raised the possibility of having to file for court protection. I did not want to consider that possibility because I was sure we would be able to pull everything together by Christmas. At some point, however, I agreed to have a meeting with our lawyers, accountants and senior staff to discuss possible strategies and look at some "what if" scenarios. When the subject of filing for court protection was put on the table, Brahm Gelfand, one of our law firm's senior partners and a close friend of my brother, was very disturbed by what was happening at Shirmax. He suggested that he might have a buyer who could be persuaded to pay $5 million for Shirmax. He urged me to consider the possibility of selling but I said:

"No, Brahm, I'm not interested. I believe we are going to pull through this without going into court protection. However, if by some chance Shirmax fails, I could live with myself if I knew I had done everything in my power to try to save it. And even if I could not save it and I lost everything, at least I would feel that I had given it everything I had. If I sold out today at $5 million, it would nag me to my grave that I had chickened out when the going got rough."

Brahm, who had a keen interest in our family's well-being, was visibly frustrated with me and he became very angry.

"Max", he said, "you are irresponsible. You have always been irresponsible because for all the years you've been in business you have never taken any money out of the business to protect yourself and your family. And now, when the ship is probably going down and you may have an opportunity — maybe — to come out of this mess with something for yourself and your family, you are saying 'No'.

"You don't seem to understand that if you have to file for protection, there's no way you can survive. Do you have any money of your own to reinvest in the company? No, you don't. Do you have anybody who is willing to put up money if you file? No, you don't. There's no way you're going to survive if you file for protection. I don't want to deal with you any more."

And he got up and left the room. You see, Brahm knew what I didn't know. He had the experience; I did not. He knew that if we got to the point of having to file for court protection, we could not survive. Fortunately, I did not understand that, because if I had, I would probably have thrown in the towel. Considering the way things turned out, I have, from time to time, been tempted to raise the subject with Brahm and brag about my decision to reject his offer, but I have never done so because I know that, at the time, he was absolutely right. It just so happened that I took the longest of all long shots and I hit a bull's eye.

What Brahm said was true. I had never taken any money out of the business and I did not have any money to reinvest in the company. The fact is, I just didn't have any money — either up to, or at that time. That calls for an explanation.

It requires enormous capital to build a retail fashion chain. In order to keep growing, I reinvested every available dollar I had back into the company over the years. Shirley and I had a very modest life style, so we did not need much. I took a salary that was not commensurate with being the CEO of a public company; I took only enough to meet our needs. In fact, for the five years that our business was downward spiraling, I reduced my salary to the point where it covered only our essential needs. And I had no savings. As a result, I had no money when the factor moved to stop credit on Shirmax in October.

The news that Shirmax had filed for court protection sent shock waves throughout the industry. I was devastated. I had been in denial, and then the whole world came crashing in on me. I never believed it would come to that. I was in shock for days. The future of Shirmax, my own welfare and that of my family, as well as the welfare of thousands of people — employees, suppliers and investors — would hang in the balance for several months.

Every large business operates on credit, and the business grows and expands based on the availability of its credit. In good times, a sound business has unlimited credit available to it and everyone is anxious to ship whatever the company wants on flexible, reasonable terms. But once you go into court protection, your credit totally dries up. One day we were running a $100 million business and had unlimited credit and bank support, but the next day, while we still had to run a $100 million business, we suddenly had no money, no access to money, no merchandise supply — and zero credit! No one was willing to ship us anything unless we paid for it up front. Actually, most people didn't even want to talk to us any more.

Even if a supplier felt inclined to support us and we promised to pay C.O.D., the supplier had to take the additional risk of making product for us with the real possibility that we would not be in business when he was ready to deliver the goods. So, along with no money, no bank support and no credit, we couldn't get product. And to add to our grief, head hunters came out in force, looking to hire our staff and if we lost very many of them we could not, under any circumstances, keep the business running effectively and it would surely die. So, given these dynamics, it is virtually impossible for a business to survive, let alone prosper, after going into court protection.

To my knowledge, in the retail fashion industry in Canada, no company has ever survived and prospered in the long term after filing for court protection without an influx of new money from the original owners or from outside investors. In those cases where new money was injected by outside investors, the original owners lost control as well as ownership. However, fate — or my guardian angel — put a host of miracles into play on our behalf.

14

THIRTEEN MIRACLES

THERE ARE SOME WHO MAY QUESTION my use of the term "miracles" here, but in light of the extraordinary circumstances that unfolded as we lived through the ordeal of bankruptcy protection, I choose to call them miracles.

When we went into court protection, the odds were that Shirmax would not survive because I had no money to inject into the business and there was no white knight or outside investor to bail us out. In order to survive, a series of miracles had to happen. If any one of them had not happened, or had not happened at the right time, we *would* have gone into bankruptcy. But they *did* happen and all of them happened when they needed to happen. From my perspective, the moon and the stars aligned in our favour and every one of those "happenings" was an individual miracle.

To a large extent, the miracles happened because Shirmax had a strong foundation of good will and a solid reputation as a fair and honourable organization. We also had excellent relationships with our employees, landlords and suppliers. As things turned out, many of them were willing to go to great lengths and take substantial risks to support us and help us survive. No one wanted to see us go down, but there was a lot of turmoil amongst our creditors.

CREDITORS

I WAS NOT THE ONLY ONE WHO WAS DEVASTATED by our being forced into bankruptcy protection. All of our suppliers were faced with the prospect of not being paid and, for some of them, that was crucial to their survival.

Phil Cohen

Phil Cohen had been in the garment industry forever. As I recall, he had retired but he and his wife had recently come back into business to help their two sons start a new company. We had recently hired a new buyer, Lisa Miller, who had done business with the Cohens in her previous job. After she joined Shirmax, she placed a large order (about $400,000) with their company. Up until then our credit rating had been excellent and we had a reputation for always paying our bills. So, as far as the Cohens knew, our credit rating was absolutely fine. Their full order was delivered the day before the axe fell.

The day after the news broke, Mr. Cohen came to see me. He was visibly distressed, and asked, "How could this happen? My wife and I and our two boys are working very hard trying to make this business work. We don't have $400,000 to lose. I do not know how we are going to survive. This could put us out of business and throw my boys out on the street. How could this happen?"

The truth is, there wasn't much I could say. I was in shock myself. Somehow, despite the circumstances, he believed me when I told him that this turn of events was totally unexpected and that I was as distressed as he was. Although Phil and I had never met before, we somehow connected amidst all the turmoil and he decided to try to help me. He became my ally and a true supporter. In fact, he made sure that he got himself onto the Creditors' Committee so that he could support me. I will always be grateful to Phil Cohen for his support.

After we came out of protection and were credit-worthy again, I made sure to direct as much business as I could to the Cohens, as I did with most of the suppliers who had been hurt as a result of our difficulties. I am pleased to say that Mr. Cohen and his sons not only survived that episode but also went on to become a thriving business.

CAMA

CAMA was a specialty store construction company owned by three brothers who had just started their business. They did beautiful work and their prices were very competitive. We were one of their first customers. W had given them a contract to build six stores to launch the new concepts we had developed for Thyme Maternity and Addition-Elle. We owed CAMA $800,000 when we went into protection. That was an enormous amount of money for a new company. They, too, knew us as a high-profile, credit-worthy company and had not asked us for a deposit before they started the project so they had not received any payment for their work.

When the axe fell, two of the brothers came to see me. They were very upset and they did not know how they would survive such a loss. I could do nothing more than sit with them and listen, and try to explain what had happened. I tried to assure them that there was never any intention to hurt them, and I guess I convinced them because again, like Mr. Cohen, they gave me their support. As soon as we started building again, I gave them all of our construction work which, in some measure, helped them to become one of the top store-construction companies in the country.

Another Supporter

A third example of support came from a supplier who will remain anonymous, but when he reads this he will know I am referring to him. I would like him to know how much I appreciated his support. He had been one of my suppliers from almost the first day I went into business, and I owed him around $500,000. On the fateful day we filed for protection, he called me and said, "Max you are going to have to make an offer to your creditors and they're going to press you to make as high an offer as they can persuade you to make. If there is any hope for you to survive this, you need to resist them and make an offer that will give you a chance to survive." Even though that advice would cost him, I guess he was convinced that I had acted with integrity and he wanted to see me survive.

These are just a few examples of the many suppliers who gave us their support at that most difficult time. There were, however, many other negative cases, too, where creditors were very angry and upset with me. Under the circumstances, I certainly understand how they felt.

THE MIRACLES

Miracle No. 1 — Amendments to the Canadian Bankruptcy Act

In the late fall of 1992, the Canadian economy was in a major recession. Many companies across Canada were going bankrupt and, in an effort to help them survive, the federal government changed the Canadian *Bankruptcy Act* to make it possible for a company to cancel a lease by paying six months' rent as a penalty. Although we didn't know it at the time, this new legislation would give us a bargaining chip with our landlords. Had that legislation not come into effect when it did, the outcome of our negotiations with our landlords would have been very different. We would probably not have received their support and they would not have made the concessions they eventually did. That legislation was our first miracle in the making and it turned out to be crucial to our survival.

Miracle No. 2 — A Bad Strategy turns Good

In an effort to minimize our losses when our business was spiraling downward, we kept reducing our inventories. However, we eventually got to the point at which our reduced inventories were contributing to the downward spiral. So, for the 1993 fall and holiday seasons, in a desperate attempt to stop the downward spiral, we decided to increase our inventories dramatically so we could offer better and different assortments to our customers. Also, we had experimented with expensive, brand-name merchandise in a few stores and it had sold well. But we made a serious mistake in thinking that we could sell that merchandise in all of our stores, and we bought lots of it. As it turned out, we could not change our customers' buying habits in one season. That expensive brand-name merchandise was not saleable to the mass market and the merchandise backed up on us. All of this excess inventory became the proverbial straw that broke the camel's back.

On the down side, buying all that merchandise used up our credit completely and precipitated the stop-credit on our account issued by the factors. However, on the up side, after we had filed for protection and could not get any new product, having all of that merchandise on hand meant we had product to sell and turn into cash, and that gave us the cash flow we needed to keep us afloat until we could start buying again. So, the miracle here was that our bad strategy actually helped to save us.

Miracle No. 3 — Jacques Rossignol

Several months before we had to file for protection, James Landry had dragged me, very reluctantly, to get some advice from a bankruptcy trustee. I was reluctant because I was convinced that such advice was unnecessary and that the Christmas season would turn things around for us. But James was worried and he insisted we have the meeting. He also felt it was important that we speak to a trustee who was outside the industry, someone who had no ties to any of our creditors and therefore had no conflict of interest.

On the day we had to file for protection, James and the trustee had to get some documents signed by our lawyers before going to the courthouse. Our lawyers were the firm of Lapointe Rosenstein, of which my brother, Alex, was a founding partner. While they were at the office, quite by accident, they ran into Jacques Rossignol, the firm's bankruptcy lawyer, who asked James what they were doing there. James told him they were on their way to court to file for protection. Jacques then cautioned James that the trustee who was with him did not have the clout to take on the fashion industry and that it would be suicide for Shirmax to file without first informing and consulting with the bank and finding a trustee with whom the bank would be comfortable. James took

Jacques' advice and immediately terminated our arrangement with the trustee. Jacques took over the case on the spot and went to court with James to file for bankruptcy protection.

In retrospect, there is absolutely no doubt that if we had gone with our original trustee we would never have got to first base with our creditors and the bank. He did not have the stature we needed. The creditors would have steamrolled over him and the bank would have closed our account. Jacques Rossignol, on the other hand, was very well-known to our creditors as a tough negotiator and a force to be reckoned with. He was just the person we needed to represent us. So, James Landry's chance meeting with Jacques Rossignol at a critical moment, Jacques' intervention, and his decision to take over was indeed a miracle. I can't imagine that we would have survived without him handling our case.

Miracle No. 4 — Credibility with the Landlords

After studying our financial situation, Jacques came to me and said, "Max, you cannot save this company without putting some money back into it. You have to put $4 million into the business. We need that much to sustain our cash flow."

I said, "Jacques, I have no money to put in. I have two homes and a few small investments, but that's all. They don't add up to nearly enough."

He then told me we couldn't even get started without the $4 million. A short time later, he came back to me and said, "Since you don't have the money, we'll have to go to the landlords and get considerations from them that are equivalent to $4 million."

"Jacques, that's impossible" I said, "I cannot get any help from the landlords. I have been asking them for rent relief for months but they won't even consider it." He replied, "Max, we have no other alternative. We just have to get $4 million from them."

Now, let me step back for a moment. In early September, just before this crisis, we were having a cash-flow problem and I had written to our landlords, telling them of our difficulties. I asked them to allow us to defer payment on our October rents to October 20th and our November rents until November 15th. I promised we would catch up in December. They all agreed. By the end of September, our cash flow turned out to be better than anticipated, so we sent out our October rent cheques on October 1st — on time — even though we had the landlords' permission to delay until the 20th.

The cheques were accompanied by a covering letter from me, thanking them for their consideration and explaining that the crunch hadn't come as early as expected and confirming that our November rent cheques would be sent on November 15th as agreed. Anyone who knows in advance that they are going into bankruptcy protection would want to protect their cash position to help them later. They certainly would not pay anything they didn't have to pay. By paying October's rent on time, instead of taking advantage of the agreed-upon deferral, we established a huge amount of credibility with our landlords. It was a clear signal that our filing for protection was not planned and that I was caught as much off guard as they were.

The miracle was that, by deciding to pay October's rent on time, we gained the trust and goodwill of the landlords, and that contributed to getting them onside when we needed them.

Miracle No. 5 — Negotiating with the Landlords

Meanwhile, at Jacques Rossignol's insistence, we prepared a plan to take to the landlords to try to get the $4 million we needed in rent relief and other considerations. Our plan included a moratorium on all rents for three months, a number of store closures without penalty and some permanent rent reductions. We knew exactly what we needed from each landlord. Jacques and I first went to see two small landlords with whom we had only a few stores. We outlined our plan to restructure Shirmax and told them what we needed in terms of support from each of them. They both told us they would get back to us, and a few days later both called to tell us they would accept our plan on condition that the landlords who held leases on no fewer than 80 per cent of our stores agreed to the plan as well.

We said, "Thank you very much. We appreciate your consideration."

We then went to Toronto to see Cambridge and TriLea, two of our three biggest landlords. We left Cadillac Fairview, our biggest landlord, and the one with whom we had the best relations and who we thought would give use the most support, for the last. Seymour Obront, our real estate broker and a dear friend, who represented us in finding locations and negotiating leases, joined Jacques and me in our meetings with the landlords. Seymour gave us great support. We met first with Cambridge and then with TriLea and presented our plan.

We got the same response from both of them, which was, "We'll consider it and let you know." We heard from both of them within a couple of days with virtually the same responses as those we had received from the two smaller landlords: "We are prepared to accept your plan, but only on the condition that the landlords of no fewer than 80 per cent of your stores accept the same plan." It was difficult to believe the same response from all of them was mere coincidence. Anyhow, after receiving those four responses we felt elated and optimistic that we would get the help we needed from our landlords. However, our optimism was short-lived.

Cadillac Fairview, the landlord that held leases on 40 per cent of our stores, had recently appointed a new CEO whom I did not know. Rossignol, Obront and I met with him and Cadillac's Chief Financial Officer, Peter Sharp, in Toronto.

We presented our case, they listened, and when we were finished, the CEO said, "Sure, we can support you, but we want shares in the company to compensate us for our shortfall." Without hesitating, I replied, "I cannot do that. If I give you shares, I will have to give the other landlords shares too, and the other creditors will also demand shares, along with the landlord of my head-office building. If I give everyone shares, I will be lucky if I end up owning five or ten per cent of the company."

He said, "Precisely."

And I said, "I'm sorry, but I cannot give you shares. As you know I am taking on an enormous challenge in trying to turn this around. I'm going to have to work very hard and put a huge effort into this if it is to succeed. I'm not going to do it if I own only five or ten per cent of the company. I would be better off just letting it go."

His tone then became very aggressive and he said, in effect, "Do you think you're going to walk away from this scot free? You think TriLea's not in trouble? You think we're not in trouble? The whole world is in trouble. Do you have any idea what all the empty stores in our malls is costing us? Where do you think we're getting our funds? You got yourself into this mess. How dare you come in here and expect us to bear the brunt of your problems? It's shares or nothing. And if you're telling me you're not giving us shares, please leave my office." And he got up and walked out.

Peter Sharp, who had always been a friend, said, "Max, he's right. We all have our troubles, so you have to decide what you want to do."

"Peter, there's nothing I can do," I responded. "I cannot give you shares. All the other landlords have stipulated 80 per cent or no deal and Cadillac-Fairview, which represents 40 per cent, is saying 'no way'. So, Peter, it's all in your hands."

Seymour, Jacques and I then left the office, and Jacques and I went back to Montreal. It looked like the game was over because, without the support of the landlords, we could not even begin to put together a plan for restructuring and reorganizing the company. When we got back to Montreal, we arranged a meeting with the trustees, accountants and lawyers for two o'clock the next afternoon to discuss how best to wind up the company.

The next morning I called Peter Sharp and told him about the meeting that afternoon to discuss winding up the business, and I wanted him to know that if I did not get the support I needed it would all be over. He said, "Max, we have nothing to come to the table with. We're asking for shares, and if you won't give us shares, all I can do is wish you the best of luck."

At 2 p.m. we convened our meeting and started to discuss putting everything in motion for an orderly wind-up of the company. The mood was very sombre. I was truly at one of my all-time lows.

At 2:30, literally at the last moment, a call came through from Peter Sharp, and he said, "OK, we are in. We accept your plan. Tell the other landlords we're on side."

I could barely speak. All I could manage to mutter to everyone was, "Cadillac-Fairview is in! We have the landlords on side."

What a difference a minute can make! One moment it is all over; the next, there's hope again. It was almost impossible for me to contain my excitement. Within minutes the entire head office went wild. There was pandemonium! People were cheering, crying, hugging and laughing. The atmosphere in the building was electrifying. All of this was typical of how I would live my life for the next six months. One evening I would come home and say to Shirley, "It looks like there's a glimmer of hope." The next evening, I would come home and say, "It's game over." We were living on an emotional roller coaster.

Getting the landlords on side to the extent that we did was truly another miracle. Without their support, we could not even have begun the process of preparing an offer for acceptance by the creditors. By the way, Peter Sharpe, who is now President and CEO of Cadillac Fairview, continued to be a good friend.

Miracle No. 6 — Timing in our Favour

As I mentioned earlier, several months before we filed for protection, the federal government had passed legislation that allowed leases to be cancelled under special circumstances. The coincidence of the timing of that legislation and our filing gave us the bargaining chip we needed with our landlords. Also, in October 1993 the country was virtually at the bottom of a recession. With many of their stores closed, shopping centres looked dismal going into the holiday season.

It was not altruism that brought the landlords around. Shirmax had a significant number of stores in shopping centers across Canada and none of the landlords wanted to add more vacancies to their centres, especially before Christmas. In their own interest, they did not want to see us go down. So, the coincidence of the timing of our filing with the recession and the holiday season just ahead worked in our favour. That was the miracle. Had the timing been otherwise, the outcome might have been very different.

Miracle No. 7 — Negotiating with the Creditors

When we filed, it caught all of our suppliers off guard because we had always paid our bills on time and we were known to be a credit-worthy company. Everyone was understandably upset. The Montreal Manufacturers' Guild called a meeting of the creditors at Ruby Foo's Hotel to discuss Shirmax's filing for protection and to develop a strategy to deal with it. I was invited to attend that meeting if I chose to do so, and I did attend.

There were hundreds of people there. Many in the crowd were very hostile and angry with me and seemed to me to be in a lynching mood. Some of them actually accused me of being a thief and of masterminding a bankruptcy for my own personal gain. Those accusations hurt me deeply because nothing could have been further from the truth.

As I said earlier, we had bought a lot of merchandise for the fall and Christmas seasons in the hope of forcing our stores to do more business. But some of the creditors interpreted that as a ploy on my part to get their merchandise and so increase my debt to them. They figured that I had anticipated filing and that, by doing so, much of the debt would be erased, and I would have acquired all that merchandise for next to nothing. At one point I went to the podium to say a few words, but the crowd would not give me a chance to say much. I must point out, however, that there were a number of creditors at the meeting who knew me well and they knew that the accusations were untrue. Several of them, in particular my very close friend, Ian Karper, as well as Jack Wiltzer, the CFO of Algo Fashions, and Abe Cohen, to name a few, tried to go to bat for me. But the din was far too loud for them to have much effect.

The objective of that meeting was to develop a strategy to deal with Shirmax. A committee was needed as the first step in negotiating a settlement offer or proposal, but there was so much confusion they couldn't organize anything. Soon after that meeting, we started trying to formulate a proposal that would be acceptable to all parties, but we had a serious problem; there was no one to negotiate with because there was no creditors' committee and the creditors could not get their acts together to appoint one. They called a series of meetings with us, but they were totally disorganized and everyone who came had his or her own agenda.

We couldn't get anything done and were literally at a stalemate. To get things moving, I hired Richter and Associates, another accounting firm, to act on behalf of the creditors. Richter was the accountant for many of the creditors and their managing partner, John Swidler, was highly respected within the fashion industry. John managed to get them organized and put together a creditors' committee.

It was clear from the outset that John was going to play a pivotal role in any successful negotiation. The first proposal from the creditors' committee was 100 cents on the dollar: 60 cents in cash, paid over two-and-a-half years, and 40 cents in shares. That became their opening position. On our side, Rossignol proposed 30 cents on the dollar over three years. He told me that if there was any chance of our surviving, we could not pay more and he was convinced that they would accept that number.

The creditors were very upset with Jacques' proposal, and insisted that they would accept no less than 100 cents on the dollar, between cash and shares. There was also a rumour at the time that Reitmans was making a play to buy the company from the creditors for 25 cents on the dollar — all cash. I was never sure whether there was any truth to that rumour or whether it was planted as a bargaining ploy by the creditors.

When Rossignol agreed to take our case, he did so on the condition that he would be in charge of the entire process and that I would follow his lead. I had agreed to those conditions, but the Reitmans rumour worried me and, one Sunday evening when Jacques was out of town, I invited John Swidler and some creditors, who were supporters and personal friends, to my home to discuss that rumour. As I remember, Ian Karper, Jack Wiltzer and Abe Cohen were there.

I must confess that I panicked at that meeting and, acting out of fear, entertained a suggestion of 60 cents on the dollar over three years. Rossignol was very annoyed when he heard what I had done and he told me I had probably thrown away any chance I had of surviving. So, I had just put our survival in jeopardy, and it was all my doing! I allowed that number to be considered — and the number stuck. That was the number we were forced to use when we submitted our proposal to the creditors' committee. Jacques was right and I was absolutely wrong. Jacques had the experience and he knew what he was doing, and I had undermined him. Pulling an end run around Rossignol and pre-empting him with a higher number was a bad move on my part. Even now, I have no excuse except that I still did not fully understand that it is almost impossible to beat the odds and survive after going into court protection and that the less you commit to pay, the better your chances are of surviving.

Now, let me put Miracle No. 7 on hold temporarily.

Miracle No. 8 — Line of Credit

When the factoring company put the stop-credit on Shirmax and we had no alternative but to file for protection, we immediately advised our bank and were told that if Shirmax hoped for any bank support throughout this process, we would have to appoint their choice of trustee, Arthur Andersen. They also insisted that we appoint Senn Delaney — one of Arthur Andersen's consulting arms that specialized in business turnarounds — to assist us in the restructuring of the company and to liaise with the bank regarding the ongoing viability of Shirmax. Here began what would turn out to be another long and drawn out, nerve-wracking experience. Although we did not know it at the time, and despite our agreeing to their demands, the bank's mandate to Arthur Andersen was to keep everything going until after Christmas, get the bank's $12 million out, and then allow the company to fold.

When you file for court protection, you do not have to pay your creditors-at-large until you come to an agreement with them. However, the bank is a preferred creditor, which means that all of the money that comes in, other than what goes to pay payroll, rent and taxes, goes to the bank first. So, as soon as Arthur Andersen took control, the bank knew it was going to get its $12 million. Even though I was still running day-to-day operations, I was no longer in charge; Arthur Andersen was. Under the circumstances, it was not surprising that everyone at Shirmax saw Arthur Andersen as "the enemy."

Meanwhile, all of the Shirmax executive team and the entire financial and accounting department were working day and night with Senn Delaney to analyze the situation and determine what was needed to produce an effective restructuring plan. Eventually, we put together a plan that we presented to Arthur Andersen showing that, if we secured our deal with the landlords, rid ourselves of our 40 low-performing stores, and recreated our business concepts as per our new test stores, there was a good chance to turn Shirmax around. Of course, this was also conditional on our making a reasonable deal with our creditors, getting the bank's support, and implementing the Senn Delaney recommendations for reorganizing and streamlining the company.

Arthur Andersen presented our plan to the bank and, in their report, wrote something to the effect that "Shirmax management, together with Arthur Andersen's consulting arm, Senn Delaney, has prepared this plan that we believe would result in turning the company around. We are confident that Shirmax can be saved, and we recommend that you give them your support." At that point, Arthur Andersen ceased being the enemy and became our ally. They were on our side.

When we finally came to an agreement with the creditors' committee, we had to satisfy two conditions. First, we had to obtain a $5 million line of credit from our bank; second, we had to reduce the annual rent for our head office and distribution facilities from $2 million to not more than $600,000. The creditors' committee submitted that proposal to the members at large for a vote to be held on December 6, 1993.

After we agreed to the committee's conditions, Rossignol, Landry and I met with the bank and advised them of the creditors' condition concerning the $5 million line of credit with our bank. We said, "You have received a letter from Arthur Andersen recommending that you support us. Will we have your support for the $5 million line of credit?" We left that meeting with the impression that we would get their support.

Now let me put Miracle No. 8 temporarily on hold, too.

Miracle No. 9 — Head Office Facility

We had closed our manufacturing division in April, so we had already mothballed one-third of our head-office building. Because we would be closing 40 stores, we estimated that would further reduce our space requirements by 30 per cent, so we needed much less space. We went shopping to price a new location and found that we could rent suitable space for $600,000 a year as opposed to the $2 million it was then costing. Thus, $600,000 became the number we used in our restructuring plan.

Rossignol, Landry and I then went to see one of the principals of the company that owned our head-office building and told him about the creditors' committee demand relating to the rent. We explained that we no longer needed the amount of space we had and that we could rent space that would satisfy our needs elsewhere for $600,000. So we asked him to either release us from our lease with a six-month penalty in accordance with the new legislation, or reduce our space and annual rent to $600,000. He told us he would look into it.

He called us back in a few days for another meeting at which he informed us that they would be willing to reduce our annual rent to $1.6 million and would also reduce the term of the lease to five years from fifteen years. We said, "We appreciate your offer but it won't work because we cannot survive paying that kind of rent. And, in any case, $600,000 is one of the conditions of the creditors accepting our proposal. If we cannot satisfy that condition, we are out of business." He said, "I'm sorry, but that's the best I can do." At that point, Rossignol responded, "Please accept six months' rent to terminate the lease without going through the hassle of going to court." His response was, "No, we won't do that. You have to honour your lease and that's the deal." And Rossignol said, "We have no alternative. I guess we'll see you in court."

That was in November 1993, but we could not get a court date until March 1994. The creditors' committee agreed to recommend our proposal, on the condition that we could get our rent reduced. That meant they would have to wait for a final decision until March. It also meant that even if the creditors-at-large accepted our proposal, we would have to live under a cloud of uncertainty until March, not knowing whether we would remain in business or not. So, even if our proposal were accepted conditionally in December, it would by no means be a *fait accompli*. Rossignol assured me we would meet to prepare our case before we went to court.

Let me now also put Miracle No. 9 aside temporarily — along with Miracles No. 7 and No. 8.

Miracle No. 8 Revisited — Line of Credit

Throughout October and November our bank loan was coming down every day. On November 29th, our account manager at the bank called a meeting with Rossignol, Landry and me, and told us that the bank had decided *not* to extend Shirmax a line of credit. She also suggested that we "take our banking elsewhere." Rossignol was outraged!

"You led us to believe we would have your support and now that you've got your money you're cutting us loose!" And without saying another word he got up, walked out of her office and left the three of us sitting there.

So there we were on a roller coaster again — but this time we were at the bottom of the loop looking into a dark hole.

James and I went back to the office and I called Rossignol. His secretary told me he wasn't available and I said, "Don't tell me he's not available. He gave me four phone numbers and told me he's available to me 24 hours a day. He's got to be available. I have to speak to him."

"Sorry", she said, "He's not available."

So I asked to be transferred to my brother, and I was told that he wasn't available either. Then I asked to speak to Brahm Gelfand, and he wasn't available. I eventually learned that they were all in a meeting and could not be disturbed. You can imagine how I felt — totally abandoned! The game was over. I had no bank, no $5 million credit line to satisfy the creditors, and I couldn't even speak to Rossignol!

As I understand it, what happened after Rossignol left the bank was more or less as follows: He went back to his office and called an emergency meeting of all the partners of the firm. He told them what had just happened at the bank and obtained their unanimous agreement to deliver a message to the bank on behalf of their firm.

That afternoon Rossignol went back to the bank and told the account manager that he was there on behalf of all the partners of his firm to tell her that the bank had acted entirely in bad faith by leading us to believe they were going to support us when all they really wanted was to get their money out. And now that they had their money, they were pulling the plug on us. The landlords were supporting us, the creditors were prepared to support us, and everything was in place — except the bank.

He said the bank would be single-handedly responsible for bringing Shirmax down and that his firm would not allow the bank to get away with that. He told her that his firm would do whatever it took to make the bank pay dearly if it caused Shirmax to fail.

Her response was, "I'll get back to you."

The next day the account manager called Rossignol and said, "With respect to the letter you need confirming a line of credit for $5 million to show to your creditors, we will give you such a letter, but the letter is all you will get. We will not advance you any money."

We passed that letter on to the creditors, and as far as they knew we had met their line of credit condition. So, another crisis was averted. Getting that letter and being able to satisfy the creditors with it, especially considering the circumstances, was truly another miracle!

Miracle No. 10 — The Vote

The next challenge was to get our proposal accepted by the creditors at large on December 6. We wanted to get an indication of whether our creditors would accept or reject our proposal so we sent everyone in the company responsible for purchasing to sound out their suppliers. The feedback was very disheartening because most of the creditors said they would not accept our proposal.

On December 6th we went to the creditors' meeting with our hearts in our throats. Our lives hung in the balance. There was nothing more to do; all the work done since October had brought us to this "judgement" day. Most of the votes were in by proxy but a number of creditors showed up to cast their vote at the last minute. There must have been 150 people in the room — Shirmax management, all of our accountants, trustees, lawyers, my wife, Shirley, my brother, Alex, and many of our friendly creditors.

When it was time for the trustees to tabulate the votes, the room was electric with tension. Based on what our suppliers had told our buyers, I truly feared the worst. Then the vote was tabulated and announced: 97 percnt voted in favour of the proposal! Truly, I cannot express how I felt. I was surprised, relieved, elated and happy — and drained. I was so overwhelmed, Shirley and I went into a corner and wept on each other's shoulders. When I regained my composure and was able to circulate in the room, the atmosphere turned into a celebration. The energy was amazing and although our future was far from secure, for a brief moment we were absolutely euphoric. My entire business life could have ended right there, but it didn't. We had won a reprieve. The creditors had accepted our proposal.

In some respects that moment was like an ending and that point marked a new beginning. The challenges of surviving, regrouping and rebuilding were still ahead of us, and they were enormous. But at least we had a chance. Another miracle!

Miracle No. 7 Revisited — Negotiating with the Creditors

I made a serious mistake when I pre-empted Jacques Rossignol by suggesting 60 cents on the dollar that Sunday evening at my home. I had put our future in jeopardy but, as things turned out, paying 60 cents as opposed to 30 cents was a miracle in disguise. Shirmax went on to become very successful and because I paid 60 cents — and not 30 cents as Jacques had wanted — I was able to hold my head high. I didn't feel guilty and I certainly did not feel I had in any way cheated the creditors. By paying them 60 cents on the dollar, they recovered virtually all of their original costs. When Shirmax was sold, in view of the price I received for the company, had I paid only 30 cents, it would have been a huge embarrassment for me and I would never again have been able to hold my head high in my community. When I chickened out, what I had done was deemed to be a bad move, but it turned out to be a blessing that benefited everyone — another miracle!

Throughout this entire episode, even though John Swidler and the Richter team were the opposition in our negotiations, we had the opportunity to see them at work, to observe their work ethic as well as their understanding of the retail fashion industry. We decided that we wanted them to be our accountants — if we had a future. Immediately after our proposal was accepted, we retained Richter and Associates as our accounting firm and they remained our accountants until the day Shirmax was sold. On a personal level, John Swidler became an advisor, a mentor, and a very good friend.

Miracle No. 9 Revisited — Head Office Facility

We still had another obstacle to overcome relating to the creditors' conditional acceptance of our proposal — the court case with respect to our head-office lease. As the weeks went by, I waited to hear from Jacques about preparing for the case, but he kept putting me off with "Don't worry, I'm taking care of it."

A week before the case was to be heard, I called him and said, "Jacques, I don't understand. You said we would meet to prepare our case before going to court, but I haven't heard from you and I don't know what's happening."

"Max," he finally said, "we cannot go to court with this case because we cannot afford to lose. If we lose, the $1.6 million and the 5-year term will be off the table, and we'll be back on the hook for $2 million a year for 15 years. The judge's ruling will deal only with whether or not we are bound to the lease; he will not reduce the rent. We cannot take the chance to go to court. I am negotiating and working behind the scenes, but I am telling you now that if we must, at the last moment we will accept their offer for $1.6 million for five years and we'll worry about the consequences later."

On court day, Rossignol, Landry and I were standing on the steps outside the courthouse when three officials representing the landlord arrived. We were ready to say, "We'll accept your proposal," but before any of us had a chance to say a word, one of them came over to us and said, "We accept your offer, with some conditions."

We couldn't believe our ears. Their conditions were acceptable and we agreed on the spot!

Rossignol later told me, "I was banking on the fact that, if I were the landlord's lawyer, I would not take this case to court because the legislation has not been tested and if Shirmax won the case, the floodgates would open and as one of the largest landlords in the country, the potential cost to them could be staggering."

That's what Rossignol was banking on and that's why they accepted. We closed down part of the building and negotiated an advantageous new lease at $600,000 a year. Another miracle!

Of all the times my guardian angel has looked out for me, one of the most crucial was when she brought Jacques Rossignol into my life. Jacques was truly amazing and I cannot imagine that I could have had better or more able support from anyone than I received from him. Many people worked very hard to save Shirmax during the court protection episode, but Jacques was the mastermind and I credit him more than anyone else with saving Shirmax and for giving us the opportunity to live another day. Had he not had the vision and the determination to take on, and get the support of, the landlords, had he not had the presence and the ability to deal with the Creditors' Committee, had he not had the boldness and tenacity to take on the bank and our head office landlord, it would have been game over for us at any one of those points. I will be forever grateful to Jacques.

Miracle No. 11 — Turnaround

I have said several times that it is almost impossible to survive after filing for protection unless new money is invested in the business by the existing shareholders or by new investors and, if there are new investors, then the existing shareholders give up both ownership and control. In my case, I had no money to invest and no intention of giving up ownership. However, soon after we filed, the winds of fortune started to blow in our favour and business began to turn around for us. We sold off the excess merchandise we had on hand and turned it into cash. That enabled us to pay off our creditors within 30 months rather than over the full three-year term of the settlement agreement, and that helped to change the mood of our creditors and our relationships with them.

When we became active buyers again, most of our former suppliers had a chance to make back what they had lost. Not only did we survive, we accomplished the impossible; we went on to prosper without any new money being invested in the company from any source! That turnaround was truly a miracle!

Miracle No. 12 — Re-establishing Sources of Supply

As soon as we filed for protection, we were faced with an enormous challenge, that of surviving day-by-day, running a $100 million business with no bank, no credit and, most important, no source of supply!

We needed merchandise in order to stay in business. But we had hurt our suppliers and persuading most of them to accept orders from us while we were still in protection was a huge challenge. Accepting orders from us was also risky because nothing we ordered would be shipped for up to five months from the date of the order, and there was a strong possibility that we would not be in business when the merchandise was ready for delivery. Also, because the merchandise we ordered was to our own specifications, it could not be sold to anyone else. The challenge was for us to get the support of our suppliers, and to bring them back on side so they would accept our orders and we could stay in business.

We had to plead, beg and do whatever it took to get them to take a further chance on us. Thankfully, enough of them decided to take that risk. One by one, supplier after supplier, including those who had called me unmentionable names, gave us their support. Slowly we were able to place orders and receive shipments, and eventually our sources of supply returned to normal. Despite the importance of all the other miracles we were blessed with, this was the key to our surviving the impossible. In fact, it was a miracle that we got their support at all.

Miracle No. 13 — Keeping our People

Employees need to know that their jobs are secure. However, as our company's survival was questionable, jobs were anything but secure. That made our employees susceptible to approaches from other companies. We had to face the daunting challenge of holding onto our people.

From the moment we filed, the head hunters were out in force trying to recruit our people; but we managed to ward off their attacks and keep our teams intact. In retrospect, I believe it was the culture we had in place, and the commitments that stemmed from that culture, that produced a fierce sense of loyalty. Also, I made it a priority to keep everyone informed and I included them in everything that was going on. I held regular telephone conferences with staff all across the country, I shared the ups and downs we were going through, and I shared my commitment to survive and live another day.

Actually, we lost only one senior member of our team throughout the whole ordeal. Jan Lourens, our construction manager came to me and said, "Max, no matter what we do, we aren't going to be building any new stores for some time, so you don't need me any more. If I stay I will be a burden on the payroll. I've had an offer, and I think I should take it." I was sorry to see Jan go, but it made sense because I, too, didn't think we would be building for a while. As things turned out, however, we were building again in four months' time, and Jan came back to Shirmax a year later, but in another position. Being able to hold onto our people as we did was the final miracle.

One miracle in a lifetime is — a miracle! But 13 miracles in a span of six months is in the realm of the impossible. Yet they all happened exactly when they needed to happen and in the proper sequence. If any one of them had not happened when it did,

Shirmax would have gone under. Skeptics might question my use of "miracles" in describing the events surrounding our ordeal, but no one can possibly deny the extraordinary obstacles and difficulties we had to overcome.

Was it luck? Divine providence? My guardian angel? Or were they, indeed, miracles?

I choose to think they were miracles.

15

REBUILDING SHIRMAX

GOING INTO BANKRUPTCY PROTECTION was truly an ordeal for everyone at Shirmax. During those difficult months, the senior executive team was preoccupied with resolving our immediate problems and had little time to devote to the day-to-day running of the business. Still, we managed to survive. However, surviving bankruptcy protection carried with it absolutely no guarantee that we would succeed in the future, but we had an ace up our sleeve.

For the three years before going into protection, we knew that our business concepts had become old and tired and we had already developed new concepts for both our Maternity and Plus-size divisions. So, when all the smoke cleared after we came out of protection, we were able to start the process of reinventing and rebuilding Shirmax immediately. We had new retail strategies and concepts to build on that were more in tune with the realities of the changing economic and social environments and when we implemented those strategies customers responded positively.

In the early spring of 1994, when the economy started to turn around, there was a marked improvement in business. We started to receive new merchandise for spring and summer, and we had a very good season. After about a year it was clear that we were no longer in survival mode. We had met the challenges of day-to-day survival and were on a roll. We were ready to move forward. We changed banks, moving to the Bank of Montreal.

As part of our restructuring program, we focused on maximizing our efficiency and effectiveness in all areas of the business. We invested strategically in people and technology, and were driven like zealots to grow our businesses and maximize our potential in the marketplace. We were driven to create "an organization that works" with the ultimate goal of maximizing shareholders' value. We focused our efforts primarily in three areas: reinventing our marketing concepts; recreating the Shirmax culture; and strengthening our management practices.

REINVENTING OUR MARKETING CONCEPTS

Reinventing the Maternity Business

When we first went into the maternity business under the Shirley K banner, maternity was considered a small specialty business, with the emphasis on "small." Even when we expanded and became a national chain, all our stores were still small in keeping with small-business thinking. By the late '80s, it was clear that our small stores and our business concept were no longer appropriate.

I have already told how Howard and Phillip changed our Shirley K maternity concept, which had been based on hiding the pregnancy, to the new Thyme Maternity concept of celebrating and showing the pregnancy. The strategy for rebuilding the maternity division was to replace all the Shirley K stores with larger, more modern and customer-friendly Thyme Maternity stores, featuring more moderately-priced merchandise.

Reinventing the Plus-size Business

Here, again, our plus-size retail concept was also old and tired. When we first went into the plus-size business, we were not sure of its potential and we were cautious. Our stores were very small, approximately 2,000 square feet, and we carried everything from pantyhose to cocktail dresses. We had bits and pieces of everything but we were "important" in nothing. And that was the way we ran our plus-size business until the early '90s, when we built a couple of new concept test-stores based on a new vision of having Addition-Elle become the store of choice for plus-size customers in Canada!

Our new concept stores, which we called combo stores, had 7,000 square feet. Each store had one store front, but the interior was separated into two parts: a career store, and a sportswear store. When I approached our Board of Directors with the new store concept, I had great difficulty getting their support. They argued that if we couldn't make 2,000 square feet work, how in the world could we expect 7,000 square feet to work? However, I eventually managed to bring them around and get their support. We opened our first 7,000-square-foot store in Place Versailles in Montreal in 1993. Customers immediately appreciated both the new store concept and the broadened merchandise assortments, and that store became the model for subsequent conversions.

Once the combo stores started to pay off, we expanded the concept by adding a plus-size lingerie department in an additional 3,000 square feet, which created a triple store. Again, it was quite a task to persuade the Board to approve 10,000 square feet but, as it turned out, going into plus-size lingerie was a great move. After a bumpy start it became a very profitable part of our business. A major aspect of rebuilding the plus-size division was the conversion to 10,000-square-foot triple stores and the development of merchandise and marketing concepts to support that expansion.

I must mention here that the "we" I have been using in discussing the plus-size business, refers to Louise Tanguay, V-P Merchandising for Addition-Elle, and me. Louise was with me from the first day we started working together to invent our plus-size business. Louise and I strategized all the changes over the years, and it was she who implemented those changes. Unquestionably, Louise was the architect and driving force in building Addition-Elle into Canada's leading plus-size brand.

RECREATING THE SHIRMAX CULTURE

Before we went into protection, I had already started a couple of management-development programs called "Discovery with the CEO" and "Shirmax Management Program: Managing Up."

176

I developed and wrote these programs and delivered them in a series of two-day training sessions to all management staff in the company. After we came out of protection, I began broadening the scope of those programs, added to their content and developed two additional programs, "Entrepreneurship" and "Team-Building."

Those four programs, which I describe in detail in Part II, formed the foundation of the very special and empowering culture we created at Shirmax. The objectives of those programs were to get everyone's commitment to our corporate vision, values and goals, imbue the Shirmax culture into all parts of the organization, and inspire everyone to operate at an extraordinary level.

STRENGTHENING OUR MANAGEMENT PRACTICES

IN ORDER TO PUT SHIRMAX on a strategic course to improve and strengthen its management practices, we acquired and installed new technologies. These quickened our response time in all aspects of our business and allowed us to become a much more effective operation.

Once we completed the implementation of these three main strategic initiatives — Reinventing our Marketing Concepts, Recreating the Shirmax Culture, and Strengthening our Management Practices — Shirmax was positioned to become very profitable and to take on whatever challenges and opportunities presented themselves.

The Inventory Dilemma

Every company has its own culture and much of that culture is determined by what I call "drivers". These drivers establish what everyone in the company is committed to, propel the decisions made and therefore govern how the company operates. At Shirmax the number one driver that defined the Shirmax culture was our key operating principle, a commitment to *maximizing your potential.*

Maximizing your potential involves taking risks. The opposite to maximizing your potential is risk aversion; it is about "playing it safe", and playing it safe does not give the same opportunities as a commitment to maximizing your potential. However, there is a down side as well as an up side to maximizing your potential. In a retail operation, the area where maximizing your potential can have the greatest positive, or negative, effect is that of inventory management. All fashion retailers struggle with a very difficult and perplexing problem when it comes to inventory: how to maximize sales during the key months of the season while minimizing the amount of stock left at the end of the season, and how much inventory is needed at all times to accomplish that.

There is a formula for merchandise management that involves "weeks of stock and stock turns." To maximize sales in the key months requires having enough stock during those months to meet the potential demand. However, that means being left with excess stock at the end of the season and that merchandise has to be written off, which in turn means a direct reduction of profits.

Thus, retailers face a dilemma. They must either:

A) maximize sales by maximizing assortments and the impact on the customer and accept the consequences of having stock left over, which has to be written off at the end of the season, or

B) give up potential sales by carrying lower inventories in season in order to have little or no inventory left over at the end of the season.

If a company is driven by option A, that calls for specific actions and behaviors that create a particular culture. Conversely, if a company is driven by option B, that calls for a different set of actions and behaviors that create another culture. Retailers must therefore choose between these two strategies.

Most retailers choose strategy B, giving up on maximizing sales in favour of having little or no inventory at the end of the season. I, on the other hand, always chose strategy A, to maximize sales by trying to impact the customer and accept the consequences of having left-over merchandise. I believed that, on balance, option A gave me the greater opportunity to maximize customer satisfaction, sales and profitability over the long term.

I am certain that the driver I adopted (maximizing potential) came from an experience I had early in my business career that influenced the way I approached merchandising and inventory management.

When we had only one store, in the Wilderton Shopping Centre, I got up one winter morning to find that we were in the midst of a blizzard, which was to last all day. I managed to get to the store and open for business. What a joke! There was no staff and there was no business! I was alone. I turned on the lights, washed the floors and, intermittently as it piled up, I shoveled the snow away from the front door. Other than that, I stood at the door with my arms folded waiting for customers.

Around four in the afternoon a car plowed its way through the parking lot and stopped in front of my store. A lady, all bundled up, got out of the car and walked through the door:

"I need a pair of navy slacks."

"What size?"

"Size 12."

"Let's check."

Wouldn't you know, I had every size in stock except size 12! For me, that meant I had wasted my entire day: I hadn't made a single sale and I didn't have the stock to make the only sale I could have made. I paid the rent and electricity, etc. for nothing!

It was from that experience that I decided if we were going to be successful over the long term, we had to make the customer our priority. We had to have merchandise assortments to ensure we had *what* the customer wanted, *when* she wanted it or she would desert us! It was from that experience that I chose to deal with the inventory dilemma by budgeting to maximize sales in the good months, and accepting the consequences of being left with too much inventory at the end of the season. That was the dilemma we lived with until we eventually stumbled onto a solution that was not only profitable, it changed (for the better) the way we managed our business.

ADDITION-ELLE FASHION OUTLET

FOR YEARS, LOUISE HAD BEEN ASKING me to open a few outlet stores where we could sell off our excess merchandise so we would not clog up the new season with old merchandise. I always refused on the grounds that outlet stores was not a business we knew. We were value-added fashion retailers and I was convinced that "outlet" was inconsistent with that image. I stuck with that decision for many years until, in 1995, I was put under tremendous pressure and was left with no alternative but to give in.

Walter Lamothe, our Executive V-P Operations, started to pressure me with, "Max, I think we are being stubborn. (He was being very diplomatic with the "we.") I suggest we reconsider and open a couple of outlet stores to help us get rid of some of our excess merchandise. It is inappropriate to use expensive space to sell off old merchandise."

"Walter," I responded, "as long as I am CEO of this company, we will never do that. That's inconsistent with who we are and it's not a business we understand. We are about excellence and outlet stores are not. It's not for us."

A few months later Walter came back to me and said, "Max, I have found a 5,000-square-foot store in a great outlet environment on Taschereau Blvd. The rent is $11 a square foot, compared to $100 a square foot that we are paying in the shopping centers. I can get a two-year lease with an eight-year option. We have enough fixtures in our warehouse to furnish the store, so it would cost us next to nothing to open the store. Let me open an Addition-Elle outlet store and see if it would work for us."

Walter had me boxed in. I did not want to be in that business, but I could not argue with his logic, so I conceded. He opened the store and it was an instant success.

A few months later Walter came to me again and said, "I have found another store, 7,500 square feet in an outlet centre in Laval. The rent is $9 a square foot and, again, I can get a two-year lease and an eight-year option. We still have plenty of merchandise to fill another store. Considering what we're doing on Taschereau, we've got to open this one too."

I approved the second store, and it was even more successful than the first.

Timing is everything. Just around this time, a new retailing concept was developing. "Power malls," also known as "outlet malls," were being built across Canada. The rents were not as low as $9 or $10 gross; they were $20, which was still a long way from the $100 we were paying in regular malls. Based on the success of our first two outlet stores, and the fact that we still had a lot of merchandise being carried over from season to season in our regular Addition-Elle stores, we started opening outlet stores in power malls to sell that merchandise at discount prices. The stores were called "Addition-Elle Fashion Outlet" and that Division was successful from day one. Within two-and-a-half years, we had 40 outlet stores generating more than $60 million in revenues. The Outlet Division attracted a different customer who really appreciated the Addition-Elle merchandise at discount prices.

Not only was the Outlet Division a viable and profitable venture on its own, it resolved Addition-Elle's inventory dilemma. Having the outlet stores to sell off our excess merchandise was a huge benefit for the Addition-Elle division, and made that division more profitable. It allowed Addition-Elle to maximize its assortments in season and still keep the merchandise clean, fresh and new by moving the excess merchandise to the outlet division where we got another kick at the can with the same merchandise.

As the outlet division grew there was not enough merchandise from Addition-Elle to support those stores. So we put together a buying team for the Outlet Division headed by a Merchandise

Manager, Jamie-Lee Goulakos, who developed and bought merchandise at discount prices to supplement our own from Addition-Elle, thus providing our customers with an excellent assortment. The combination of having those two divisions working together and supporting each other was a great formula that resolved our inventory dilemma. It was having our cake and eating it, too!

It is noteworthy that the Addition-Elle Outlet Division became the catalyst for the eventual sale of Shirmax. Our Outlet Division was in direct competition with Penningtons, one of Reitmans premier divisions at the time, and we were a thorn in their side. Reitmans' saw the opportunity to own and control the competition and I believe that was a key consideration in Reitmans' decision to acquire Shirmax. So, developing the Outlet Division, which I had so resisted, turned out to be a stroke of great good fortune. The Outlet Division was the goose that laid the golden egg!

Once again, I credit my guardian angel for manipulating events and circumstances to force me to change my decision and go into the outlet business.

16

ENTREPRENEUR OF THE YEAR

WE WERE PROFITABLE FROM THE FIRST QUARTER after coming out of protection and we increased our profitability every quarter after that. By the mid-'90s we had paid off our creditors six months in advance of the due date and it was clear that Shirmax was on a roll. The negative fall-out from our proposal disappeared and was replaced with praise and acknowledgement for what we were accomplishing, especially from the retail fashion and financial business communities. Everyone was impressed with our achievements, not only for surviving court protection, but also for accomplishing a dramatic turnaround and becoming profitable again in such a short time. We became more and more high profile.

Each year an award is given to acknowledge the most outstanding CEO in Canada. In 1996, as a result of the recognition Shirmax was receiving, I was nominated for CEO of the Year. The Shirmax people prepared a comprehensive submission in support of the nomination and, although I did not win the award, being nominated was a huge compliment, and a boost to the morale of everyone in the company. This was especially gratifying inasmuch as only three years earlier morale had been at an all-time low.

One year later, in 1997, Pierre Beauchamp, the Senior Vice-President of our new bank, the Bank of Montreal, nominated me for consideration as Entrepreneur of the Year in Quebec, in the category of Turnaround Entrepreneur. He had watched our performance and the work I did in establishing the Shirmax culture, and was very impressed with our management philosophy, the way we empowered our people, and the job we did turning Shirmax around.

The Entrepreneur of the Year award is an international event sponsored annually by Ernst & Young in collaboration with other organizations in each province, state and country. Again, being nominated was a huge compliment, but I was not very interested in pursuing it because of our experience with the CEO of the Year award. Our people had done a lot of work and spent valuable time preparing our submission for that nomination and I did not want them to take on that work load again. However, most of them insisted that I accept the nomination, arguing that since I was entered in the category of Turnaround Entrepreneur, and we were getting so much recognition specifically for the Shirmax turnaround, they felt that I should let the nomination stand. So I agreed to let my name go forward.

In addition to our submission, the officials from the Entrepreneur of the Year organization did a lot of work on their own. They interviewed me, as well as many people who knew me both inside and outside the company. Several weeks before the awards event, however, I received a call from an official of the organization who informed me that the "Turnaround" category had been cancelled because I was the only nominee in that category. Instead, I had been entered in the larger, broad-based category of Wholesaling, Retailing and Manufacturing.

I immediately wanted to withdraw my nomination because, while I thought I might have had some chance in the Turnaround category, I was certain that I did not have a chance in the much broader category. It seemed obvious to me that I could not compete with all the major companies in Quebec and all the accomplishments of the presidents and CEOs who ran them. I was sure I could not win and I did not want to put our people through the trauma of being losers again. Filing for bankruptcy protection had been a huge challenge to our people and we had managed to bring them back to feeling like winners again. I felt it would serve no purpose to set up an unrealistic, un-winnable expectation. But I was overruled. Most of our people argued that the work had already been done and, again, they urged me to let the nomination stand. So I reluctantly agreed, and the process went forward.

About a month before the awards ceremony, a short list of up to five nominees was announced in each of eight categories. To my surprise, my name was on the short list for my category of Wholesaling, Retailing and Manufacturing, but I held my emotions in check because I was certain there was no way I could win the award.

In the meantime, the idea of their CEO winning the Entrepreneur of the Year Award caught on like wildfire and caused great excitement among Shirmax staff, both at Head Office and in all our stores across the country. I began to feel very uneasy because I was sure that everyone was being set up for a letdown. On the day of the awards dinner I received literally dozens of phone calls from friends and staff members right across the country wishing me good luck. This bothered me even more because I dreaded the prospect of having to call them the next day with the news that I had not won.

The awards ceremony was a very elegant affair attended by over a thousand people and was held in the huge ballroom of the *Palais de Congrès de Montreal*. The evening started with a cocktail party followed by dinner, then the announcements and presentation of the awards. All of the nominees were encouraged to have people from their companies attend, so we had a table of ten at the event. All were Shirmax people except for my wife, Shirley, and my younger daughter, Rachelle.

At the cocktail party, James Landry asked me if I had prepared an acceptance speech and I told him I hadn't because there was no way in the world that I could win. He responded, "But what will happen if you do win? You will be unprepared." And I teased him by asking, "What kind of support is this - to ask me now? If you had asked me about a speech three days ago, maybe I would have taken your suggestion and prepared one. But don't worry, there's no way I'm going to win." And so, all of us went into the ballroom, sat down at our table and had dinner. Then the awards ceremony began.

The event was staged like the Academy Awards. All of the nominees had been asked to prepare a slide show about their companies, and when the nominee's name was announced in each category, their company's slide show was shown on the big screen. The organizers knew where each nominee was sitting and when a winner was announced, the music started and the spotlights were directed to the winner's table. It was a very exciting evening. Of the eight categories, the presentation for our category was seventh on the program.

The winners in the first three categories were all from francophone companies. Naya Water had been a huge success in Quebec in 1997 and they were one of the nominees in the fourth category. It was obvious to me that Naya would win, but when the winner was announced, it was not Naya Water, it was a small unknown francophone company that made cranberry juice! At that point, not only was I certain I did not have a chance in the broad category of Wholesaling, Manufacturing and Retailing, I was absolutely convinced I could not win because I was not francophone. So, I felt no tension at all sitting there as the evening progressed.

Finally, it was time for our category, and they announced the five nominees, while showing the slide shows for each nominee on the big screen including Max Konigsberg, CEO from Shirmax. The music started blaring, the spotlights were flaring back and forth, and then the announcement: "The winner is..." and all the spotlights turned on our table... "Max Konigsberg!" I was *stunned!* I just sat there, too shocked to move. Suddenly, everybody at the table started jumping and cheering. Shirley was speechless. My daughter Rachelle went totally wild. Now I was in trouble! I had not prepared an acceptance speech and I had no time to think. With the spotlight on me I had to walk the whole length of the hall and up on to the stage to accept my award and make an acceptance speech. As I made the long walk to the stage that seemed to take forever, I kept telling myself to just think clearly and speak slowly.

When I got on stage, there were handshakes all around and I was presented with the award plaque. Then I went over to the microphone. I cannot repeat exactly what I said because I had nothing prepared, but it was something like, "Thank you ladies and gentlemen. I am in shock. I am overwhelmed to be receiving this kind of acknowledgement from my peers and from the Quebec business community. I am truly honored to accept this award, but I do not consider it to be simply a personal acknowledgement. Rather, it is an acknowledgement of the entire Shirmax team. So many people have worked so hard for many years to bring Shirmax to the point where it is now. If Shirmax is recognized as an outstanding company today, it is because they made it so. I am therefore accepting this award on behalf of all the people at Shirmax. Thank you."

Something very special for me personally happened as a result of winning that award and from my acceptance speech. The next morning, I got a call from Herb Siblin, one of the partners at Ernst & Young. Herb is a very high-profile member of the Jewish community in Montreal and Herb and I had had a long-standing relationship. He had been one of my mentors and I have enormous respect for him. He said to me, "Max, you are a credit to your community and to our people. Your words were very inspiring. We are all so proud of you." Until that evening my image of myself had always been that of an "also ran." I never thought of myself as a "winner." Winning that award was very special for me because, for the first time in my life, I knew how it felt to be a winner.

Throughout this entire episode, everything that happened, the nomination, accepting the nomination, the change of categories, the decision to refuse the nomination, then deciding to

Accepting the Entrepreneur of the Year Award

With Howard at the Entrepreneur of the Year Awards Ceremony.

With Philip at the Entrepreneur of the Year Awards Ceremony

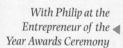

accept, the news of becoming a finalist, had all been comm unicated to everyone in the company. Everyone at Shirmax knew what was going on and everyone was excited. I had the tangible support of a couple of thousand people. Everyone was involved in the run-up to the event and they made me feel that they had an investment in my winning the award. What a great day it was when I went to the office and announced to everyone that we had won, and then I started making my phone calls across the country. Thankfully, my concern that we would not win and so deprive everyone of the feeling of being a winner proved to be unwarranted. Winning the award was the ultimate acknowledgement that we were well on our way to achieving what we had set out to do — and had worked so hard to accomplish — to create an "organization that works."

This entire episode was a wonderful experience, and I still get a great thrill when I think back on it. Having said that, I have never taken that recognition for granted, and I hope I never will.

I read a business book recently titled *Good to Great* by Jim Collins and Jerry I. Porras, which makes a strong case that most great companies have not become great simply as a result of having been good. The authors claim that most great companies have reached that level by going from the brink of disaster to great, NOT by going from good to great. They argue that to become a great company requires that it push its boundaries, take risks, take dramatic actions, and constantly reinvent its business concepts. When everything is going well, a "good" company is not inclined to do any of these. They don't make waves or rock the boat. Even when a company is clearly in serious trouble, management rarely takes drastic action until it is facing the prospect of absolute disaster. I support the authors' claim because I had the same experience at Shirmax. The company became great only after it had reached the brink of disaster.

I consider the two events, filing for protection in 1993 and winning the Entrepreneur of the Year Award in 1997, as one event because they were entirely interrelated. It was only by coming to the brink of disaster that we were motivated to examine our business in every detail, face the brutal truths about who we were, and take the necessary risks and bold actions that resulted in becoming the company that earned the award.

17

A NEW VISION
FOR SHIRMAX

AFTER COMING OUT OF BANKRUPTCY PROTECTION, as part of the process of rebuilding Shirmax, we began to develop a new vision for building a much bigger business and for creating a powerful new organization that could expand successfully anywhere in the world, with or without me at the helm. By the spring of 1996 I and all of the Shirmax management team had that objective clearly set in our minds and we became totally preoccupied with and driven to achieve that end result. We were all operating from a vision to create an organization that would stand out above all others.

I should explain why I have added "with or without me at the helm."

I had always been the driving force for growing the company and for taking risks, and our people were pleased to accept the challenges and follow me. They were ambitious and they shared my vision for exploring all possible avenues to grow. Now we were capitalizing on our vision. All of our business concepts were reaching their potential and we were having great success in satisfying our customers and building profitable sales. We were managing effectively and were in a very strong financial position.

So, there was a new world of opportunities for taking Shirmax to an entirely new level. Everyone was inspired to spread their wings and embark on a period of aggressive growth. But *I became a problem*. I was beginning to hold the organization back! My goal had been to build an organization that was so effective it would be capable of operating new businesses in both Canadian and international markets. And now that our goal could be realized, I was saying "No." I did not want to be responsible for taking the company to the next level. I had reached a stage in my life where I was not willing to take on additional responsibility or assume additional risk. In all my years at Shirmax there had never been a difference between my personal vision and my vision for the business. But now the two visions were in conflict and something had to give. I had to get out of the way and free up the company to pursue its full potential. That left me with two options: either merge with another company, or sell Shirmax outright.

VISION

I HAVE USED THE TERM "VISION" many times in this discussion. Let me digress once again and explain how and why the whole concept of vision plays a very important role in the way I manage my life.

When I say that I have a vision for, or of, something, I mean simply that I can see or visualize it in my consciousness — in my mind's eye — and it becomes real for me. There is a formula relating to vision that I consider to be a formula for the way things work. I call it one of the laws of the universe. The formula is:

I can create anything I have a vision for, the courage to declare,
and the willingness to stay responsible for.
The formula also has a corollary:
I cannot create what I do not have a vision for.

"I can create anything I have a vision for" is anything I can see or visualize in my consciousness or in my mind's eye.

"The courage to declare" is the courage to make my vision public, putting it out into the universe as a commitment.

"The willingness to stay responsible for" is staying responsible for the outcome and not quitting, despite the fact that the universe will always find ways to throw obstacles in my way.

One of the best examples of the power of this formula occurred on May 25th, 1961, when President Kennedy declared that the United States would "put a man on the moon within ten years." He had the vision, he declared it to the world, and he stayed responsible for the outcome. He did everything consistent with making it happen despite the fact that, when he made his declaration, there was no evidence that man could ever go to the moon. The United States put a man on the moon in fewer than ten years. Miracles can result from a vision!

As for the corollary, *I cannot create what I do not have a vision for; I can create only to my vision.* I cannot create to another person's vision and another person cannot create to my vision; we can create only to our own vision.

Most people have difficulty with this concept. After all, when we make a request of someone, we expect a specific outcome, and we are always surprised when it doesn't happen! Invariably we don't get the results because we haven't done a good enough job sharing our vision. I had an experience at Shirmax that clearly illustrates this.

When we started building the Addition-Elle Fashion Outlet stores in power malls, that division's management team and I shared a common vision for the kind of store environment we wanted. We built a model store in Toronto according to that vision, and all of us went to the store opening to approve the concept before we built any more stores. Everyone was thrilled with the new model and we gave it our stamp of approval.

The team went back to Montreal while I stayed in Toronto to visit some of the newest power malls to check the latest trends. During that tour, I saw that a shift was taking place. Power malls were changing from being primarily outlet malls to complexes for a different kind of retailing — not discount stores but lower-cost and higher-value retailing!

As a result of that visit, my vision for Addition-Elle Fashion Outlet changed and I came up with a different concept for what our business should be and a vision for an entirely different environment for our stores. Consequently, for me, the model store we had just built, loved and approved, was no longer appropriate.

At the management meeting the following Monday, I opened the meeting with the statement: "That store we all loved and approved last week is all wrong. It needs to be something very different."

You can imagine the reaction! Everyone looked at me as if I had lost my mind. As much as I tried to explain my new vision to them, they just couldn't "get" it. At first, I was very disappointed that they could not see what was so obvious to me. But after I got past my irritation, I realized that they had not seen what I had seen and so they could not conceptualize what I was talking about. I was asking them to execute to a new vision that was not their own; they could not do that. They could not design and develop a store concept according to my vision. So I arranged for the entire team to go back to Toronto, and I met them there. I took them, two at a time, to the complexes I had visited and showed them what I had seen, exposing them to the same conditions and allowing them to have the same experience that had triggered my new vision. The light went on for them as it had for me and they saw what I had seen, but now it was their own vision and they could execute according to that vision. From that experience the Addition-Elle Fashion Outlet division was transformed to a new and more relevant retail concept and it happened because everyone was operating from a shared vision.

This is an example of how the formula for the power of vision works. I have found this formula to be a great working tool and I have internalized its principles to the point where it dictates the way I think and the way I manage my life.

18

PERSONAL VISIONS

S O FAR, WE HAVE EXPLORED THE POWER OF VISION in the context of business but it also plays a very important role in our personal lives. The following are some examples of the power of vision taken from some family experiences.

Philip

The power of vision was illustrated earlier in the chapter titled "King of Maternity" where I described the contribution that my son, Philip, and my nephew, Howard, made to Shirmax by developing the Thyme Maternity concept. Their vision for a new maternity retail concept ultimately contributed enormously to the growth of the company. I resisted it because it was not my vision and I didn't "get" it. It was only after they built and merchandised the stores and they became very successful that I was able to see and "get" the concept, and then it became my vision, too. I could never have created that concept — I simply didn't have the vision for it — and Shirmax would have been the poorer without it.

Rachelle

From the time Rachelle was very young, she wanted to have a career in which she could contribute to, and "make a difference" in people's lives. However, she had no idea of what that could be. Rachelle attended St. George's High School in Montreal, which is very well known for its theatre program. She became involved in that program and, in her final year, she played Helena in *A Midsummer Night's Dream*. She was outstanding in the role and from that experience she developed a vision for a life in theatre. She enrolled in the Theatre Arts program at York University in Toronto, and earned a Bachelor of Fine Arts degree, specializing in directing.

Life in the theatre was hard and created an upside-down lifestyle for her — sleeping by day, working by night, moving from one gig to another — never sure of what was coming next. Although she had some success in the theatre, she was never really happy with that lifestyle and, even more important, she did not see how a career in theatre would fulfill her vision of contributing to and make a meaningful difference in people's lives. Then she met Paul Gold, who was to become her husband.

Paul had been practicing Yoga for some time and introduced her to the philosophy. She went to Bekram Yoga School in California for three months of intensive training. Although it was the most difficult and challenging three months of her life, she took to it like the proverbial duck to water. Yoga became her passion and she developed a new vision for herself as a yoga teacher. She saw that, as a yoga teacher, she could fulfill her childhood dream to contribute and "make a difference" in people's lives. Rachelle left the theatre and started to teach Bekram Yoga.

In the meantime, Paul was doing a much more demanding form of Yoga called Ashtanga Yoga. Eventually Rachelle also moved on to practice that discipline and together they developed the vision of becoming Ashtanga Yoga teachers and opening a school of their own.

They went to India for three months to study with the living master of Ashtanga Yoga, K. Pattabhi Jois, then came back to Toronto and opened their Yoga school called Ashtanga Yoga Shala. Since then, they have returned to India annually to further their training with Pattabhi Jois. So far, they have been to India several times and are among a small group of about 100 people worldwide who are authorized to teach Ashtanga Yoga.

Again, I have related this story in the context of the formula relating to vision — "I can do anything I have a vision for, the courage to declare and the willingness to stay responsible for." Rachelle had a vision to make a difference in people's lives. Yoga became her new vision, she had the courage to declare that vision to the world, and stay responsible for the outcome. She did whatever it took to overcome all obstacles and to turn that vision into reality. Rachelle has fulfilled her dream.

Esther

When my elder daughter, Esther, was in her early teens, her vision was to be a nurse. At that time there were few female doctors, so being a doctor was not an option that had occurred to her.

When Esther was about 14, we were on a family vacation and stopped off in Chicago to visit our friends, Robert and Mary Krugman. Coincidentally, their niece who was 18 years old was visiting them at the same time. She told Esther that she was going to study medicine and become a doctor. Esther's eyes lit up. In a flash, she had a new option. She had never considered the possibility of becoming a physician — and that young woman opened up a new world for her. Her vision for who she could be, changed from being a nurse to being a doctor — and she never wavered from that golden dream.

She finished high school, pursued undergraduate studies in Science at McGill, and was accepted in medicine at McMaster University a year before she completed her B.Sc. Esther graduated from McMaster as a family physician. For the next fifteen years she had a very successful practice with two other female physicians. She had the vision, and she made it happen.

In the mid-'90s, Esther began to feel dissatisfied with the way she was practicing medicine. She felt that, given our health care system, she was unable to give enough time to her patients and as a physician schooled only in western medicine she felt limited in what she was able to offer to her patients. She was introduced to Dr. Deepak Chopra's philosophy and teachings, and became intrigued with his approach to health and healing which is very much based on practicing preventative medicine. Esther subsequently developed a close professional relationship with Dr. Chopra and became licensed to give a number of his courses, including "Primordial Sound Meditation."

From her association with Dr. Chopra, she developed a new vision of herself as a physician. She saw the possibility of adding an entirely new dimension to her medical practice, combining traditional western medicine with alternative medicine. As this new vision was crystallizing, Esther learned of a new two-year program in alternative medicine offered at the University of Arizona in Tucson. That program was developed by Dr. Andrew Weil, who is world famous for his teachings in alternative medicine.

The program is offered to qualified medical practitioners through a combination of residency and extension courses. Esther enrolled in the program in the second year it was offered and, when she graduated in 2003, she was class valedictorian at her graduation ceremonies. She now shares Dr. Weil's approach and practices "Integrated Medicine," a combination of traditional western medicine and alternative medicine.

Esther left her practice with her two associates in family medicine in 2003 and, in real terms, became an entrepreneur, investing in, building and establishing a clinic; The Family Practice Centre of Integrative Health and Healing in Burlington, Ontario. The clinic offers patients a variety of alternative health and healing disciplines, including homeopathy, naturopathy, Chinese medicine, acupuncture, chiropractic, and massage therapy. This is the first such practice in Canada and was born out of Esther's need to be able to offer her patients much more than she had previously been able to provide. She shares Dr. Weil's lofty vision to change the face of health care and healing on the planet.

Our Family on my beach in Barbados
Philip, Rachelle, Paul, me, Jordana, Shirley, Alana, Harrison, Esther and Keith

Philip and his wife,
Marie-France
(They were not yet
married when we took
this photograph.)

Shirley and me with Esther,
Philip and Rachelle

199

I am truly in awe of Esther for having the courage and making the commitments she has had throughout her life. It took a lot of courage to give up an established, fifteen-year-old practice to head into uncharted waters and to invest a significant amount of her life savings in a new entrepreneurial venture. She put everything at risk to realize her dream. It also required a huge commitment to go back to school as a mature student. She made regular visits to a medical school campus more than 2,000 miles away, while at the same time maintaining her medical practice, continuing to give her meditation courses, and being a wife, mother and homemaker.

I know that Esther could not have accomplished all of this without the commitment and support of her husband, Keith. In addition to the moral support he gave her as a fellow physician, he put her needs ahead of his own and was there for her during those years.

Esther's clinic has been very successful to date. She has received recognition from her peers, as well as from her patients who truly appreciate what she now offers them. She has also received academic recognition through her appointment as an Associate Professor in Family Medicine at McMaster University as well as Clinical Assistant Professor in the Department of Medicine at the University of Arizona.

I have told this story in the context of the formula relating to vision: "I can do anything I have a vision for, the courage to declare, and the willingness to stay responsible for." Esther had a vision, she had the courage to declare that belief to the world, and she took responsibility to do whatever it took, overcoming all obstacles, to turn her dream into reality.

We feel truly blessed.

19

A MATTER OF FAITH

I have been asked many times, "What, more than anything else, has contributed to your success?" I don't have to think hard for an answer: All my life I have been what I call "an opening for contribution."

By this I mean I have always looked for, embraced and welcomed help and contributions from any source, including from my guardian angel. I believe that, because I was an opening for contribution, people have always shown up to contribute to me. So, much of what I have achieved has been due largely to the offerings I received from so many throughout my life. I don't mean to suggest that I had no part at all in my own success, because it was always my responsibility to evaluate and use — or not use — what was offered to me. It was always up to me to make things happen, and that's what I did: *I made things happen.* So I do take some credit.

In the context of being an opening for contribution, I have referred again and again to my guardian angel. I believe, and have faith, that she will show up to direct me whenever necessary, whether I am aware that I need to be directed at the time or not.

When I look back on the many times I have credited my guardian angel for directing me, I can see that it has always been marked by events and circumstances that she manipulated in my favour.

She saw to it that I got out of Holland, which saved my life. She saw to it that my uncle John came to Barbados, which re-directed me from Israel to Montreal. She saw to it that I met Irving Haznof, who took me to the Young People's Club where I became president, started building my self-esteem, and met Shirley, who has made the greatest contribution of all to my life. My guardian angel saw to it that I failed my auditing exam, which redirected me from accounting into a life as an entrepreneur. She saw to it that the factors pulled the plug on our credit, which set off a chain of events that gave me the opportunity to re-invent Shirmax. She saw to it that Howard and Philip showed up to invent Thyme Maternity, which became the financial engine that helped to rebuild Shirmax. She manipulated the events and circumstances that resulted in the sale of Shirmax — and on and on. Although I can take credit for how I responded to and capitalized on all of these events, I cannot take credit for creating any of them. They were manipulated in my favour (I say) by my guardian angel.

I have already acknowledged that having a guardian angel is my interpretation of whatever it may be that directs my life. Many may not agree with that interpretation. After all, everyone has been affected by events and circumstances that have turned out well for them, but they may be more likely to credit their own good judgement for the happy outcome than something as offbeat as a guardian angel. However, for me, I cannot honestly credit my own good judgement for all the consistently "good" things that have happened to me. They were more than mere coincidences. So, I feel blessed in having a guiding force in my life that I choose to call my guardian angel.

I have often asked myself why it is that my guardian angel seems to have been there for me at almost every turn. I always come up with the same answer, it must have something to do with believing and having faith that she is there for me and that she will always show up when I need her, or when the time is right. My faith in my guardian angel creates an opening for her to exert her influence.

Soul Searching

Speaking of faith, I struggled with my relationship with my God for a long time. I subscribe to the widely held belief that God is the

Creator and, as the Creator, He has created everything. I accept that good things happen, and that bad things happen and I can accept that there is sickness and death and that natural catastrophes occur. I have had no quarrel with my God with respect to any of them. I accept them all as being part of the natural order. However, for a long time I had a quarrel with my God in connection with man's inhumanity to man. I could not accept that God, who created man, could allow man to perpetrate the atrocities that men commit.

In the spring of 2004, I visited the concentration camps of Auschwitz and Birkenau in Poland. The horror of what went on there tormented me and I was genuinely haunted by the questions: Where is God? How could God allow this to happen? How could God allow all of this evil and inhumanity? I could not come to terms with a God that could endow man with such evil capabilities. Until recently, that was my relationship with my God — distrusting my faith, and troubling questions with no answers.

Traditionally, the Jewish holy day of Yom Kippur, the Day of Atonement, is celebrated by a full night and day of fasting and services in the Synagogue. Yom Kippur ends with the blowing of the *shoffar* — the ram's horn. In 2004, at the end of the services, after fasting for about 27 hours, everyone was in a rush to leave the Synagogue, when the Rabbi asked us to sit down. He told us the following story:

A teacher asks his students, "Tell me, class, is there a God?"
They reply, "Yes."
"Is God the Creator?"
"Yes."
"Does that mean that God has created everything?"
"Yes"
"You're sure that God has created absolutely everything?"
"Yes."
"Is there evil in the world?"
"Yes."
"So, if there is evil and if God has created everything, then it follows that God has also created evil."

The students pondered this for a while but could not rebut it so the teacher felt satisfied that he had managed to prove his own personal bias — that God is the creator of evil.

One of the students then stood up and asked, "Teacher, can I ask you a few questions?

And the teacher said, "Of course."

"Teacher, is there cold?"

"Yes."

"No teacher, there is no cold. There is just an absence of heat.

And the teacher said, "I guess so. Yes, I agree."

And the student continued, "Teacher, is there darkness?"

"Sure."

"No, teacher, there is no darkness, there is just an absence of light. With a total absence of light there is nothingness. So there is no darkness, there is just an absence of light."

And the teacher said, "Again, I must agree."

"Teacher, is there evil?"

And the teacher said, "We all just agreed that there is evil."

The student then said, "No, teacher, there is no evil. There is just an absence of God."

That student was Albert Einstein!

It took me some time to internalize that story. But the more I thought about it, the more I began to realize that the story provided me with the key to answering the questions that had been plaguing me with regard to my God. I reasoned that God created man and gave him a special gift — the ability to think for himself and make choices. But free choice is an "imperfect" gift. It is like a double-edged sword: man is free to make bad choices as well as good choices. Since God is the Creator of all things, I held Him responsible and accountable for all the bad choices man has made and all the evil man has perpetrated on his fellow man.

Now, after internalizing the Rabbi's story, my perception is that people who perpetrate evil on their fellow man make a choice and they make that choice out of an absence of God in their lives. *It is not God who is responsible for the evil and horror that man perpetrates on his fellow man. It is people who have not embraced God; it is the absence of God!*

Because of this interpretation, my relationship with my God has changed. I no longer hold my God responsible or accountable for all the evil men do. I am now at peace with my God.

BRUSHES WITH DEATH

AT THIS POINT, ALLOW ME TO RELATE a couple of personal experiences that put me in touch with my mortality...and even closer to my God. These experiences certainly helped me get my priorities straight and have affected how I live my life.

The Swimming Incident

Barbados has a tremendous pull on me and I have been returning to the Island regularly since I left in 1953. I love Barbados and particularly Accra Beach, where I spent much of my youth. When I'm there I feel as if I'm 18 again. I am a strong swimmer and, when I am at my beach I take every opportunity to swim.

I've always been a high-energy person and every morning when I am there, I get up at 6 o'clock and go into the ocean for a 60-minute swim. I've been doing that for years. I start at a good pace for the first 50 minutes and then I swim flat out for the last 10 minutes. When I'm through I'm totally exhausted. It takes me a little while to get my wind back, then I'm fine. I find that swim exhilarating.

In 1998, our entire family — children, grandchildren, everyone — went to Barbados over the Christmas holidays. We stayed in an apartment right on "my beach" and, of course, I did my morning swim every day.

The water is usually very calm there, but on the last day of our stay, it was very rough. I had some reservations as to whether I should go into the rough waters, but I did not want give up my last opportunity to swim before going home. So I put on my goggles and went into the water. It was a tough swim because the waves were unusually high and they were tossing me around a lot, but I persevered.

As usual, I did my first 50 minutes, and then I let it all out for the last 10 minutes. I gave it everything I had. Now, with the rough water and all, I had drifted off my usual course and I finished too far from shore and in an area where there is often an undertow. The waves were very high, I was exhausted and breathing heavily. In fact, I was hyperventilating, which meant that I was breathing through my mouth to get the oxygen I needed. The waves kept splashing water into my mouth and I started to swallow water, which made me choke. To make matters worse, the tide was pulling me out to sea. I knew I was in trouble.

It was about a quarter to seven in the morning and there were very few people on the beach. I called for help but I was too far out to be heard, so I started waving my hands to attract attention. However, every time I tried to wave I couldn't hold myself up and I went under and swallowed more water! At that point I knew I was in serious trouble and I saw no way out.

I actually came to terms with the fact that I was going to drown. The only thing I could think of was that everybody's going to say, "Max loved the water so much. Isn't it fitting that the way he went was in the water."

That's what I was thinking when I decided to let go, to give up. However, just as I was waving my last couple of waves, my son-in-law, Keith, came onto the beach and he saw me. In an instant he realized I was in trouble and I saw him come into the water. Now, Keith is not a strong swimmer and I knew that if he came in after me that far out, he would also get into trouble and he would drown too.

I thought to myself, "This is not acceptable. It's bad enough that one of the family goes, but two of us is intolerable."

At that point I put my head down into the water, stopped breathing and I started to propel my arms with an energy that I had no idea I had. My mind was numb. I just kept propelling my arms for what seemed like an eternity and somehow got myself out of the tide and made it to shore. In retrospect, it was a super-human effort. I felt as if I was having an "out of body" experience. Had Keith not come into the water, I would have given up, but the prospect of both of us drowning was intolerable to me, and that saved my life.

Once again, my guardian angel showed up for me that morning by sending Keith out onto the beach. Thank you, guardian angel.

The Heart Incident

Back home in Montreal, a few days after my swimming experience, I began to have discomfort in my chest, much like indigestion. The discomfort was not severe, but it was persistent and somewhat disconcerting. After tolerating it for a couple of days, I went to the hospital and was sent immediately to have an angiogram. The cardiologist determined that, although my arteries were generally clean, I had a blockage at one spot.

As I understand it, what often happens is that a piece of plaque breaks off in an artery and lodges somewhere up the line and causes a blockage. I wondered if that had happened to me as a result of my superhuman effort and experience in Barbados, or was it a mere coincidence that I should have the problem one week later. The doctors acknowledged that it was possible, but that they had no way of knowing. Anyway, they did an angioplasty, which involves inserting a stent into the artery to open the blockage. A few days later I felt fine and I quickly forgot about the incident.

Two years later, I began having that same feeling of indigestion in my chest and, because of my previous experience, I went to see my doctor. He told me he could find nothing wrong, but that, given the symptoms and my history, he thought I should go straight to the hospital. At the hospital they take no chances with what might be a cardiac problem, so they took me right in, put me on a monitor and did some tests. They told me they didn't see anything wrong, but as long as I was there, they thought it was a good idea for me to stay for a few hours so they could keep me on a monitor.

Shirley went out and picked up some supper and the two of us ate in the little cubicle I had in the emergency room. Around 9:30 I told Shirley that as long as I was already there, I might as well lie down and rest, and I suggested she go home and I would call her when they released me. So she left, and I lay down very comfortably, not concerned any more and ready to go to sleep.

A little after ten, all hell broke loose in the emergency room. The loudspeaker started blaring "Code blue! Code blue!" and several people came running into my cubicle. They unhooked me in a hurry, wheeled me into a code blue room. A doctor rushed in and told me that the readings on the monitor were going wild and that I was having a massive heart attack.

As soon as the alarms went off, a nurse had called Shirley and told her that I was having a heart attack and that she should come back to the hospital immediately. She told her not to drive herself but to take a taxi. She also told her to call any family members and have them come in as well. So Shirley and all my family came to the hospital. Philip, Alex and his wife Vivian, Betty and Jack, and Ellen and Peter. When I saw Shirley, I said, "Honey, we've got a problem."

Meanwhile, the chief cardiologist was called at home and asked to come in. So he, the doctor in charge of the emergency room, and a few other doctors got into a huddle discussing my case.

At one point, the chief cardiologist came over to me and said, "We've got a difficult decision to make. You're having a serious heart attack and we are considering two options. One is to go in and do an angioplasty and unblock the artery. However, our angiogram team has gone home and it will take us a few hours to get them together to do the procedure. By that time most of your heart will be damaged. The other option is to give you a medication that can open up your arteries, but there's a very good chance that it will cause a stroke."

In the meantime, I was not feeling much of anything, except that I was numb from what was going on around me. Alex, who is my lawyer, was pacing back and forth and at one point asked, "Max is there anything you want to tell me, want me to do or take care of?" And I said, "No, we've already done all that." Eventually, one of the doctors came in and said, "We've decided that we cannot take a chance with the medication so we're doing our best to pull a team together as soon as possible to do an angiogram."

While we were waiting, I asked for a telephone so I could call my elder daughter, Esther. I had a message for her. I told her, "I don't know what's going to happen here, but I want you to know that if I do go I have no regrets, except that I would be leaving Mommy alone. I would hate to go thinking she will be left alone and I hope she can find someone to spend the rest of her life with. I don't want you or the others to give her a hard time." And Esther said, "I got it."

It took another hour or so for them to pull the team together to do the angiogram. They wheeled me out of the code blue room, along a corridor, and down to the operating room where all my family were standing outside looking very grim and sombre.

They don't put you to sleep when they do an angiogram. There was a monitor over my head and I could see everything that was happening. They inserted a long probe with a tiny camera on the end of it through an incision in my groin and I watched it go up through my arteries, I think right into my heart.

The doctor who was performing the procedure said to me, "I don't know what they're talking about. You're as clean as a baby. There's not a damn thing going on with your heart. Max, just forget that this ever happened and get on with your life", and they wheeled me out.

Everyone was overwhelmed with relief. We didn't know whether to laugh or cry. I had to lie flat on my back for about five hours after the procedure so the incision in my groin could close up. The next morning I was back at work.

Before I left the hospital, the doctor who was the attending physician in the emergency room, came to see me and she said, "I cannot tell you how happy I am to see you. I was sure I was losing you last night." That was one hell of an experience for me and my family. Although this episode was more of a false alarm than a brush with death, it certainly had the same effect. It helped me get my priorities straight.

As a postscript, I went to see a series of specialists to try to find out what had happened — why was I diagnosed as having a heart attack when I wasn't. Everyone gave me the same answer, "We don't know. We can only assume that it was triggered by some kind of electrical "short" in your heart that caused the electrocardiogram to register what looked like a massive heart attack."

The hospital gave me a copy of that electrocardiogram so I could show it to the doctor if something like that ever happened again.

20

SELLING SHIRMAX

Iₙ the late fall of 1998 I received a call from Stephen Reitman, one of the two brothers who run the Reitman organization, inviting me to join him for lunch. Now, to put this call into perspective, I should explain that Shirmax and Reitmans were fierce competitors and had been so for many years — not only competing as retailers locking horns in the marketplace for customers, but also competing for staff and real estate. Also, many years before that phone call, Stephen and I had been embroiled in a conflict and we had had no contact since. I will relate the circumstances of that conflict here because it brings an interesting dimension to what happened next.

Many years ago, when we were a much smaller company, the idea of taking care of, or empowering, our staff was as foreign to me as the thought of speaking Japanese. Certainly, I had good relationships with some of our people, but we were struggling to survive from day to day and we paid no attention to nurturing or taking care of our general population of employees. A chain of events occurred that caused all that to change.

In 1978, when Laurie Lewin joined Shirmax, he came to us from a fashion retailer, MIA Fashions, that had just gone bankrupt. Laurie brought a number of people from MIA with him. At MIA, Laurie had had a very good merchandise manager whose name was Barbara Lyons-Tremblay. We tried to persuade Barbara to join us as well, but she declined. She had had an offer from Reitmans, and she felt it would look better on her CV in the future if she had worked for a large company like Reitmans rather than a small maternity retailer, as Shirmax was at that time. So she accepted the Reitmans offer. I was disappointed, but I told her that if she ever decided to make a change I would appreciate if she would call me first. She joined Reitmans and worked for them for several years. We had an ongoing friendly relationship during that period partly because she had worked with many of the people who were now with Shirmax,

In 1982, Barbara called me to say that she was ready to make a change, and asked if we could talk. We did, and she joined Shirmax as Merchandise Manager for our maternity division.

Very soon after Barbara joined us, I got a call from Stephen Reitman. This was interesting inasmuch as I had never met or spoken to Stephen so I had absolutely no relationship with him. He told me that he understood that I had hired Barbara, he congratulated me on that hire and let me know that she was very capable and he was sure she would do a great job for Shirmax. He wished me the best of luck, but then he went on to say that often when people leave a company to join another in the same business, they are tempted to take other employees with them. He asked me, point blank, not to approach any of his people and to make his wishes clearly known to Barbara.

I responded, "Fair enough, Stephen. Thank you for your call."

I spoke to Barbara, she understood the agreement, and that was that.

A couple of years later, in 1984, Barbara came to me and said, "Max, there is a very good buyer at Reitmans, Roslyn Ross, who worked with me while I was there. She called to tell me she has decided to leave Reitmans and I would like to have her join us. I know about the arrangement you have with Stephen, but she is going to be leaving them anyway and it would be a shame to have her go somewhere else. I did not approach her, she called me. Under the circumstances, I would like to hire her."

I told Barbara that I would have to clear it with Stephen first, but to go ahead and meet with Roslyn and to see if there was a basis for a mutually acceptable agreement. I also cautioned her to make it absolutely clear to Roslyn that we would not hire her until after I had cleared it with Stephen. Barbara met with Roslyn and they came to an understanding. Barbara then came to me and said, "OK, Max, call Stephen."

Barbara assured me that she had made a point of telling Roslyn that she should not discuss any of their conversation with anyone until I had cleared it. I called Stephen but he was out of town, so I left a message asking him to call me back as soon as he returned.

The next day, before Stephen could return my call, Roslyn, assuming I had already spoken to Stephen, went to him to acknowledge that she was leaving and joining Shirmax. Not surprisingly, Stephen called me almost immediately. He was incensed and all hell broke loose!

I don't remember his exact words but he said something to the effect of: "Max, you are not a man of your word. We had an agreement and you went behind my back and hired one of my people. I promise, you will pay dearly for this."

I tried to break in on his tirade, but he wouldn't stop and he continued with, "You have nothing to say that I want to hear." And he hung up on me.

I was very upset. In fact, I was in great distress because Reitmans was a much larger company than Shirmax, and I knew that Reitmans had the wherewithal to do us great harm. I called him back several times but he would not take my calls.

Within days Stephen hired away our entire Store Operations management team — including Ruth Asher, our V-P Store Operations. A short time later we started getting calls from our people in the field telling us that Ruth, (who was now V-P Store Operations for Reitmans), was planning a trip across Canada and that she wanted to meet with them. Having just lost most of our senior management team for store operations, we could not afford to lose anyone else. Harry Wilson, who was then our Senior V-P

Operations, and I decided on a defensive maneuver. We orchestrated an emergency meeting at Head Office for all our key store and field managers. So. when Ruth Asher took her trip, there were very few people she could meet with and she came back empty handed — but Stephen had made his point.

I have not told this story to make Stephen wrong. We were both caught up in an unfortunate chain of events. I am telling it to credit Stephen with being the catalyst that moved us to create the culture we had at Shirmax. Because of that experience with Stephen, I came face to face with the fact that we had done very little to encourage loyalty and foster commitment from our employees — and I saw just how vulnerable we were.

That experience was the wake-up call that inspired me to create a new culture at Shirmax, a culture that fostered fierce loyalty and commitment. Thank you, Stephen Reitman.

I did not hear from Stephen again until he called and invited me to lunch in November 1998. At that lunch, our conversation went something like this:

"Max, we are both in the same business, investing and competing in the same markets and duplicating costs. It would simplify life for both of us if Reitmans acquired Shirmax. So, we would like to buy Shirmax."

To which I responded, "That's interesting, Stephen, but Shirmax is not for sale."

"Let's talk about that," he said.

"It's not that I wouldn't consider selling," I replied, "but I don't believe the company is saleable today at a price I would want to get for it. I have a vision of taking this company to a point where it will have that value, but it's not there today. So, today, Shirmax is not for sale."

But he persisted. "What price are you thinking about? Give me the number."

And I said, "No, Stephen, I won't put out my number because I cannot justify it today."

We parted company and agreed that we would talk again another day. Stephen called me back a few days later and told me his brother, Jeremy, would like to talk with me. I agreed and we met. After a few pleasantries, Jeremy came right to the point. Our conversation went approximately as follows:

"Put your number on the table."

"Jeremy, I cannot justify the price I want at this time...."

"Put your number on the table."

"OK, the number I'm looking at is $5.50 a share."

"You're right, it's not worth that."

"Thank you."

And that was that.

Although, Reitmans was a logical buyer for Shirmax, they had a history of always looking for bargains and I was sure that Shirmax would never meet their criterion of a "bargain." So, I pretty well wrote them off as ever becoming a serious buyer. My strategy was to build a business that would appeal to a potential U.S. buyer. I believed that the greatest value would be to an American company who could use Shirmax to enter the Canadian market and who could also take our business concepts and expand them into the United States. No Canadian buyer could take our concepts into the U.S. market as readily as an American company that was already established in that market. As far as I was concerned, our target buyer was a U.S. fashion retailer.

For the next four years Shirmax continued to do well. We were building a business that I was very proud of and we were becoming more and more profitable. I was confident I would eventually be able to say to a prospective buyer, "This business is worth what I want for it, and a lot more." We stayed the course. We built the Addition-Elle Fashion Outlet Division to complement our established Addition-Elle operation, and that added further value to the company.

In the meantime, my brother Alex and John Swidler, acting as intermediaries, kept an informal dialogue going with Reitmans. From time to time the Reitman brothers reiterated their interest in acquiring Shirmax, but since I didn't believe that would ever happen, my focus remained on attracting an American buyer.

At some point in the year 2000, at one of our Board meetings, the number of $4.50 a share came up during a discussion in connection with Reitmans. I am not sure if it came from Reitmans, or if it was just speculation on our part. In any case, I found myself under tremendous pressure from my mentors and the Shirmax Board to consider the possibility of selling, perhaps not at $4.50, but maybe at $5 a share.

I refused. I was adamant. I said "No." Even James Landry, my closest working associate and who had a huge influence on me, pressed me to consider the possibility of $5 a share. His reasoning was that even though it may have had the value I believed it had, it would be worth only what a buyer was prepared to pay when I was ready to sell — the old "bird in the hand" adage.

I remember saying to him, "James, I promise you, when we're ready to sell, there will be a buyer at the price we want. *The universe will deliver.* You know, James, the universe always delivers for us. All we have to do is to put our intention on the result we want and stay focused on that result. *When the time is right, and we are really ready, I promise you a buyer will show up.*"

THE UNIVERSE WILL DELIVER

ANYONE WHO KNOWS ME WELL has heard me use the phrase, "The universe will deliver." For me, this is a very empowering concept I embrace and use in all aspects of my life. In fact it is not just a belief, it is real for me that the universe will deliver to me any result I am looking for and stay focused on. I have complete trust that the universe will deliver for me, and it has been my experience that it does.

About 20 years ago, I began to notice that every time I intended to have something happen — that is, every time I focused on a

"James, I promise you, when we're ready to sell, there will be a buyer at the price we want. The universe will deliver!"

specific objective — information and/or help came my way to facilitate achieving that objective.

I noticed that this happened over and over again, and I wondered whether I was really that lucky. Were these coincidences that constantly stacked up in my favour, or were they other examples of my guardian angel being there for me? While I was considering these questions, I had several experiences that made me realize that the universe "delivering" for me had nothing to do with luck or coincidence or guardian angels. It had simply to do with how the universe works.

When I first began to understand the concept of the universe delivering, I knew what that meant for me, but I was still very careful with whom I used the expression because I could not easily explain how and why it worked. I was concerned that it made me sound off-the-wall and mystical and that it called my credibility into question. Today, however, I use the expression freely because I understand how and why it works, and that it is not at all mystical. To explain, it is, perhaps, easiest to cite an example.

A Trip to India

In the late '80s, stemming from a conversation I had with my daughter, Rachelle, I started to understand how the universe delivers. Rachelle and I have always had a special rapport. When she was in her late teens she thought that she would like to go to India and spend time in the mountains there with a guru. She told me she would love to have me go with her and share the adventure and experience.

The idea intrigued me, but I could not go with her at the time because I was deeply involved in my business. However, I told her that it was something I would very much like to do and that we would go to India together as soon as I could free myself up. The following evening, Shirley and I went to a movie with another couple. The four of us were deep in conversation while we waited in line for the ticket booth to open.

While we were chatting, my ears picked up a conversation between two young men standing behind us. One of them had just come back from India after spending three months in the mountains with a guru. I turned around and said to him, "Excuse me, but I could not help but overhear you say that you had just come back from studying with a guru in India. I am very interested in doing the same thing, and I would like to talk to you about your trip. Would you mind giving me your phone number so I can get in touch with you?" He gave me his number.

The significance of the incident did not really register with me immediately but when I got home that evening I had time to think about it and I wondered, "How is this possible? Two days ago the idea of a trip to India was nowhere in my mind, but tonight, twenty-four hours after having my conversation with Rachelle, I find myself standing next to a total stranger who has just come back from India and who could give me information I needed."

I had difficulty explaining how or why the incident happened. First, I told myself that I was very lucky and that the encounter was just coincidence. But I rejected that idea because incidents like this, where I put my intention on something and *voilà* it's delivered, have happened to me many times before. There had to be an explanation.

Eventually, I realized there was a pattern to these apparent coincidences. They always began with a clear intention I was focused on or a declaration I made. In this case, my focus was to go to India and the information I would need was made available to me just like that. Why did that happen? How did that happen? How could I explain it? From pondering these questions, I began to understand how the concept of "the universe will deliver" works.

I saw that it was not a matter of luck or coincidence. Rather, there was a sea of unlimited information swirling around us all the time. That information is always there, but we don't notice it. In fact, we're not even aware of its existence. But when we put our intention and focus on something, it's as though we put up an antenna or throw out a "hook", looking to snag information that supports our intention.

Sooner or later that information shows up and, because we are now conscious of it, we hook it and reel it in. So, those two young men who were standing in the line behind us were going to be there having their conversation whether I was there or not, or whether I was interested or not. Had I not had my conversation with Rachelle the day before about going to India, I would not have overheard them. The conversation would have been there regardless, but it would have had no relevance to me; it would not have existed for me. It was only because I had declared my intention that my ears perked up when I heard the word "India." And I hooked on to that bit of conversation out of all of the other bits and pieces of information that were swirling around me at the time.

So, information or help is always available to us, or will become available. All we have to do is stay focused on our intention and the universe will deliver — perhaps not immediately, but certainly when the time is appropriate. That is simply the way the universe works.

Now, despite making this case, I must say I cannot prove categorically that it is so. Nonetheless, I know it works for me. I believe it works for me because I am confident it will. I expect it, I trust that it will, and I am conscious of it when it does.

I have often asked myself why it is that the universe appears to deliver for me so much more often than it appears to deliver for others? Again, my answer is simple — it does not!

The universe can and does deliver for everyone. I believe it is just that I am more conscious of it than most people. All it requires is that I be aware that it is available, that we be open to it, have confidence in it, expect it, and take notice of it when it does deliver.

The Lost Wallet

Another example of the universe delivering for me is rather amusing now — but it certainly wasn't amusing at the time.

After Rachelle moved to Toronto and met Paul Gold, they eventually became engaged and we started making wedding plans. Paul's parents, who live in Toronto, suggested that the four of them come to Montreal to help plan the wedding. So, one Saturday in the early spring, Rachelle, Paul and his parents flew to Montreal for the weekend. We had a number of decisions to make, one of which was to choose a band for the reception. We had heard about a band playing at the Grey Rocks Hotel in the Laurentians, and we decided to drive up to hear them and to see if they would be suitable to hire for the wedding.

I rented a van and the six of us drove up north. At the hotel, we had a couple of drinks, ate some nibbles and listened to the band. When it was time to leave, I reached for my wallet to pay for the drinks but it was missing. I looked everywhere, but my wallet was nowhere to be found. It was gone! Understandably, everyone was upset. Anyhow, we drove back to Montreal, I took Paul and his parents to their hotel and the rest of us came home and went to bed.

What I refer to as my wallet was actually a credit card case, which contained my driver's license, my medicare card and all of my credit cards. That wallet was crucial to my day-to-day functioning. It just didn't make sense to me that I could lose something as important as my credit-card wallet. It really bothered me, and I couldn't sleep.

I got up around five in the morning and I started to play back the day before in my mind. I remembered that just before we got onto the Autoroute on our way up north, I had stopped for gas and had paid for it with my credit card. Obviously, I had had my wallet in the car. I didn't get out of the car when we gassed up, so I could not have left it at the gas station. What could have happened? Then I remembered that while we were on the Autoroute the passengers in the back of the van were cold because they were a long way from the heater, and I turned the heat up to high in order to get the heat back to them. However, I was sitting right in front of the vent and I was very warm, so I pulled over onto the shoulder, got out and took off my jacket.

The only thing that made sense to me was that my credit card wallet must have fallen out of my jacket pocket when I took it off. I woke Shirley and said, "Come with me."

"Where? It's 6:30 in the morning. What are you doing?"

"We're going to get my wallet."

"What are you talking about, you're going to get your wallet?"

"My wallet is somewhere on the Autoroute and we're going to get it."

Shirley just looked at me and shook her head. We threw on some clothes, got into the car and backed out of the garage. As soon as we got onto the driveway, I realized that there had been a light snowfall overnight. At that point, I began to take stock of the situation. Number one, I had no idea where on the 90 kilometres of the Autoroute I had stopped to take off my jacket. Number two, even if I had dropped my wallet, as I reasoned, it would now be covered with snow, so how was I going to find it? (Talk about finding a needle in a haystack!)

Meanwhile, Shirley was giving me static. "Where are we going? This is nuts. You're out of your mind." But it didn't work for me that I should lose such a valuable object and do nothing about it. That was just not an option.

We drove for about 30 kilometres on the Autoroute and I said, "This looks like as good a place as any where I could have stopped to take off my jacket." I pulled over onto the shoulder and said to Shirley, "You walk south, I'll go north, and we'll see if we spot anything." I got out and took, maybe, 30 steps and saw something like a gold light shining up from under the snow. I bent down and brushed away the snow and there was my wallet!

Evidently when it dropped it landed fully open with my gold Visa card on top, and that was what I saw shining through the snow. I picked up the wallet and started back to the car. What a feeling of relief and delight! I motioned for Shirley to come back and I said to her, "Here's my wallet." Shirley said, "You've got to be kidding. Where did you find it?" I was going to play this for all it was worth, so I answered, "Where do you think? Exactly where I expected to find it!" Before we could get back into the car to drive away, a police car pulled up.

"What are you doing here? Is there a problem?"

"I came to find my wallet" — which I showed him in my hand.

He looked at me, shook his head, and said, "I don't even want to go there. Would you just drive your car away, please?"

For me, there is simple explanation: because I believed that the universe would deliver for me, I went back and found my wallet. Without that belief — or faith — I would have stayed in bed and would never have seen my wallet again.

So, referring back to my conversation with James, when I refused to consider $5 a share, I said "No" because I could see that my vision for where I wanted to take the company was becoming a reality, and I had a new number in mind. I believed that when we were ready to sell, the universe would deliver a buyer who would pay that price, and that's what I stayed focused on.

TIME TO SELL

I CONTINUED TO SAY "NO, NO, NO" until the end of 2001, when I decided that the time had come to put the company on the market. My vision for where I wanted to take the company had become a reality. I believed that our two retail concepts of maternity and plus-sizes were now ready to compete successfully in markets outside Canada and North America. Shirmax was a well-oiled machine that was running smoothly. We were profitable and there was great future potential. We had an effective infrastructure with an incredible team capable of managing not only our ongoing operations, but also a much larger operation.

I was confident that a U.S. company could come into Canada, buy Shirmax and leave the Canadian operation intact. The new owners would not have to worry about running Shirmax, and if they were prepared to implement our strategies for growing the business in the United States, it would greatly enhance the value for them. I believed this was a winning formula for a U.S. buyer.

We approached Bear Stearns, a prominent U.S. investment banker, and gave them a mandate to market Shirmax.

A SOBERING EXPERIENCE

IN ALL MY YEARS IN BUSINESS, one of the things I have been most proud of is the personal relationships I've had with so many people, both inside and outside of Shirmax, and that I have been able to retain many of those relationships even after the business relationship ended. I felt sure there were very few who harbored any ill feelings toward me or the company. I guess believing that served me well. But the universe has a way of bringing us down to earth. While we were involved in the process of selling Shirmax, I had a sobering experience, that brought me down to earth with a crash.

After a series of coincidences, I got in touch with an old friend, Mickey Ross, whom I had not seen for nearly 25 years. Mickey went all the way back to the very beginning when I started in business. He owned the company that did our window dressing in our very first store. But the window dressing part was really incidental to the fact that Mickey became a very good friend to Shirley and me and to most of my family. In fact, he always said he felt the same about my father as he felt about his own. For him, the relationship was not about making money, it was about friendship.

For example, one evening when he and three of his employees were dressing our windows and store interior, we all worked until after 10 o'clock. Mickey then took everyone, including Shirley, Jack and me, out for a Chinese dinner, which must have cost him $80 at the time, even though he was paid only $25 for the work he had done that evening. In retrospect, I'm sure there was nothing I could have asked of Mickey that he would not have done for me.

As our business grew and we became a national chain, Mickey also grew his business nationally to accommodate our growth. In that context, our affiliation, and our friendship, spanned over twenty years. However, our business relationship eventually came to an end, and with it came the end of our friendship. With the passage of time I had only a very dim recollection of how our association ended. I knew that Shirmax had grown to the point where it made sense for us to bring our window dressing in-house. We were spread across the country and it was cheaper and more effective to have our own window dressing staff. I assumed that our business relationship just came to an end and that we simply went our separate ways, and so lost touch with each other.

Anyhow, I was thrilled when we made contact again, and I invited Mickey and his companion to brunch at our home with Shirley and me and Betty and Jack. Mickey said he would get back to me, which he did the next day. He declined my invitation to brunch but suggested that he and I go out for lunch alone. The reason he gave me was that the women did not know each other and, in the circumstances, his friend might find it a little awkward when the rest of us were trying to catch up. That made sense to me, so I agreed to meet him for lunch.

I was delighted to see Mickey again after such a long time. When we met, I wanted to give him a hug, but he turned away my advance. I was a little taken aback but, anyway, we sat down and started talking. Instead of reminiscing about the good old days, Mickey proceeded to tell me there were some people from his past who had done him wrong. He was waiting to meet them in the hereafter to give them a piece of his mind, and of all the people he was waiting to meet on the other side, he most wanted to meet Max Konigsberg so he could tell him what he thought of him! He then proceeded to tell me how badly I had hurt him, and that he had been carrying a personal grudge against me for more than 25 years. I was shocked and embarrassed by what he told me because, until that moment, I had no idea that I had hurt him or that he had been living with such bitterness and anger toward me.

Apparently, what had happened was that Harry Wilson, our Vice-President of Operations who was responsible for merchandise presentation, decided that it was no longer viable for us to use outside services and that we should bring window dressing in-house.

Unquestionably, I would have agreed to that. So, when Harry informed Mickey that we no longer required his services, Mickey asked:

"Did you hire me?"

"No."

"Who hired me?"

"Max did."

"OK, if Max hired me, let Max fire me."

So I was called in and I said to Mickey, "I am not responsible for this department any more. It is Harry's area of responsibility and I support his decision."

Clearly, I copped out of my responsibility to Mickey as a friend. I took the easy way out by passing the buck to Harry. Not only did my action hurt him personally — that a friend could do that to him — it also hurt him financially because he was stuck with the national infrastructure he had built to service us and all the costs related to it without any revenues to offset them. I knew that Mickey had put an infrastructure together to take care of our account, but, until our luncheon meeting, I had never considered the implications or the consequences to him of our taking our account away from him.

I have no excuse for inflicting such harm on a valued friend and supplier. Mickey had always been a true and loyal friend and he had done nothing to deserve such treatment. Had I faced the issue directly with Mickey at the time, I am sure we could have made an arrangement that would have been more acceptable, or at least less damaging, to him and his organization.

I sat across from Mickey, embarrassed and completely ashamed that I could have allowed that to happen. I acknowledged that no amount of my saying "I'm sorry" was enough to excuse what had happened. What I did was inexcusable and I hoped that he could forgive me. Thankfully, I had the opportunity to apologize to Mickey. My sense is that we put that whole episode behind us and, once again, Mickey and I have an ongoing relationship.

As a result of that humbling experience, I now realize that there may well be others out there who have an axe to grind with me or with their Shirmax experience. So, to whomever they may be, I apologize.

THE SALE

BECAUSE OF THE OPEN COMMUNICATION we had at Shirmax, everyone in the company knew that we were trying to build an organization that could expand into the United States and that it was my intention either to try to sell Shirmax outright or to merge, preferably with a U.S. company. In fact, I had declared that intention in my addresses to shareholders at the last three Shirmax annual meetings. So, it came as no surprise to anyone when we gave Bear Stearns their mandate.

Before proceeding with Bear Stearns, however, my brother, Alex, and John Swidler spoke to Reitmans, told them what we were planning, and suggested that, before Shirmax signed a costly contract with Bear Stearns, Reitmans might want to come to the table. But Reitmans declined. So we signed an agreement with Bear Stearns and they prepared a "blue book", a document designed to promote and market the sale of a company.

Shortly after Bear Stearns sent out the blue book to a select group of prospective buyers inviting their interest, Reitmans came back and asked us to put a hold on the Bear Stearns proceedings. They wanted an exclusive option for a short period of time to take a serious look at Shirmax and to come up with an offer. I agreed. In light of the possibility of a quick sale without the emotional turmoil of an auction and keeping the company Canadian, even though I might have got more from a U.S. company, I decided to accept $7 a share. Great value!

I told Alex and John to tell Reitmans that the price was $7 a share, non-negotiable. Reitmans did their due diligence and, without any further discussion about price, came back to us and said, "We're on. We're willing to pay $7 a share." And so it was that Shirmax was sold. I got the price I wanted and I think that Reitmans got a great deal. In fact, it was a good deal for both of us.

It is my belief that this was a marriage made in heaven for Reitmans because it put them in a position to realize tremendous synergies and economies of scale from their acquisition. So, by acquiring Shirmax, Reitmans was in a position to manage their new organization so that both businesses were properly focused and would not step on each other's toes.

From my perspective, this entire episode, starting with my luncheon with Stephen right up to the actual sale, all supported my belief that the universe will deliver. I had put out my intention to sell at my price, I stayed focused on that outcome and the universe delivered. I must also acknowledge my guardian angel for manipulating the many events and circumstances that resulted in the sale.

Thank you again, guardian angel.

21

AFTER THE SALE

Naively, I suppose, I assumed Reitmans would capitalize on what I considered to be Shirmax's major strengths and assets. In my opinion, these were its senior and middle management teams, all the incredibly gifted and committed head-office and field personnel across the country, the company's corporate culture, and its management philosophy and system that had proven to be so successful over the years. I had heard that several of the Reitmans advisors and their Board had recommended that they capitalize on those strengths and assets and not destroy them, but that is hearsay.

I expected Shirmax to continue to operate pretty well intact for at least two years. Again, I assumed that once the new owners had the opportunity to see how Shirmax "really worked" they would adopt the best practices of both companies. Based on those assumptions, I signed a two-year contract and expected to be with Reitmans contributing to that process for at least that time. I also accepted an invitation to become a member of the Reitmans Board of Directors. I even persuaded the established Shirmax team that we would continue to be a team, working together, albeit as part of the larger Reitmans organization, with all the benefits that could accrue from being part of a much larger company. But it was not to be.

I would like to be able to say that everybody "lived happily ever after" especially because for me, personally, the timing was exactly right. I could not have asked for a better ending to an incredible journey. But there was also a lot of sadness. It was heartbreaking that, within three months of the sale, Shirmax had literally disintegrated.

Shirmax was a unique company with a unique culture driven by a number of powerful business concepts and an extraordinary team of talented individuals. It was a huge disappointment to me when Reitmans decided to integrate the Addition-Elle and the Thyme Maternity Divisions into their own operations, and allow Shirmax and everything it represented to disappear. However, it is well known in business circles that merging two companies is a difficult task, and that the merging of two corporate cultures borders on the impossible. The Reitmans and Shirmax cultures were so different that, in retrospect, I recognize that Reitmans took the only course — integrating the two companies — that made sense. Any other strategy would have only prolonged the agony and would probably have had the same outcome. Having praised the strengths and virtues of the Shirmax organization, in retrospect I must also acknowledge that Reitmans, too, is a very well-managed company. In fact, it is a great company!

After the sale was concluded, I planned a dinner party at my home for 40 members of the Shirmax team with whom I had worked very closely. I had formal invitations printed that said something to the effect, "To thank and acknowledge you for helping to bring the Shirmax ship home." That wording turned out to be inappropriate and I was caught off-guard. Just at the time the invitations were being printed, massive layoffs of Shirmax employees were announced. When the invitees received their invitations, the mood became "Your ship came home, but ours sank." I truly believed what I said when the sale was announced — that Shirmax would stay intact for two years, that Reitmans was a growing company and would need good people and, given the quality of our people, that most jobs would be safe. I had not anticipated the level of hurt that would result as a consequence of my good fortune. To this day, I feel very sad about that turn of events.

The party went ahead as planned, although a few of those invited were upset with me and did not attend. Some even told me that they felt I had sold them out. Despite this, everyone who attended did so with good grace. My intention was to acknowledge and honour my guests for their contributions to me and to Shirmax. As things turned out, despite their concern for their future, they took the opportunity to honour me. They all came with touching words of appreciation for the years we had worked together, and for the contributions they said I had made to their lives. It was an evening filled with both joy and sadness. I will always remember and cherish their words.

For me, the sale of Shirmax was bittersweet. It was bitter because of what happened to most of the people who were part of the extended Shirmax family. Shirmax had become the home and family for so many people who expected to live out their working lives with the company. But the rug was pulled out from under them. It was sweet because it brought financial security to me and my family. I had spent 45 years building Shirmax and it was time for me to move on.

Within a couple of months of the sale, it became obvious to me that I was in no position to contribute either to the transition or to ongoing operations. I was powerless and I was only getting in the way. So I went to Jeremy Reitman and told him how I felt and that, although we had a two-year contract, he should not feel bound by it and I was prepared to leave at any time he thought it appropriate. He came back to me in a few days and said he agreed and I was free to go whenever I was ready. I stuck around for a few weeks to clean up my personal files, and then I left. As I said before, I have stayed on as a member of the Reitmans Board of Directors and I am truly honoured to be on their Board.

And so ended my career as a fashion retailer. For my part, my life at Shirmax was a fabulous journey and by any measure it is a success story. I spent 45 years building the business, and I built a wonderful life around that business. For all the years that

Shirmax was part of my life I could say that Shirmax was like a mistress; but she was more than that — she was truly another love in my life.

There were good years, not-so-good years, and bad years. But despite the difficult times and all the challenges I had to overcome, on balance, it was an amazing ride and I loved every moment of it. Shirmax afforded me incredible opportunities to travel and to meet and associate with amazing people; and my years in business contributed to and were the catalyst for my metamorphosis as a person, as a businessman, and as a leader.

There are times when I feel I want to get up on the rooftop and shout to the whole world how lucky I am and to thank the universe for blessing me the way it has, and to thank my guardian angel for taking such impeccable care of me.

I came to the end of that journey, but that is by no means the end of my travels. I had this book to write, and, I hope I have other contributions to make. I look forward with great anticipation to where my guardian angel will direct me and to what the future has in store for me!

PART TWO

BUILDING AN ORGANIZATION THAT WORKS

NOTE TO READER

It occurred to me after I was well into the writing of Part Two that "Building an Organization that Works" has a business context and that some readers, whose interests are not focused primarily on business, may think that this section will be of little interest to them. I am concerned that at some point they may stop reading and, perhaps, not get to Part Three.

I am certain that Part Two will interest, and may even be of great value to many business people. However, the fact remains that many of the discoveries I made and the lessons I learned in the process of building Shirmax can be applied with equal success to building a powerful personal life. Here, in Part Two, I share those discoveries and lessons learned, so I urge you to "soldier on" through Part Two because it is an important preamble to Part Three.

I truly believe that Part Three has great value because it is relevant to all aspects of our lives. It may even make a difference in yours!

M.K.

22

AN EXTRAORDINARY
ORGANIZATION

I HAVE CLAIMED MANY TIMES that Shirmax was an extraordinary organization. I would even go so far as to say that Shirmax was a great organization! It exuded energy and excitement, and it had spirit and many other qualities that most other organizations do not have. Admittedly, extraordinary and great are qualities and so you cannot point to them as you would to a building, a product, or any other physical object. Nonetheless, I assert that Shirmax was an organization that was beyond ordinary; it was therefore *extraordinary*.

I make my claim based on the accomplishments of the Shirmax team in achieving the unprecedented turnaround of taking the company from the brink of disaster in 1993 to the position of one of Canada's leading retail fashion organizations. I also believe my claim is supported by the recognition we received when I was nominated for the CEO of the Year award in 1995, the Entrepreneur of the Year Award in Quebec (which I won) in 1998, and the sale of Shirmax, at a premium price, to Reitmans, Canada's largest specialty store retailer, in 2002. Finally, I believe the overwhelming sadness of 3,000 Shirmax employees who were distressed by the breakup of what they called the Shirmax family when the company was sold, also supports my claim.

Shirmax did not become extraordinary by accident. What made it unique was the culture we created that inspired our people to operate at extraordinary levels; it was the culture that made it possible for everyone to maximize their own potential as well as to contribute to Shirmax maximizing its potential.

ORGANIZATIONS DO NOT WORK

I REFERRED TO AN "ORGANIZATION THAT WORKS" several times in Part One. My definition of an organization that works is: *an organization that maximizes its potential,* i.e., the potential of *all* its assets, human, financial, property, etc., as well as its potential in the marketplace. Given this definition, I assert that organizations do not work because they are inherently inefficient and ineffective. They miss opportunities, waste resources, and allow far too much to fall through the cracks.

Of course, many companies are financially successful, but that success is achieved despite the missed opportunities, built-in inefficiencies and ineffectiveness, etc. They do not maximize their potential. Therefore, they do not satisfy my definition of "an organization that works."

Airlines are a good example of organizations that do not maximize their potential. They may be efficient and effective in many areas, but they are unbelievably inept in others. For instance, virtually all airlines are grossly inefficient in the way they handle baggage. When passengers check their bags for a flight, they cannot be sure that their bags will arrive at their destination when they do.

The direct costs to the airlines of recording, searching for, handling and delivering misdirected and misplaced baggage is enormous, not to mention the indirect costs caused by the irritation, inconvenience and anxiety of the passengers. As a frequent flyer I must assume that the airlines' commitments to equipment maintenance and aircrew training are very different from their commitment to the handling of baggage. If I did not make that assumption, I would never get on a plane again.

I allow as how airlines do many things right and, before the catastrophe of 9/11, many of them were profitable. But as long as they continue to manage baggage the way they do, they will not maximize their potential. This pattern is not unique to airlines. It exists to a greater or lesser degree in all organizations. So, again, I assert that organizations do not maximize their potential and, therefore, *organizations do not work*. With this as a background, I claim that Shirmax came very close to maximizing its potential and so, to being an "organization that works."

This part of the book is intended to give readers a sense of what was involved in our effort to turn Shirmax into an organization that maximized its potential.

Shirmax: Close to being an "Organization that Works"

As the business grew, it became obvious to me that if I were to have any chance of creating an organization that worked, I had to become a better manager and a more effective leader.

Despite the time I spent at McGill and working as an accountant, none of my formal education provided me with much background in business management or leadership. I did not have the knowledge, or receive the training I needed, to take the company to another level. I had been acknowledged as an entrepreneur, I had also been warned that it is nearly impossible to make the transition from entrepreneur to professional manager. However, I had no alternative, so I took on the challenge and set out to get the education and training I needed to make the transition successfully.

Part of that process involved my reading many books, taking courses and attending seminars, all of which contributed to the metamorphosis I went through in my effort to become an effective CEO and leader. All of that instruction contributed to my gaining a better understanding of business principles and techniques and helped me develop my vision of an organization that maximizes its potential — *an organization that works*.

Now, I acknowledge that maximizing a company's potential involves setting an almost impossible goal because it *is* impossible for an organization to maximize its potential across all fronts all the time. So, my vision of an organization that works was never about achieving perfection; it was about continuous improvement — getting better and better all the time across as many fronts as possible. At Shirmax, we strove for continuous improvement every day of our business life. The principle of maximizing our potential drove everything we did. It dictated the way we thought about and how we evaluated our business. It became the foundation of our corporate culture and it defined how we made every decision. Everyone was focused on maximizing the company's, as well as their own, potential.

Creating an organization that maximizes its potential is a daunting task because there are so many opportunities for things to fall through the cracks, get missed, overlooked or forgotten, all of which are by-products of the way people work. So, creating an organization that maximizes its potential requires that everyone operate at extraordinary levels of efficiency, involvement, commitment, intensity, integrity and responsibility in order to achieve the organization's goals.

A HIGHER CALLING

FOR PEOPLE TO PERFORM AT AN EXTRAORDINARY LEVEL requires that they be inspired to respond to what I call a "higher calling." I allow that a higher calling is usually applied to professions and pursuits that have spiritual or moral ideals attached to them. However, I am not using higher calling here in that context. What I mean by that expression is *being motivated to participate or perform at a higher level than one's own personal agenda.*

In some professions, it comes easily to step up to a higher calling. For example, health care workers are motivated by the idea of saving lives; teaching professionals are motivated by the ideal of molding young minds and the lives of future generations; firemen are dedicated to protecting others and saving them from danger; and clergy are driven to save souls. It is easy for people in these fields to see that they are contributing to something important, certainly more important than their own personal agendas.

It is much more difficult for workers in the steel or automotive industries, the sanitation department or the retail clothing business

238

to be similarly inspired because people in those fields cannot see that what they do makes a difference or that they contribute to humanity the way a doctor or a fireman does. However, unless such workers can be inspired to perform at an extraordinary level, the best one can expect is an ordinary organization. I assert that only those organizations where the leaders can inspire their people to a higher calling can go beyond being ordinary to become extraordinary.

At Shirmax we were able to do just that in a fashion retailing environment. We provided our people with a foundation and a working environment that allowed them to satisfy their personal as well as their professional goals. We introduced our people to a corporate culture and value system that empowered them and enriched their lives. We had worthy goals and aspirations that our people could easily identify with and embrace. Every employee was part of a team that was striving to build a unique retail fashion organization in which we could all take pride. And everyone could participate at a level where they understood, and could see, that they truly made a difference. As a result, they strove to be the best.

That was the culture we had at Shirmax. It inspired our people to step up to a higher calling and perform at extraordinary levels.

Some skeptics might suggest that I am over-stating my case, and argue that it is impossible to get ordinary people in ordinary businesses to step up to a higher calling. However, I had an experience recently that I think should dispel such skepticism.

Over the years, Shirley and I have taken many cruises, three of which were with Princess Cruise Lines. The service was always excellent and I always thought that what motivated that service was the customary practice of tipping. I assumed that the *maitre'd*, the waiters, busboys and cabin stewards all bent over backwards to impress passengers so as to get maximum tips. However, I have since changed my opinion.

In 2005, Shirley and I took our three children, their spouses and our three grandchildren, on a cruise aboard the *Caribbean Princess* to celebrate Shirley's and my 70th birthdays. As we were settling into our cabin, we learned from the cruise literature that there had been a change in a Princess policies: tipping was no longer discretionary. Instead, there was an automatic, daily, per-person charge for gratuities. Under this new arrangement, the tips the service staff receive do not depend on the passenger's appreciation of the quality of service. Staff are "rewarded" whether passengers are pleased or not. Initially, I assumed that under this arrangement we would not receive the same level of service as in the past, and I feared the worst.

There were eleven people at our table and I cannot imagine a more difficult group to satisfy. It included two vegans, who eat no animal products whatsoever and who are also wheat and lactose intolerant. This left very few options. Special food had to be bought and stocked and special meals had to be prepared for them. Two exceptions out of 3,300 passengers!

In addition, four others in the group are very fussy eaters. Despite these factors, I cannot begin to describe the service we received. It was beyond outstanding; *it was superb!* From the *maitre'd* down, *everyone* literally jumped through hoops to take care of us according to our individual tastes and needs. The kind of service we received was made possible only because the people who were providing it were committed to rendering service at the highest level. Obviously, Princess Cruise Lines found a way to get their staff — 1,200 people from 45 different countries and cultures — to step up to a higher calling. Certainly it was a higher calling than their own individual agendas.

It was obvious to me that the agenda of the Princess Cruise Line was also the staff's agenda. Certainly, if Princess was able to achieve that in the cruise business, it was equally possible for Shirmax to do the same in the retail fashion industry. And we did!

In the last few decades, many business gurus and business books have taken the position that a manager's prime responsibility is to motivate his or her people. That is not true. In fact, I believe it is one of the biggest misrepresentations ever inflicted on managers.

The truth is that, for the most part, people come to us motivated. They come to us wanting to do a good job, wanting to go home at the end of the day saying, "I did a great job today. I made a contribution. I made a difference. Something is going to be better or different because of me." The problem is that most people become *de-motivated* by the corporate culture, the rules and regulations, the system and their inability to feel that they are making a difference.

So, it is not up to managers to motivate their people; their task is to ensure that they do not de-motivate them! It is their responsibility to inspire their people to be as good as they can possibly be by having worthy goals that call them to a higher calling. Managers must honour their people by having high expectations of them and by creating an environment where they can see themselves making a difference and a meaningful contribution. Obviously, that's what they did at Princess and that's what I believe we did at Shirmax.

To imbue the Shirmax culture into the organization and inspire our people to step up to a higher calling, I developed a series of programs and gave them as seminars to Shirmax management staff across the country.

The programs included:
> Discovery with the CEO
> The Shirmax Management Program (Managing Up)
> Entrepreneurship
> Team Building

The remainder of this part of the book highlights the key elements of these programs.

23

DISCOVERY WITH THE CEO

DISCOVERY WITH THE CEO IS THE TITLE of the first management-related program I developed at Shirmax.

From the outset, building Shirmax and managing the company was a matter of meeting one challenge after another. In the process of meeting those challenges I learned many lessons and made some important discoveries as to how things work, what contributes to things working and what inhibits things from working. The objective of the Discovery with the CEO Program was to share those lessons and discoveries with participants and have them benefit from the knowledge base that had evolved within the company.

The Discovery with the CEO program was given together with the Shirmax Management Program (which I discuss later) in a two-day session to as many as sixty participants at a time, four or five times a year, for more than 12 years. Participants were store managers, assistant store managers, and all field-operations and head-office management personnel. Through these programs we shared our mission and values, our purpose, goals, plans and accomplishments, with the objective of getting participants to "buy into" and embrace them.

Participants started the sessions with one understanding of who we were as a company, what we were committed to and what their jobs and responsibilities were. After two days they were deeply immersed in the Shirmax culture and had a very different understanding of the company, their jobs and their responsibilities. I believe they left the program responding to a higher calling.

The following are the five key elements of the program.

Defining the Business
The Power of Setting Context
Drivers
The Power of Culture
The Formula for Success

DEFINING THE BUSINESS

IT WAS NOT UNTIL THE LATE '80s, after I had been in business for more than thirty years, that I really understood what business we were in. That understanding led to a very important change in the focus and, consequently, the culture of the Shirmax organization.

When I took the Owners and Presidents Management course at Harvard, our marketing professor, Marty Marshall, began one of his sessions with the question, "What business are you in?"

Without exception, everyone answered in terms of their business sector. For example, a doctor said, "I am in the health care profession." A manufacturer said, "I am in the business of manufacturing building tools." I said, "I am in the fashion retail business."

Professor Marshall's reaction to our responses was, "If you really operate your businesses the way you've described them, you won't be in business for very long. If you expect to be successful in business, you had better make sure that you know what your customers want from you. That will force you to define your business so it focuses on your customers."

After some discussion, everyone changed their definitions. The physician said, "What my patients want most from me is the confidence that I know what I am doing and that they are in the best hands, so I am in the business of providing peace of mind." The building tools manufacturer said, "My customers want me to help make their jobs easier. so, I am in the business of making carpentry easy."

I thought about my customers and realized that both pregnant and plus-size women tend not to feel good about their bodies or how they look, so our focus had to be "to honour them for who they are and help them feel good about themselves." I then announced that, "We are in the *feel good* business."

From that experience we made a context shift at Shirmax that focused on helping our customer feel good about themselves, and from that context shift, everything changed. Our purpose and all of our priorities were redirected to focus on the customer and that gave all of our people another perspective on how to address the customer. For example, from that context we adopted a marketing slogan for our plus-size business, "Big is Beautiful" and we operated entirely out of that context.

Retailers must also define their businesses in terms of the market segment in which they choose to compete. They have two options: they can choose to focus on and be driven by lowest cost and lowest price, **or** they can choose to be driven by adding value.

Shirmax could not compete as a low-price operator because we did not have the buying power or the economies of scale that come with size, to compete in the lowest-price market. We had no option but to compete in the value-added market where it is necessary to enhance or *add value* to the product. So everyone at Shirmax had to understand and be focused on adding value, but more than that, *we had to be outstanding* at adding value.

The following is an example of what can happen when we do not understand what business we are really in.

I have always been obsessed with visual presentation. From the time we opened our first store, I was committed to having merchandise presented in a way that was well-coordinated and enticing — visual presentation that "spoke" to the customer. A customer's time is precious and it should be easy for her to make her choice. She should not have to waste her time digging through merchandise to find a golden nugget. I was convinced that having outstanding visual presentation would create more customer satisfaction and generate more sales. It was not difficult for a head-office person who understood the merchandise to set up one store that spoke visually to the customer. It was, however, very difficult to get all the stores in the chain to do the same. Everyone was aware of my commitment to visual presentation, so it was a top priority in the company.

One day, Moira Mooney, one of our senior area managers, called me and said, "Max, we are putting too much emphasis on visual presentation and it's putting undue pressure on the teams in the stores. Everyone is so focused on presentation that we don't have time to serve the customers. I think we should consider loosening this visual presentation noose. Would you please think about this?"

This was not the first time I had heard this concern about visual presentation and I said, "Thanks for bringing this up. I understand what you're saying and it makes sense. Let me think about it and I'll get back to you."

As I thought about it, my first reaction was that it was not acceptable to have the store staff focusing on anything other than the customer, so we should loosen up on our commitment to visual presentation. However, while I was in that mode of thinking, I had an experience that helped me understand, in concrete terms, the business we were in. I went shopping at Costco.*

Shirley and I entertain at our country house most weekends, so we buy groceries in quantity and we often shop at Costco. One evening, while we were at Costco on our way to the grocery section, I saw a table piled high with Oxford cloth, button-down shirts by Arrow priced at $18. Now, that happened to be my favorite shirt. Until then, I had always bought my shirts at Sears and had paid $48, but Costco was now selling them for $18. I did what any consumer would do; I bought four shirts, all I could find in my size.

Now, if I had not been from the fashion industry, I would simply have bought the shirts, complained to whoever would listen to me about how Sears had ripped me off and, maybe, I would have gone back grudgingly to Sears as an unhappy customer when I needed

*I want to make it clear before proceeding, that I have made up many of the details in what follows. My account is not based on any inside information; it is, generally, how I understand the businesses operate.

more shirts (because Costco wouldn't necessarily have them when I wanted them again). But since I was from the fashion industry, I wanted to understand how Costco could sell a shirt so much more cheaply than Sears.

I studied the operations of three retailers, each representing a different sector of fashion retailing: Costco, Sears, and a shopping centre retailer operating smaller specialty stores like Shirmax. In this example, Costco represents the lowest price sector, Sears represents the department store sector, and Shirmax represents the smaller specialty store, shopping centre sector. Let's look first at Costco.

Costco is a very low cost operation:
- cost of occupancy (rent, taxes, etc.) is very low — basic, minimal structures built in the suburbs
- cost of service is very low — totally self-service environment
- cost of management per dollar of sales is very low — very high sales volumes per store
- cost of product is very low — in many cases Costco appears to buy only what they can get deals on and because of their huge buying power, deals are readily available
- mark-up is very low — because of their very low cost structure and very high volumes, as well as their practice of charging customers a membership fee, they are able to operate with a very low mark-up.

Taken together, all of these factors make it possible for Costco to sell my shirt for $18 and still make a profit while giving the customer excellent value. So, Costco and other similar operations set the price/value bar. For me, the value of my shirt that had previously been $48 was then set at $18. Now, let's look at Sears.

Sears cannot compete with Costco on price. Their costs are much higher:
- cost of occupancy is much higher — they build beautiful stores in shopping centres and pay a much higher rent

- cost of service is much higher — they have some sales staff, and they do give some service
- cost of management per dollar of sales is much higher — they have a more complex operation to manage and they generate much lower volumes per store
- cost of product is much higher — Sears has a commitment to have my button-down Oxford cloth shirt in stock all the time, while Costco buys when they can get a deal. So, Costco buys the shirt at favoured prices and Sears pays full price
- mark-up is much higher — Sears must take a higher mark-up to cover higher costs. Because of higher overheads, higher cost of product and higher mark-up, Sears must sell my shirt for $48.

I am using a button-down Oxford cloth shirt as an example, but the same applies to almost all products. Costco and other similar operations set the price/value bars for all products.

So, how can Sears justify their higher prices? Certainly not on the basis of product alone. They can justify their prices only by adding value to the products — *by doing a better job than Costco at adding value* — so customers perceive that they are getting value that is equivalent to the price.

In terms of my button-down Oxford cloth shirt, if all Sears gives me is the product for my $48, then I will perceive that Sears is ripping me off. So, the challenge for Sears is to set themselves apart from Costco and get me to perceive that I am getting good value, despite the fact that I am paying more. They do this by creating "Sears" and Sears products as brands, offering more choice, and by providing better marketing, store environment, customer service, presentation, ease of shopping, etc. These represent added value and help to create the customer's perception that they are getting value.

All of this begs the question, "What business is Sears really in?" If Sears thinks of itself essentially as being in the business of buying and selling product, they will miss the boat because Sears cannot compete on product alone. They must add value to the product. They must understand that they are in the value-added business, and that they have to operate out of that context.

Now, let's consider a shopping-centre specialty store retailer like Shirmax.

A retailer like Shirmax cannot compete with Costco or Sears on price. The relative costs of operating a smaller specialty store in a high-cost shopping centre are much higher than they are for Sears and Costco:

- costs of occupancy, service, management and production are much higher, so mark-up has to be much higher, consequently mark-up has to be much higher, and the price to the customer is also much higher.

So, compared to both Sears and Costco, if all Shirmax gave to the customer was the product for the price, Shirmax would have been seen as ripping off the customer. The only way Shirmax could compete was to do a more outstanding job than Sears at adding value. (One could argue that this was not an issue, because Shirmax did not carry *exactly* the same merchandise as Costco or Sears, and therefore the products were not comparable. But the fact remains, Costco and businesses like Costco, set the price/value bar for all categories of merchandise).

My experience with the Oxford cloth shirt helped me to understand that we were really in the *value-added business* and, in fact, that we were at the *high end* of the value-added business! We could win only if we were outstanding at adding value and we did a better job at it than the competition. We had to see ourselves as being in show business; we had to put on a great show. We had to get our customers to appreciate their total shopping experience — to appreciate our retail concepts as brands, our outstanding store environment, visual presentation and the highest standard of customer service provided by professional, knowledgeable staff. *We had to be outstanding in all of these key value-added areas all the time.* The only way we could give our customer true value was to ensure that she appreciated her total shopping experience.

Now, let's get back to Moira Mooney and her request to ease up on visual presentation.

The fact that Moira made her request, and that I said I would consider her request, shows clearly that, at the time, neither Moira nor I understood what business we were in. We did not understand that we were in the value-added business and that satisfying our customers was not about adding value in just one of the key value-added areas, we had to add value to everything that affected the customer. *We had to be outstanding in all of the key value-added areas all the time*, because if we did nine things right for the customer, but let her down on the tenth, we would lose her.

From my Costco experience, I realized that both Moira and I were asking the wrong question. The question should not have been, "Can we relax on visual presentation?" Giving up on visual presentation, or any other key value-added area, was not an option. The question should have been, "What do we have to do to impress the customer in all the key value-added areas and ensure that she has an outstanding shopping experience all the time?"

As a result of that experience, we made another context shift; "Our customer must perceive that she is getting value for her money and time spent. Shirmax is in the value-added business and we must be outstanding at adding value." That became our *modus operandi*.

THE POWER OF SETTING CONTEXT

I HAVE REFERRED TO CONTEXT A NUMBER OF TIMES and it is essential that we explore the Power of Context before we go any further. Setting a context is a very powerful working tool because it is a way to focus everyone's attention on a common objective and get them to pull in the same direction. My definition of setting a context is:

Making a declaration to do something or make something happen without any evidence that it is possible.

Setting a context is making a declaration out of a leap of faith. Turning that declaration into reality involves "living into" or doing everything that is required and consistent with making it happen.

An outstanding example of the power of setting a context occurred on May 25th, 1961, when President Kennedy declared: "The United States will go to the moon in ten years." When he made that statement there was no evidence that it was possible, or that it would ever be possible, for humans to go to the moon. But Kennedy set the context when he made his declaration, then he lived into making it happen.

More often than not, something that seems impossible can be made to happen by setting a context and living into it. In President Kennedy's case, he set the context and he did everything consistent with making it happen — and the United States put a man on the moon in less than ten years! That's the power of setting a context.

There are two approaches we can take when we set a context:

- we can set a context by playing it safe, **or**
- we can set a context with stretch.

Playing it safe means we can look at the past and extend it into the future. It is safe because, based on our past experience, we are confident we can accomplish what we say we will do. We know we can keep our word and that our integrity will remain intact. Setting a context that plays it safe certainly works, but setting a context with stretch is much more powerful. Setting a context with stretch means setting a context out of *a vision of what might be possible*, and then "living into" making it happen. Consider a simple example:

Based on past experiences of regular three-to-five percent annual sales increases, we can set a context to increase sales next year by another five percent and live into making that happen. Everything we do will be consistent with achieving a five percent increase. We can be comfortable with that. There is very little risk, and we feel safe and reasonably confident that we can achieve that goal. Alternatively, we can set a context for a fifteen percent sales increase and live into making that happen. Everything we do will then be consistent with achieving that goal, and we will have to do many things differently from living into a five percent increase.

With a five percent goal, chances are that we may miss it by plus or minus two percent. We may also miss our fifteen percent goal by, say, plus or minus four percent. However, even if we do miss our higher goal by four percent we will still have achieved an eleven percent increase compared to the seven percent we might have achieved with the five percent goal. There is also the possibility that we might achieve up to a nineteen percent increase! Certainly, there is more risk in the fifteen percent goal, but there is also more potential reward.

Setting a safe context perpetuates the *status quo* and contributes to mediocrity, whereas setting a context with stretch has the potential to produce extraordinary results. Setting a context with stretch is how breakthroughs and miracles happen. The following is an example of the power of setting a context on a personal level.

Everyone who knows me knows that I have always been something of a workaholic. After Shirmax was sold, many people, especially my children, asked me what I was going to do now. Because I felt they had high expectations of me and I didn't want to disappoint them, I felt I had to come up with a "worthy" project. Without thinking of how I would do it, I started saying, "I'm going to write a book." Of course, I am not a writer and I had no idea what was involved. But after I said this to several people, my feet were nailed to the floor and I was committed.

Under any circumstances, writing a book is a daunting task, but besides not being a writer, I have another more serious handicap. I am legally blind. I have an eye condition called macular degeneration and although I continue to function well generally, because of my condition I am no longer able to read, write or drive. Being unable to read and write adds several layers of complication when one is writing a book.

Writers usually draft, re-draft, change, scratch out, move paragraphs around, and re-write, and then go through that process again and again. I could not do any of that. I worked with two editors, I dictated and they transcribed and read my words back to me. I had to depend entirely on my memory and my ability to visualize what was read to me and make changes in my head. Then we re-worked the material through several edits to the point where we had an acceptable manuscript. This was difficult for me, but it was also difficult for my editors — as well as for my wife, Shirley, who helped me enormously.

By the time this book is in print, I will have been at it for nearly four years. But I set a context, made a declaration without any evidence that I could do what I declared, and I lived into making it happen. I overcame all the obstacles I encountered and here you are, reading this book. That's the power of setting a context!

At Shirmax, we understood the power of setting contexts. It was part of our modus operandi, we used it as a very effective operating tool, and with it we made extraordinary things happen.

DRIVERS

EVERY ORGANIZATION, BUSINESS AND WORKING GROUP has its own unique culture, which is derived from and driven by its own unique principles and context statements. I call those principles and context statements "drivers" because they drive the way everyone in the organization thinks and behaves, and the way all decisions are made. Now, let me elaborate on drivers using some examples from Shirmax.

Shirmax had several documents that articulated our values and commitments and reflected the essence of what Shirmax was. These context statements were the drivers that drove how we operated. They included:

Shirmax Mission Statement
    Statement of Corporate Values
    Statement of Customer Entitlements
    Statement of Staff Entitlements
    Departmental Mission Statements*
    Key Operating Principles

The texts of the above documents appear in the Appendices on pages 381-383. Collectively, they contain most of the key words and phrases that constituted the drivers at Shirmax. The drivers have been highlighted in those documents and the following are some examples:

- Maximize our potential
- Surpass customers' expectations
- Be the premier marketplace
- Be profitable
- Operate from a context of excellence and quality
- The Truth
- Teamwork
- Pro-active communication
- Highest standard of professional customer service
- Highest standards of visual presentation
- Nurturing corporate culture
- Shirmax people are its most valuable asset
- All employees have the opportunity to grow
- Contribute to employees maximizing their potential
- Every square foot of every store must be productive and profitable every hour of every day
- Shirmax' definition of success is: maximize our potential
- Shirmax will always strive to be an organization that works
- Shirmax will operate out of a context of "the glass is half empty" and "Living in the Gap."

---

* Each department had its own mission statement. The HR mission statement shown in the Appendices is representative of all the departmental mission statements.

Everything we did at Shirmax and every decision we made flowed from these drivers. For example, "maximizing our potential" was our principal driver and was the key benchmark against which we measured how we were doing. It was the driver that kept us committed to striving for continuous improvement.

Another key driver at Shirmax was "living in the world of the glass is half empty." For us, a glass that is half full implied that a half-a-glass (of anything) was somehow acceptable or that "things were good enough" and so did not call for much action, if any, action. Conversely, for us, "a glass that is half empty" implied that a half-a-glass (of anything) is NOT acceptable. Having only half-a-glass was NOT good enough"; it meant that "something was missing. The point is that we were unwilling to settle for only half-a-glass; we wanted *more!* The idea behind this driver kept us striving for continuous improvement.

These drivers were our equivalent of "...to the moon in ten years." They were what we "lived into." They drove how the organization operated, and affected everything we did. They drove our commitments, our priorities and behaviors. Together, these drivers shaped the unique culture at Shirmax. When I finally understood culture and that drivers are the source of a culture, it was a huge breakthrough for me: it enabled me to ensure that our drivers were consistent with our vision of who we wanted to be.

In addition to these drivers we lived the inquiry of; "What is it that contributes to things working?" and "What is it that inhibits things from working?" We applied those questions to just about everything we did at Shirmax. Those questions, and our continuous search for answers to them, kept us focused on the important issues and helped us to identify the appropriate actions we needed to take in order to generate continuous improvement. The questions took on a life of their own and became an integral part of the Shirmax culture.

It was through a common understanding of our drivers and the power of those questions that we were able to engender everyone's commitment to them. That was amazing power — 3,000 people with the same understanding, all with the same commitment, and all pulling in the same direction!

The following outlines what motivated our commitment to such drivers as "maximizing our potential", "living in the world of the glass is half empty", etc. and to living with such questions as "What's missing?" and "What is it that contributes to things working?".

Because Shirmax operated approximately 250 stores and had total annual sales approaching $250 million, it is easy to think of Shirmax as a large company. However, in the context of the marketplace in which we operated, we were actually quite small and we were therefore saddled with the limitations of a smaller company.

Our revenues came from two smaller divisions, butt we were competing in the major leagues. We had to do everything as well as, or better than, companies that were three and four times our size. I have already made the case that in order to compete, we had no option but to be outstanding in adding value, and that is very costly.

Technology, for example, was a key element in running a successful enterprise. Technology is also very costly, but in order to compete in the marketplace we had to put the same investment into technology as companies that were three and four times our size. This meant we were running a high-cost operation with limited revenues to absorb those costs.

In addition to the cost factor, we were limited with regard to our ability to source product. Being able to source product direct from overseas is a key element for success in fashion retailing. Our divisions were not large enough, and therefore did not have the buying power, to source directly. We had to go through intermediaries, so our cost for product was higher and, consequently, our mark-ups had to be higher than those of our competitors.

Because we did not have the economies of scale we could not afford to be inefficient or ineffective. We had to maximize the potential of every dollar we spent and make sure that every strategy paid off. We had to ensure that whatever we invested in had a maximum payback. We had to understand why things were working or not working and ensure that we were addressing the right issues. Given our cost/revenue ratio, we had no option but to do everything in our power to maximize our potential.

THE POWER OF CULTURE

GENERALLY, WHEN PEOPLE USE THE TERM "CULTURE", they are referring to the arts or the customs and institutions of a society, a nation or an ethnic group. However, every organization or group has its own unique culture, which emerges from the values and principles embraced by its members. Those values and principles are expressed in the organization's context statements. Those statements become the drivers that shape the culture. It was in this sense that the Shirmax culture emerged from our values and principles.

I first encountered the concept of corporate culture when I attended the AMA President's course. It was there that I began to understand culture as it relates to a corporation. Over the years, with that background, I learned how a company's unique culture is formed and the role that drivers play in creating that culture. I also learned that understanding a company's culture and the role of drivers enables us to manage the culture and ensure that it is consistent with the vision that has been set for the organization.

I allow as how some may find the idea of managing a culture to be questionable. However, as we proceed, it should become clear that it is not only possible, *it is essential to manage the culture if one hopes to build an organization that works.*

In some respects, a business organization is like a computer. A computer has two distinct components: hardware and software. The hardware of an organization, or the "hard stuff", includes its business concepts, systems, processes and procedures, technologies, machinery, real estate, etc. Essentially, all of these are things we can see and touch. The software, or the "soft stuff", is the culture: the values, behaviours, beliefs and standards, the effect the organization has on its people, the effect individuals have on each other and on the organization, etc. In most respects, the soft stuff is about people and their "ways of being" in the organization.

As with a computer, an organization functions effectively only when the hard stuff and the soft stuff work together in harmony. A company can have an excellent business concept, great processes and procedures, real estate, technology and machinery but if it does not have the culture, that is, the beliefs and behaviours, or ways of being, that contribute to everyone working together, supporting each other and pulling in the same direction, the company will not be successful.

Conversely, a company can have the best culture in the world, but if it has a poor business concept, inadequate processes, procedures, technology, real estate, etc., it, too, will not be successful. One without the other does not work. Yet, most organizations spend the bulk of their time, money and effort concentrating on the hard stuff and very little on the soft stuff. However, unless management understands the effect that the soft stuff has on the functioning of the organization and ensures that the soft stuff is appropriate and in place, the organization will not maximize its potential.

In summary, the culture of an organization evolves out of a set of beliefs and values and from a set of principles that are articulated in its context statements. The context statements are the "drivers" that determine the behaviours in the company, drive all the decisions made and ultimately create the very essence — the culture — of the company. Managing a corporate culture is essential if one hopes to build an outstanding organization that works.

THE FORMULA FOR SUCCESS

THE FORMULA FOR SUCCESS IS A FORMULA FOR WORKABILITY, and workability contributes to success. In our discussion so far we have considered living in the questions, "What is it that contributes to things working?" and "What is it that inhibits things from working?" Living in these questions led me to try to determine whether or not there *is* a pattern that contributes to things working or not working, and I discovered that, in fact, there is a pattern. I also discovered that when we operate according to that pattern, things work, and when we do not, they do not work. For me, that pattern was a formula for workability. I call it a formula for success.

The formula has four elements:

The Truth
The Gap
The Source
Intolerance

THE TRUTH

The truth will set you free.
The lie will shackle you to a life of misery

I HAVE USED THE TERM "OUTSTANDING" SEVERAL TIMES in the context of adding value but, frankly, I don't know how to measure outstanding and I can't really tell when it has been achieved. I perceive outstanding as striving to get better and better. But things do not get better just because we want them to; they get better only when we take action to make them better. However, we are not motivated to take action until we acknowledge that something can and should be better. So, to make things better requires that we see and tell ourselves the truth that something is missing or not working. But we are often unable to see and tell ourselves the truth about what's missing or not working and therefore we cannot fix it or make it better.

Now, the reason we are unable to see and tell ourselves the truth is because we are programmed to defend what we've created or are responsible for. As a result, it is very difficult for us to acknowledge and accept that something we have created, or are responsible for, is not working, not good enough, ineffective or inappropriate. Also, we are defensive about what we've created or are responsible for because we tend to collapse *what we do* into *who we are*. What we do and who we are become one and the same thing for us and we cannot separate them. To admit that something we have worked hard to create is not good enough or is ineffective is the same as admitting that *we* are not good enough. That's our interpretation, and for most of us, that idea is intolerable.

We have a built-in survival mechanism that protects us. If we constantly tell ourselves that what we have created is not good enough, and we internalize that to mean "I am not good enough", we will eventually destroy our image of ourselves and our self-worth. Our survival mechanism won't allow us to do that. So, our survival mechanism often prevents us from seeing and telling ourselves the truth.

Telling ourselves the truth can be very difficult. In fact, our inability to tell ourselves the truth is the key factor that inhibits us from making things better and prevents us from being outstanding and successful in both our business and personal lives.

In Part One, I explained how my maternity business, the business I had nurtured, developed, loved and was so passionate about, was in decline. My survival mechanism prevented me from seeing and telling myself the truth about what was causing the decline. I could not see that our original business concept had become old and outdated. Because I was unable to see the truth I could not take appropriate action to change what needed to be changed. But my nephew, Howard, and my son, Philip, were able to see what I could not; they did not have the same history and emotional investment to defend and were not blinded as I was. They could see the truth so they were able to do what was needed to turn our maternity business around and make it an enormous success.

Our manufacturing division is another example of my inability to see and tell the truth. When we built that facility it was one of the most modern and advanced manufacturing operations in Canada and I was very proud of it. It gave us a strategic advantage that helped our retail divisions build their businesses. However, that strategic advantage eventually turned into a strategic disadvantage; it became a liability. But I could not see that. Again, I was unable to see and tell the truth that its time had passed. I kept that division alive for many years at a huge cost. Clearly, the potential cost of being unable to see and tell the truth can be staggering.

I had two other experiences that also opened my eyes and made me intensely aware of the power of the truth and the implications of not telling the truth.

In the mid '80s, Mike Kershaw joined Shirmax as President and Chief Operating Officer, while I held the position of CEO. In a desperate move, motivated by our declining business, we decided to buy a company that was in the process of going bankrupt. That company had two divisions: GIGI, a chain of 12 high-end women's dress stores, and Anthony Sax, a chain of 24 junior sophisticate sportswear stores.

When we bought the company it was our intention to keep a small part of its management team to look after buying and store operations, and to eliminate all of their other overhead costs by absorbing them into the Shirmax operation. The retail profiles of the company's two divisions and the possibility of eliminating much of its overhead costs made it seem like a good buy. Carole Rosenstein, the owner of the company, was an experienced retailer and we brought her in as Vice President to run the GIGI and Anthony Sax divisions.

After a few weeks with Shirmax, I asked Carole to take Mike and me on a tour of her stores so we could become more familiar with her operations. As we visited each store, Carole proceeded to point out all the great attributes of each one. She saw everything as being wonderful and the best. Now, my wife had been a GIGI customer and my daughters had been customers of Anthony Sax, so I was familiar with the two operations. I knew that their merchandise assortments were always outstanding, but I also knew that other things fell short.

When we finished our tour we headed back to the office. Carole was driving, Mike was in the passenger seat and I was in the back. I started to think about our day together and I became upset with Carole because I thought she was doing us a disservice by not telling the truth. I knew we had to make some significant changes if those two divisions were going to become successful. But if Carole would not acknowledge that there were deficiencies, then she would not take action to change anything, and since she was running the divisions, nothing would change. I realized I had bought a company that I could not run and Carole, by not acknowledging what was not working or what was missing would not take the action necessary to improve the operation. I felt helpless and frustrated.

As I was becoming more and more uncomfortable, I became aware of Mike sitting next to her. And then it hit me. Mike was essentially the same as Carole. He was a very accomplished executive with a high profile in the Canadian retail fashion industry. His background and expertise were primarily in mass market retailing, not specialty stores, and he had implemented a number of strategic changes to our way of operating. However, not all of Mike's strategies worked. Some did, but others were clearly inappropriate for specialty store retailing. As with Carole, I felt that Mike, too, was unwilling to acknowledge — to tell the truth — that some of his strategies were not working and were actually contributing to the downward spiral. I was certain that because of their unwillingness to face the truth, we would be stuck in the *status quo* and nothing would change.

I then asked myself, "Why are these two very accomplished executives unwilling to acknowledge the truth?"

That was a magic moment for me because, suddenly, sitting there looking at the backs of their heads, Carole and Mike became mirrors for me to see myself and the light went on! "Max", I said to myself, "You are no different from them. It is not that they are trying to hide the truth or unwilling to tell the truth, *they are unable to see the truth!*"

I realized that I had the same problem; I, too, was often unable to see and tell myself the truth. My mind immediately flashed back to the maternity and manufacturing facility episodes when I could not see and tell the truth. From that experience I realized that those of us who are most passionate and in love with what we do, and are most committed and work the hardest, have the greatest difficulty seeing and telling ourselves the truth about those things we have created or are responsible for. It was not that Carole and Mike were trying to hide the truth. They were blind to the truth, just as I had been. I saw that all of us suffer from the same handicap!

As a postscript, Carole was an entrepreneur and had always had her own business. She and her team were not comfortable operating in our corporate environment, so they left to start a new business, which I understand has been successful. We were never able to make Anthony Sax or GIGI profitable. In fact, they cost us many millions of dollars before we closed down Anthony Sax entirely and sold GIGI for a token amount.

Although Mike and I had a great relationship and great respect for each other, I could never really bring myself to give up the role of President so he, too, eventually moved on to other opportunities.

The second experience that contributed to my understanding of the power of the truth had to do with an experienced buyer for our Addition-Elle division. She had spent six months putting together the season's dress line, but when those dresses hit the stores they didn't sell. All across the country, our store staff complained bitterly that our customers did not like anything about them — they did not like the fashions, the colours, or the fabrics. Every time I went to the stores, I was bombarded with, "These dresses are terrible."

My response was always, "Listen. You've got to understand that these dresses are in line with the fashion direction for this season. They are what all the dress manufacturers are making, and that's where we've been directed. If the customers don't like the fashion trends this season, then I understand it's going to be a bad dress season for all retailers, but we have to be in step with the current fashion."

I came up with that answer and justification because I had an investment in the buyer's success — I was the one who had hired her. I was defensive and I made up an excuse that did not reflect negatively on her ability or my credibility. Nonetheless, I kept being bombarded with the same complaints, and I kept sticking to my argument and justifications.

Eventually, I encountered a store manager who stood up to me. She said, "Look, that is not the truth. These dresses are *not* in step with today's fashion. Please come with me and we will see the dresses other retailers are showing." We went to a number of stores, and she forced me to face the truth: our dresses were not consistent with the dresses being shown in other stores. She made me see that I had made up an excuse to justify the buyer and myself. I had not done my homework. Rather, I had fabricated a story that was plausible but which, in fact, had nothing to do with the truth. I was blinded by my investment in the buyer and in having her be seen as "right."

Armed with my new truth, the following Monday afternoon during our weekly management meeting, I asked the buyer,

"How are the dresses selling this season?"

"They're not doing well at all."

"Oh, why is that?"

"Well, as you know, we are in a recession. People are not flush with money. They are making every effort to maximize what they're getting for the money they spend. A dress is a highly visible fashion, and it's always the same. If you wear a dress once, you cannot wear it again the next day, so your investment doesn't go very far. But if you invest in coordinated sportswear, you can have multiple outfits; you can mix and match and get more mileage for your money. So, in today's economy, customers are investing in coordinated sportswear and not in dresses."

Her explanation certainly sounded plausible, but it was not the truth. She had made it up, and she believed it herself. The truth was that the dresses were wrong, but she could not acknowledge that fact to anyone, especially to herself. By not acknowledging that the dresses were wrong, she did not/could not ask the kind of questions that would have led her to take the necessary action to make the dresses better next season. Questions such as: "Why are the dresses wrong? What's causing me to be so out of step with fashion? Am I getting wrong information? Am I researching in the wrong places?"

Had she asked those questions, she might have seen, for example, that Europe may be relevant for researching sportswear, but it is not appropriate for dresses worn in North America. (This is not necessarily true, incidentally.) Perhaps that would have led her to change her venue of research. The point is that as long as she did not/could not acknowledge that the dresses were wrong, there was no chance that she would make the dresses better next season. Although I knew that and the store staff knew that, the dresses were not going to get better unless the dress buyer saw and acknowledged that truth herself.

Why was the dress buyer so blind that she could not see what was so obvious to everyone else? Consider the investment she had made in creating that dress line. When she started putting the line together six months earlier, she analyzed the performance from the previous season to decide how much she would invest in dresses for the coming season. She knew there had been some significant missed opportunities in the previous season, so she decided to be aggressive and plan an aggressive sales increase, and she persuaded management to approve her plan. Her task then was to create a dress line that would generate such an increase.

It was standard practice for Shirmax buyers and merchandisers to travel to most of the major fashion centers in Europe twice a year to do fashion research. Most of those junkets were six-day trips — two days each in three different countries. So, our dress buyer packs a pair of running shoes, leaves her family, and off she goes to Europe on a research trip. She needs the running shoes because there is a lot of ground to cover. There are dozens of stores to shop and to check out.

When she arrives in a city she goes directly to store number one, looks around and sees nothing interesting. She tells herself, "There's nothing new here and nothing I like." Then she goes to store number two and again has the same reaction. However, by the time she gets to store number eight, she starts noticing that all the stores are showing orange! So, she decides that orange is a trend and it starts to look good to her. She visits a few more stores and notices that she is seeing the empire cut over and over again. Again she decides that the empire cut is one of the new fashion trends. As she goes on to other stores she notices that all the sleeves are bell sleeves and that all the slacks have belts on them — more new trends.

By the time she gets to the twentieth store, she recognizes the same things over and over again. She is literally being conditioned to love what she is being exposed to and she believes that what she has fallen in love with will be the new fashion statements for the next season.

My interpretation of these research trips was that it was a form of brainwashing and when I talked about our merchandisers going on research trips, I used to say that they were going to get brainwashed. I said that as a joke, but it really wasn't a joke because it was actually the process.

After her trip to Europe, conditioned by her brainwashing and her new inspirations, the dress buyer spends the next six months totally focused and absorbed in putting together a dress line for Shirmax. She has no time for her children or for her husband. She is totally committed to getting the line out, making sure it is on time and having the dresses be what customers will want. Now the dresses end up in the stores, and they are all wrong. Can we really expect her to look at the dresses and say they are all wrong? That's too much to ask. After all, she's an experienced dress buyer, she loves her job and she is committed to do it well. The way she relates to her world is as a dress buyer — that's who she is. How can she now, after spending six months buried in creating that line, say that the dresses are all wrong?

To make matters worse, she now goes further and makes up a very plausible story that buries the truth even deeper. That is another trap we all fall into. Not only are we blinded from seeing the truth, but we also make things worse by making up stories to justify that we are "right."

Those experiences showed me how enormous the cost to an organization can be if everyone from the CEO down is unable to see and tell the truth. Indeed, searching for the truth became the key factor that influenced my thinking and the way we operated at Shirmax. It became obvious to me that I had to find a way to get everyone in the organization to understand the power of the truth and the cost of not telling the truth. I had to find a way to imbue "looking for and telling the truth" into the culture of the company if we hoped to maximize our efficiency, effectiveness and potential. As a result, I wrote a piece on the Truth as the foundation for the Formula for Success, which I presented in my "Discovery with the CEO" program.

For me, the concept of the truth became, and remains, the single most important ingredient for success in personal and business endeavors. Not being able to see and tell the truth affects everything in life.

From that background, we created an ongoing dialogue about telling the truth and imbued it into the Shirmax culture. That culture caused everyone in the company to be constantly aware of how difficult it is to see the truth and how important it is to always search for and uncover the truth. *To search for and tell the truth became the Shirmax golden rule.*

Our inability to tell ourselves the truth is not easy to accept because it challenges our perception of who we are. We consider ourselves to be honest and truthful, so to consider the possibility that we are often unable to see and tell ourselves the truth is confronting. Let me be clear that we are not addressing honesty or dishonesty here. We are not talking about telling the truth to someone else. We are talking about our inability to see and tell the truth to *ourselves!* In fact, that inability is part of our human condition. We all suffer from it and it affects every part of our lives. Nonetheless, overcoming this human *disability* and being able to see and tell oneself the truth is fundamental to living a powerful life, to creating an organization that works and to living a life that works.

To complete my thoughts on the Truth, I would like to include a prayer we read from our prayer book on Rosh Hashanah (the Jewish New Year) that I believe supports, the notion of how difficult it is to see and tell the truth from another perspective.

A Prayer

Lord our God, many are the evasions and deceits which we practice upon others and upon ourselves. We long to speak and hear truth only, yet time and again, from fear of loss, or hope of gain, from dull habit, or cruel deliberation, we speak half-truths, we twist facts, we are silent when others lie, and we lie to ourselves. But we stand now before You, and our words and thoughts speak to One who knows them before we utter them. We know we cannot lie in Your presence. May our worship teach us to practice truths in speech and in thought before You and before one another.

Before continuing with the Formula for Success, allow me to digress briefly with a personal story. Because of the negative connotations associated with brainwashing, I'm not sure that our buyers appreciated my interpretation of their research trips as being a form of brainwashing, so I often told them the following story about brainwashing "with a twist"to lighten things up. It tells of an experience I had with brainwashing myself, not entirely in a negative sense, but it was brainwashing nonetheless. It always got a chuckle and I believe made my interpretation more palatable to them.

Shirley and I have two very close friends, Judy and Irving Katsof, who share our love of travel. The four of us have been traveling together since our first trip in 1981. From our standpoint, Judy and Irving are a nearly perfect "fit" as travelling companions because we enjoy the same kind of travel. Both couples enjoy the outdoors, hiking, biking, adventures, etc., and all four of us are more interested in visiting out of the way places than traditional cities and countries.

We've taken some very exciting hiking trips together, including Waterton Lake in Alberta, which is touted as one of the ten best hikes in the world. We did a major wilderness hike in Canyon Lands and Zion in Utah. We have taken biking trips in Vermont, Mississippi and Niagara-on-the-Lake, biking and scuba diving trips in Tartola and the British Virgin Islands. We took a cruise together to South America around Cape Horn and have also traveled to some pretty exotic places, including Kenya, Tanzania, Turkey, Ecuador, Australia, New Zealand and Papua New Guinea

Irving loves to plan our trips. He has the soul of a travel agent, and he spends months researching and planning a trip. That's not my thing, so it's a genuine bonus for Shirley and me to have Irving look after everything. He tells us where we're going, when we're leaving, what kind of clothes to take, how much it's going to cost and when to show up at the airport.

When I said that Judy and Irving are a nearly perfect "fit" as travelling companions, I used the word "nearly" because, as much as we like many of the same things, there is one thing the two couples do not have in common. Judy and Irving are antiquers. They particularly love primitive art and artifacts. Shirley and I have almost no appreciation for that stuff. The truth is, and I have told Judy and Irving this directly, I think they have some pretty weird tastes, especially in primitive art. They have some pretty unusual, and, I think, ugly things in their home; in fact, sometimes I wonder why their grandchildren aren't frightened by them.

Anyhow, this story is about a trip the four of us took to Papua New Guinea and New Zealand. We spent three weeks in each country. On our way to Papua New Guinea, we stopped in Cairns, on the east coast of Australia, at the Great Barrier Reef. Now, the Great Barrier Reef is a natural wonder of the world. You might think it would be the prime attraction and that everyone would be anxious to go to the Great Barrier Reef, but not Judy and Irving.

We arrived in Cairns late in the afternoon, and the first thing next morning, Judy and Irving had to visit a warehouse they'd heard about that sold artifacts from Papua New Guinea. They couldn't wait to get to Papua, New Guinea to shop for artifacts and primitive art. So, on our first morning in Cairns, with the Great Barrier Reef beckoning, we had to go artifact shopping — and when I say "we", I mean they were going and we opted to go with them.

So, there we were in this huge barn full of ugly, stinky, bug-infested stuff, and Judy and Irving were like a couple of kids in a candy shop. In no time they had bought three big, ugly carvings and had arranged to have them shipped back to Montreal. Shirley and I had walked behind them, watching them choose this stuff, shaking our heads and thinking, "My god, these people are even more weird than we thought."

Eventually, we arrived in Papua New Guinea, which is truly one of the most primitive places in the world. Even when we stayed at four- and five-star hotels, we were locked in after dark as protection from the "rogues and rascals." As part of the trip, we took a small boat that travels up and down the Sepik River. ('Septic' would have been a better name for it because it was so dirty and muddy.) That boat was our home for four days. As we travelled along the river, we stopped at one isolated primitive village after another. The natives rarely see people from the outside world other than when this boat comes by, maybe three times a year, bringing a few visitors to their village.

As we came to the first village and docked the boat, the villagers see came out in their traditional clothing of ass grass (sic), loin cloths and beads, and they brought the wares they wanted to sell and spread them out on the ground for the visitors to browse through. And what were their wares? Carvings. In their culture, the women do all the work. They build the houses, do all the cooking, raise the family, and the men sit and carve. Their carvings are really very primitive and very, very ugly. In fact, they make their carvings as ugly as possible because they put them on their houses over doors and windows to scare off evil spirits.

When we got off the boat at the first village, we were walking along looking at their offerings, and in no time Judy and Irving bought three items. Again, Shirley and I scratched our heads. What are these people doing? Where are they going to put this stuff?

At the third village I saw a carving of a crocodile, and I said to Shirley, "Look at that, that's a pretty good looking carving." So I bought the crocodile. At the next village, there was a man selling a dilapidated, messy drum, and I'll be damned if we didn't buy the drum. We went to another village and there was a mask on display, and I said, "Gee, there's a mask that's really ugly"...and we bought the mask. And at the next village we bought three more items.

Now, we had bought all these things, but we were not allowed to take them into our room on the boat because they were infested with bugs, so we had to put them down in the engine room where it is very hot. Apparently, the heat makes the bugs in the wood dormant (but it doesn't kill them). More villages and more purchases to go into the engine room.

When the time came for us to leave the boat, we asked the crew to bring our stuff up and put it in our cabin (presumably the bugs were dormant by now), so we could pack for the next stage of our trip. Then we went to lunch. When we came back from lunch, I tried to open the door to our cabin, but I couldn't swing it open into the room. We finally managed to push some stuff aside and got the door open. The room was full of all the stuff we had bought, stuff that a few days ago we would not have given a second look. I counted 21 pieces. I went next door to Irving's cabin, and he had only 17!

When we finally got all this stuff home, we had to leave everything outside all winter, because the only way to kill the bugs is to freeze them. In the spring, we brought them all into the house, and suddenly our house was overrun with artifacts that were just as ugly as those in Judy and Irving's home — those ugly artifacts that had caused me to think my friends were so weird.

That was a fabulous trip, and so are all our mementos from it. And you know what? My friends Judy and Irving do not seem so weird any more — or maybe we have become just as weird as they are.

That's my follow-up story of getting brainwashed — being exposed over and over again to something until the thing you didn't notice or didn't like three days ago all of a sudden becomes very appealing and ends up in your living room.

Now, let's get back to the Formula for Success.

THE GAP

THE "GAP" IS THE SPACE OR DISTANCE between two points — point A, where I am, and point B, where I want (or need) to be. To make something better I must close the gap. That is, I must move from where I am to where I want to be, from point A to point B. If we think about it, that's the way we live our lives. Everything we do is about closing gaps, about getting from one point to another. That's how the world functions.

Gaps do not close and things do not get better simply because we wish them to get better. *Gaps close and things get better only when we take action to close a gap.* But before we take action we must know the *size* of the action and the *kind of action* required. (It is important to note here that *the size of the action relates to the size of the gap*, whereas *the kind of action relates to the cause of, or the "source" of the gap.*

To repeat, the gap identifies only the *size* of the action needed to close it. It does not identify the *kind* of action required. We will deal with the kind of action required when we discuss the Source, but first let's stay with the gap and the size of the action required.

A small gap requires only a small action to close it, whereas *a large gap requires a large action.* If we take a small action to close what we think is a small gap, but it is really a large gap, it will have no effect and nothing will change. A small action will not close a large gap. Now, there is a trap here, because in order to identify the true size of a gap we must be able to acknowledge and tell ourselves the truth as to where we really are (point A) and where we really need to be (point B). We have already discussed how difficult telling the truth can be, so if we are unable to see and tell ourselves the truth, we may identify a small gap when, in fact, the gap is much larger. As a result, we will not take the correct size of action needed to close the gap.

For example, if I asked a store manager, "On a scale of one to ten, how do you rate customer service in your store?" and she told me it was eight out of ten, she has identified a small gap (the "distance" between eight and ten). That requires only a small action to close it. Perhaps all she has to do is make it a priority that everyone in her store focus on taking care of customers. She might post signs at the cash, in the fitting rooms, and in the employees' lunch room to the effect that "Customer Service is our Number One Priority." These would remind staff to focus on customer service. That is not a very large action, but it would probably be enough to close a small gap.

If, however, she is unable to see and tell the truth, and she says that customer service is an eight, when it is really a three, then the gap is very large (seven) and posting a few signs will not be enough to close it. Such a large gap probably mean there are serious problems that require much larger actions. Maybe some of her staff members should be replaced. That requires a large action. However, as long as she identifies only small gap she will not take a large action and, therefore, nothing will change. That's the way things work in all aspects of our lives — both business and personal. A small action will not close a large gap.

Referring to my conversation with Maria Moutzov, when she asked me how I would rate Shirmax on a scale of one to ten, I rated it as a seven. I identified a small gap (three) which would have required only a small action. However, a small action would have made no difference because the true gap was much larger. As soon as I saw and acknowledged the truth, that we were only a two out of ten, everything changed. For the first time I acknowledged reality and recognized the enormity of the job ahead of me. That set me off on a journey to transform myself as a CEO and in turn to transform the company — very large actions, indeed! That conversation with Maria, acknowledging the true size of the gap, marked a breakthrough for me and a new beginning for Shirmax. In fact, it was the first of several new beginnings in the history of Shirmax.

One of the key factors that contributed to the company's downward slide in the late '80s and early '90s was our failure to see and acknowledge that there was a gap between how we were doing and how we should have been doing. The following is a true account of a nearly disastrous experience we had at Shirmax that illustrates how and why we were unable to see and acknowledge a gap.

After our sales had declined steadily for many months, Ian Vincent, our Director of Store Operations at the time, came to Mike Kershaw and me and told us that the store staff were demoralized because they were not achieving their sales targets and so were not earning bonuses. At the time I was very conscious of the fact that our store staff, our people on the front line, were our most valuable asset and if they were demoralized the consequences could be disastrous. Demoralized staff do not do their best and certainly not their best by the customers. Mike agreed and proposed that we lower the sales targets to make them easier to achieve. So we lowered the sales targets and made bonus money available.

I traveled around the country as a one-man pep rally, visiting our stores, telling the staff we were lowering their sales targets and that they could expect to earn bonuses again. However, the following month, most of the stores again failed to meet their targets and, again, Ian came back and told us that the situation had become even worse. We had raised the expectation that things would get better and they had not. Staff were now even more demoralized.

The following month we lowered our targets even further, and again they were not met. The same thing happened the next month and the next. We became so focused on making our staff feel better that we did not ask, "Why is the business downward spiraling month after month? What's missing? What's not working? What are we doing wrong? What are our sales and what should they be? What is the gap? What actions should we take to stop the downward spiral and close the gap?"

Now, let's consider what was going on here.

In order to produce buying plans, we first had to develop sales plans, then buy the quantities of merchandise required to meet those sales plans. So, every time we lowered the sales plan, we correspondingly reduced the amount of merchandise we bought, which in turn reduced the assortments in the stores. Having smaller assortments caused sales to drop and as sales dropped we further lowered both the sales and buying plans. This meant there was even fewer assortments and customers had even fewer options, thus further reducing sales. We eventually woke up to what was happening and realized that by continually lowering our sales plans we were not acknowledging that something was missing. We did not identify a gap. By not identifying a gap, we did not ask the questions that would have called for appropriate actions to turn the situation around and we practically downward spiraled ourselves out of business!

There is a saying: *The quality of our lives relates directly to the quality of the questions we ask.* In our case, not only were we *not* asking the right questions, we weren't asking questions at all! At the time, we did not understand the concept of the gap, so we did not ask questions that could lead us to discover the reason for the gap, and so we could not take corrective action to close it.

In retrospect, it's embarrassing for me to tell this story and to admit that I was at the helm when all this was happening. But it is what happened and it underlines how easy it is to be side-tracked and not see a gap. It was because of this episode that we adopted the concept of the gap as a key operating principle and as part of an ongoing conversation at Shirmax.

In a business context, there is a powerful way to apply the concept of the gap that can catapult us out of the realm of ordinary into the realm of extraordinary. I call it "living in the gap." Living in the gap involves a mind set and a discipline that focuses continually on making things better and better. It is about constantly looking for what's missing and/or what's not working and taking action to fix it. Living in the gap is about never being satisfied. It is about things never being good enough, about living in the world of "the glass is half empty" and about pushing boundaries. It is about constantly identifying new gaps and taking action to close them. "Living in the gap" was how we operated at Shirmax and contributed to creating the organization Shirmax became.

At this point, I must draw your attention to an important *distinction.* I have said that our inability to tell the truth and identify a gap affects both our business and personal lives. I must make the distinction between living in the gap in a business context and living in the gap in a personal context.

To be successful in business, we must constantly strive to improve on the *status quo* and that requires that we never be satisfied. It means we are always looking for what's missing, etc.

Now, although that is a prerequisite for success in business, it could be disastrous if we lived that way in all aspects of our personal lives. In our personal lives, we must distinguish between those things we have the power to change and make better, and those things we do not have the power to change. We must to come to terms with those things we cannot change and appreciate them for what they are.

I believe the following prayer used by Alcoholics Anonymous makes this very clear.

> *"God grant me the serenity to accept the things I cannot change,*
> *the courage to change the things I can,*
> *and the wisdom to know the difference."*

THE SOURCE

EVEN IF WE TELL THE TRUTH, identify the true size of a gap and the size of the action required to close it, we still have to determine what *kind* of action is required to close the gap. To do so, we must know the cause or the source of the gap. Once we have identified the true source, we can then decide on the kind of action that is needed.

It is often difficult for us to get to and address the real source because, more often than not, the true source is hidden, or it is not obvious. As a result, it is easy, and potentially dangerous, to identify a symptom as being the source and then take action to correct that symptom. The point is that addressing a symptom has little or no effect on closing a gap. So we must keep digging until we find the true source and only then can we know what kind of action is required to close the gap. Also, if we identify the wrong source, we will take the wrong action and we will not only not close the gap, we may well make things worse.

Consider the following hypothetical case:

> *Bob is not feeling well. He has a fever and must decide what action to take to nurse the fever. He recalls that the night before when he walked the dog, he hadn't worn a jacket. It was colder than he expected it to be and he caught a chill. He concludes that the chill is the source of his fever. From his grandmother he knows that*

when he has a fever he should take two aspirins with some rum, go to bed and sweat it out. He has identified the chill as the source of his fever and has taken what he thinks is appropriate action.

However, the next morning he wakes up with terrible pains in his stomach. He goes to his doctor and tells him about the chill and the aspirin and rum remedy. The doctor examines him, presses on his stomach, and he yells "Ouch!" and the doctor says, "You have an ulcer. Your fever is not the result of a chill, it is being caused by an infection due to an ulcer. Aspirin and rum are probably the worst things you can take if you have an ulcer." So, Bob has incorrectly identified a symptom (the chill) as the source, taken the wrong action, and has aggravated his ulcer.

Now the ulcer has become the source of the fever and Bob must take appropriate action to treat it. He opts for surgery. A few months go by and the stomach pain comes back. Back to the doctor, who presses his stomach, "Ouch!" "You have another ulcer. What is going on with you? Are you stressed? Maybe stress is the real source of the ulcers. See a psychiatrist."

So stress is now the source and the ulcer is only another symptom. After many sessions with the psychiatrist they decide that Bob's marriage is causing him stress. Nothing he does pleases his wife. She is very demanding and they fight every morning before he leaves the house.

Now his wife is the source and the stress is only a symptom.

Time to visit a marriage counselor. After a number of sessions with the two of them, the marriage counselor suggests that their differences are irreconcilable. They part and soon divorce. Finally Bob is free of his wife, his nemesis, and the source of his problems.

Time passes, he meets a lovely lady and they marry. A few months later, pains in his stomach again. Another ulcer! Back to the psychiatrist. What's the problem now?

Eventually the psychiatrist determines that Bob is selfish, inconsiderate, aloof and demanding. He is impossible to live with. He is not suitable for marriage or for any kind of serious relationship. He is the problem. In fact, he is the source of all his problems.

And all of those other (what he thought were) sources were really only symptoms and all the actions he took for the chill, the ulcer, stress, and to fix his marriage had to fail. They were only addressing symptoms. The only action that could possibly work was to fix the real source — he had to fix himself.

To repeat: *If we address the wrong source we will not only not make things better, there is a good chance we will make them worse. It is essential, therefore, to identify and address the true source of a problem, not the symptoms, in order to take the correct action.*

In 1987, at the top of the economic cycle just before the major recession, we had an experience that highlighted the difficulties that can occur when we identify the wrong source. We signed leases for 40 new stores at very high rental rates. When the recession hit and our business began to spiral downward, we could not afford to continue paying those high rents and our rental rates became a serious problem for us. Mike Kershaw and I decided we would go to our landlords and ask them to reduce our rents. We prepared a schedule for each landlord, listing our stores in their shopping centre portfolio, showing sales for each store before the recession and at the time of the meeting. We went to Toronto to visit our three major landlords, and in summary what we said to them went something like this: "We are suffering from the recession and we cannot afford to continue paying these rents, please help us."

Our first meeting was with Peter Sharp of Cadillac Fairview. He listened respectfully and said he would speak to the powers that be and call us back. As we were leaving, he stopped us with, "By the way, I know we are in a recession and that business is down. Our Eaton Centre was down four percent last year and is down five percent this year, which for us is very poor. But why was your Addition-Elle store in the Eaton Centre down 20 percent last year and 30 percent this year? Surely there is something more than the recession that is wrong."

Mike responded immediately with, "It's cannibalization. You see, when the Eaton Centre store was doing well for us it was the only plus-size store in the area. But since then we have opened stores in Sherway, Square One, Oakville, and other centres. Also, Antells have opened a number of plus-size stores. There are too many stores for the customer population and we have cannibalized our business."

"Oh", he said, "Too bad."

We next went to see an executive at Cambridge. Same conversation. Same response, followed by much the same question, "How come your stores in our centres are hurting so much more than the centres are?"

This time I didn't give Mike a chance to respond. I jumped right in with, "It's cannibalization," and I gave the same explanation.

"Oh. OK. Thank you."

As a rule, Mike and I did not fly together. On that occasion he took an Air Canada flight home and I took Canadian Airlines. My plane taxied out onto the runway and stopped. The Captain then announced that we would have a two-hour delay because of a defective part. I was sitting in the first row in Economy, with a tapestry divider in front of my face. I had nowhere to go and nothing to do, so I replayed the day in my head and proceeded to get very upset. I asked myself how I could have let this happen. I had an established base of very good stores and in my greed I had opened other stores that cannibalized our established stores and destroyed our business. I realized that if there were too many stores for the customer base, there was nothing I could do to correct it. I was in big trouble!

An hour passed, and I kept digging myself deeper and deeper into a hole. "Why did I open Sherway, Square One and Oakville? Why didn't I see that they would cannibalize the sales of Eaton Centre?...Just a minute! In those years when our Eaton Centre store was at its peak, Sherway, Square One and Oakville were also at their peaks. All of those stores were open and doing well at the same time. Antells had stores in other parts of the country, but they had only one store in Toronto, and it was in Fairview Mall, in the north end of the city. It couldn't have any effect on our Eaton Centre store. So, where did this story about cannibalization come from?"

There was no cannibalization!

Mike needed a quick answer to an unexpected question and he created one — which identified the wrong source! And then I jumped onto the bandwagon and repeated the same story to Cambridge.

From our conversations with Cadillac Fairview and Cambridge, I was then armed with new information: I knew that the recession was responsible for only a part of our lost sales and that there must be other reasons, *sources*, for the deterioration. I could no longer blame the recession alone for our downward spiral and I was forced to start asking the right questions. What's really causing this downward spiral? What are we not doing? What are we doing wrong? What do we have to do more of, better or differently?

When we started asking these kind of questions we began to uncover the truth. We saw that the source of the decline had mostly to do with internal issues and that many of our strategies (including the sales/bonus plan fiasco) were inappropriate and had contributed to the downward spiral. It was from those questions that we discovered another startling truth; our business concepts had grown old and tired and needed to be reinvented. As long as we believed that the source of our problems were external, such as the recession, which was beyond our control, there was no action to be taken; it was all out of our hands. However, by being able to see and tell the truth, identify a gap and the true source of the gap, we could take appropriate corrective action.

This account illustrates the enormous potential cost and consequences of being unable to see and tell the truth, identify a gap and the true source of a gap.

DISCOVERY WITH THE CEO

INTOLERANCE

WE HAVE ALREADY DETERMINED that it is not easy to identify the true gap and the true source of the gap. But even if we do, often things still do not work and we do not get the results we want because we *tolerate* the gap.

Once in a while we don't want to deal with a gap because it is too big, too confronting, too difficult or too painful — so we tolerate it. Or, the gap is too small and we have bigger fish to fry so, again, we tolerate it. Now, I'm not arguing whether tolerating the gap is good or bad or right or wrong, but I am saying that when we tolerate a gap we cannot maximize our potential. So, if we are committed to maximizing our potential, we must be intolerant of the gap.

Here, I must be clear and differentiate between being intolerant of the gap and being intolerant of people. When I suggest that we be intolerant, I am absolutely not talking about being intolerant of people; rather, I am talking about being intolerant of the gap. It is true that in a business context most gaps are caused by people's inability to "get the job done." So, being intolerant of the gap may mean that if, after supporting a person, he/she is still unable to get the job done, that is, to do the job and therefore close the gap, then we may have to part company. If that is necessary, I am comfortable that it is because of my intolerance of the gap, not because I am intolerant of the person. Dismissing an employee is always difficult and is, therefore, an area where managers often tolerate the gap.

The following is a hypothetical case I used in our Management program to illustrate how difficult being intolerant of the gap can be.

Imagine you are a 24-year-old manager of one of our maternity stores. You came to this country a few years ago with some experience working in a small jewelry store in Switzerland. You were a newcomer to Canada, you applied for a job as a store manager with Thyme Maternity and, despite the fact that you had no related experience, you got the job.

There is an older woman on staff who has been working in your store for many years. She sees you are struggling and she takes you under her wing. Even though you are her boss, she teaches you the ropes about the business and that greatly accelerates your learning curve. She also takes a motherly interest in you and invites you to her home and introduces you to a young man.

You and the young man hit it off and soon you are married. Then there is a baby. You need a godmother for the baby. Who else would you ask to be godmother? Obviously your older friend.

Now, you come to this seminar, and your CEO impresses you with his prediction that very few Canadian businesses that are around today will be able to compete, survive and prosper over the next five years. The few that will survive and prosper will be those that are outstanding in everything they do and have learned to maximize their potential.

In fashion retailing, customers demand outstanding service by people they can relate to and whose fashion sense they trust. The age group of the pregnant woman is generally in the 20s and 30s, so the sales staff serving pregnant customers should also be in that age bracket if the customers are going to relate to them.

You buy into your CEO's message. You go back to your store all fired up to maximize its potential. Then you come face to face with the woman who has made such a meaningful difference in your life. You know your younger pregnant customers will not relate to her. There is a gap. What do you do?

Given the dynamics of your relationship, chances are you will make up excuses to justify keeping her and you will tolerate the gap — the issue is just too personal. However, if you tolerate the gap, you will not be maximizing the potential of your store.

Now, I sympathize with your dilemma; I would have the same problem and I might also tolerate the gap. But we have to understand that if we tolerate the gap there is a price to pay — we are not honouring our commitment to maximize our potential and if, within our company, we have too many instances of tolerating the gap and we do not maximize our potential, we will not be in business for very long.

Being intolerant of the gap is the driver that makes the Formula for Success work. It is true that the Truth, the Gap and the Source are key components of the Formula, but it is Intolerance of the Gap that ensures that the Formula works. So, if we expect to be successful over the long term, we must be intolerant of the gap

I said earlier that the quality of our life relates directly to the quality of the questions we ask. Using the Formula for Success forces us to ask questions that keep us focused on the right issues. I am not saying that using this formula guarantees success, but I am saying that if we don't use this formula, we will not be focused on the right issues, and we will not be successful.

If we can see and acknowledge the Truth,

if we can identify the true size of the Gap,

if we can identify the true Source of the Gap, and

if we are Intolerant of the Gap,

there is a good chance we can maximize our potential and be successful.

So, that's the Formula for Success and the final element in the Discovery with the CEO program. At Shirmax, we lived and breathed the Formula for Success. It was an integral part of the Shirmax culture and it drove the way we thought and the way we approached and analyzed all issues. Although I have discussed the Formula in the context of business, I want to be very clear that the Formula for Success — for workability — also applies to all aspects of our personal lives. When we apply it, things work; when we don't apply it, they don't work. I express the formula as:

Truth $\longrightarrow$ Gap $\longrightarrow$ Source $\longrightarrow$ Intolerance = Success

24

THE SHIRMAX MANAGEMENT PROGRAM

The origins of the Shirmax Management Program go back to the night I couldn't sleep after talking to Maria Moutzov during the Six-day Course. It was from that experience that I realized we were not a seven out of ten; we were a two out of ten! The company was not being managed effectively, we had no proper infrastructure or management structure, and an enormous number of things were not working or were missing.

As the CEO, I was carrying everything on my shoulders and I felt I was responsible for everything. I felt that every criticism of the organization, everything that went wrong and everything that wasn't working was my fault. I knew that if we were to stay in business and be successful, all of that would have to change and that if we did not develop the ability to manage the company effectively, we would go out of business.

Perhaps the most graphic example of the importance of effective management, and the consequences of not having it, was made clear to me when I studied the following business case at Harvard.

An ophthalmologist and a physics professor invented a revolutionary new contact lens that was different and better than anything else on the market. It was a thin, soft lens that could fit 75 percent of all wearers. At the time, all contact lenses were made to special order only. The inventors studied the standard business model of the contact lens manufacturers and saw that they functioned in the following manner:

• A client visits the optometrist, usually by appointment.

- *The optometrist determines the particular specifications of the contact lenses for the client.*
- *The optometrist orders the required lenses from the manufacturer.*
- *The manufacturer then custom makes the particular lenses and ships them to the optometrist.*
- *The optometrist then calls the client who makes another trip to their office to pick up the lenses. The inventors considered this to be a cumbersome process and they developed the following more efficient business model.*
- *The inventors' lenses could satisfy the requirements of 75 percent of all lens wearers. Because the investment and costs associated with manufacturing were all in the development stage, the actual (unit) cost of production was just pennies. The manufacturer could therefore offer optometrists a full inventory of lenses at very little cost.*
- *Customers could come in, have their eyes tested and leave with their lenses, all in one visit (no return visits and no additional management costs).*
- *The optometrists would then phone in replacement orders to keep their base inventory intact.*

The optometrists appreciated the quality of the lenses, loved the business model, and were happy to channel their business to the new supplier. The inventors raised venture capital and set up shop as a contact lens manufacturer and supplier. The optometrists received their initial inventories of lenses, started selling and began calling in their replacement orders.

In order to receive calls and fill orders, the new company needed a sophisticated telephone switching system that was on back order with the telephone company for six months. (There was no internet or e-mail at the time.) When the optometrists tried to call in their orders, they could not get through because there were not enough telephone lines, and when they finally did get through, they spoke to inexperienced, untrained order-takers who did not understand the product. They messed up orders and shipped the wrong lenses.

The optometrists quickly became frustrated and returned to their original suppliers.

In a very short time, the two inventors went out of business, never to be heard from again.

They had a great product and a great business concept with enormous potential, but they blew it because they were unable to manage *their new business so that all the things that needed to happen to make it viable did happen.*

This case is a good example of what can happen to a company that is unable to manage effectively even though it has an outstanding business concept and an excellent product line.

At Shirmax, our success also depended on our ability to manage effectively. Our stores were spread across 3,400 miles. We had 3,000 employees and we were operating three divisions serving customers from many different social and economic backgrounds. For a company as diversified as ours, the challenge was management.

More often than not, what makes a business successful is its ability to manage. Even though a company has a good business concept, it will fail if it does not have effective management. That is, if it cannot manage (ensure) that all the things that need to happen to be competitive and profitable *do* happen.

So, it became very clear to me that we needed some kind of management framework and structure that would allow us to manage the company effectively — and the universe delivered!

Martin Richter suggested that I attend the President's Course given by the American Management Association (AMA). It was there that I learned a management system that I could install at Shirmax.

The AMA Management System

THE AMA HAS A STRUCTURED management system that is used by most medium- and large-size companies everywhere in the world.

The objectives of the AMA System are to identify the business a company is in, articulate its main objectives, and provide it with an organizational model and operating framework that enables everyone in the organization to pull in the same direction to achieve those objectives. The elements of the system are:

A Mission Statement
A Statement of Corporate Values
A Strategic Plan
An Annual Plan and Budget, and
The AMA Productivity Formula, which contains:
    a) Position descriptions
    b) Performance standards
    c) Progress reviews
    d) Plans for development

At Shirmax, we used the AMA Management System very successfully. These elements were not mere documents that sat in drawers; we kept them alive by reviewing, revisiting and re-exploring them frequently at various departmental meetings and seminars held during the year. These documents were the drivers that drove the way we operated at Shirmax. They articulated the objectives against which everything we did in the company was measured.

The AMA Management System is an excellent system, and when organizations reach a certain size, they must use it, or a version of it, otherwise there will be chaos. Nevertheless, I assert that the AMA system is imperfect because it allows for too many inefficiencies and for too many things to get missed or overlooked; it does not prevent things from falling through the cracks. From my point of view, the critical shortcoming of the AMA system is that it is based on a standard hierarchal organizational structure and the responsibility for managing a company is entirely from the top down. So, if we wanted to build an organization that works, that is, an organization that maximizes its potential, we had to find something to complement the AMA System that would enable us to manage the company more effectively.

I understood that I, the CEO, and senior management and department heads at Shirmax were responsible for setting direction, formulating policy, establishing rules and regulations, and developing and managing processes and procedures, but we were too far removed from the front lines and could not see the effects and results of our actions and decisions. Consequently, our decisions were often not good ones, and the policies, processes and procedures were often not conducive to empowering staff and influencing customers to choose Shirmax. In short, we were not managing effectively. Understanding this led me to ask some difficult and important questions:

- How can we manage the company so that we're effective, so that very little falls through the cracks and we don't miss opportunities?
- How can we fix everything that needs fixing, moment by moment?
- Is it possible for me and my management team to manage every detail in a complex organization like Shirmax so that it maximizes its potential? Is it even doable?

I struggled with these questions for a long time, then one day the light went on and I realized it was *not doable*. It was not because we were inadequate or incapable, it was just not doable! It was simply not possible for me and my management team to ensure, to manage, that everything that was going on in all parts of the company was effective at all times. That realization changed my perception of management forever. I began to understand that an organization structured strictly as a traditional management hierarchy, no matter how successful the organization appears to be, cannot manage effectively. Management is too far removed from the front lines, they cannot identify what's missing or not working in all areas of the company every moment of the day and fix everything moment by moment. Such an organization can not maximize its potential.

For me, understanding this was a huge breakthrough and it led me to ask further questions.

- If a traditional management hierarchy does not work, what will work?
- What would it take to manage the company effectively?
- What do we have to do more of, better or differently?
- What would it take for us to know, moment-by-moment, what's missing, what's not working and then fix it?
- If the senior management team cannot manage the company effectively, who can?
- What kind of organizational structure would be needed?

While I was wrestling with these questions, we engaged a Halifax company, Proactive Communications, to develop a training program to help our store staff have a greater impact on our customers and also bring them closer to head office. Given that mandate, Proactive did a great job. Their Program was primarily about how to sell and how to manage a store. I knew it had value but I was still uneasy. I felt there was something missing but I didn't know what it was.

As part of their program, Proactive decided to produce a video that would help store staff to identify with and feel connected to management and Head Office. They interviewed me as part of that video. One of the questions they asked was, "What message do you want to give to your store staff?" — and Mrs. Keys came to mind.

Mrs. Keys

Back in the early '60s, we had two small maternity stores in Toronto, one in the Yorkdale Shopping Centre, the other in Fairview Mall. They were both excellent stores, each with annual sales of approximately $500,000. That was a lot of business for small maternity stores in those days. When it was announced that a new shopping centre, Sherway Gardens, was to be built in a developing area of Etobicoke, I took a store in the new mall. I assumed it would take a long time to develop but I didn't want to leave room for someone else to open a maternity store in the Toronto region. I stocked the store thinking it would have a slow start and a long building period. In the first year, our sales were $35,000. Mrs. Keys was the store manager. I had hired her personally and we had a very good relationship. In fact, we were on a first name basis.

One day, during the store's second year of operation, I got a call from Mrs. Keys, but instead of calling me Max as she always did, it was "Mr. Konigsberg" (I knew right away I was in trouble.) "Yesterday was my day off, and I went to visit our stores in Yorkdale and Fairview. I saw wonderful merchandise in those stores that I don't have in my store. Why don't I have that merchandise?"

"Mrs. Keys, sales in Yorkdale and Fairview are $500,000 a year. Last year your sales were $35,000. We have to merchandise a store according to the sales that store can do. If we give you all of that merchandise, it will sit in your store and die. We cannot afford to do that. We cannot give you more merchandise than is needed to do your projected sales. We know the Sherway mall will take time to develop, so we need to be patient."

"OK, thank you very much."

The next week, Mrs. Keys called again.

"Mr. Konigsberg, I went back to the Yorkdale and Fairview stores last week end. I studied their merchandise and I simply don't know how I can compete with them if you don't give me the same merchandise."

"Mrs. Keys, I understand that you cannot compete with them, but you're not in a mall that has the same potential they have. You don't have the same customer base. It would be a huge cost to the company if I gave you that merchandise and it died in your store."

"Well, alright, I guess so."

A week later, "Mr. Konigsberg, I'm calling to give you my notice. I'm resigning."

"What are you talking about Mrs. Keys? You can't resign. You're part of our family. You're a great asset, and we cherish having you here."

"I understand, Mr. Konigsberg, and I too have been very happy to be part of this company. However, I cannot make the kind of difference here that I am capable of and I am not interested in working in a store that does only $35,000 a year. I am sure that I could do a lot more business but I cannot do it with the merchandise assortment you are giving me and you've made it clear that you cannot afford to give me more. I will stay and help you find a replacement, and then I will move on."

"Mrs. Keys, I don't accept your resignation. I will get you the merchandise."

I went to our inventory management people, and said, "Look, you've got to get this woman off my back. She says she can do a lot better and she wants the same merchandise as Yorkdale and Fairview. Please give her what she is asking for."

Their immediate response was, "Mr. Konigsberg, we cannot do that. That is suicide. We have a responsibility to turn our inventory, and giving her all that merchandise will hurt us terribly."

"Let's try and make it work. Let's satisfy her by giving her the merchandise she wants, but we will use her store as a warehouse in Toronto. As Yorkdale and Fairview sell out of any style, we will transfer to them from her store. That way Mrs. Keys will have her initial stock but it won't die there."

In the twelve months immediately after we put that strategy into effect, Sherway became our number one store in Toronto! Then it was:

"Mr. Konigsberg, I have been looking at the other stores in our mall, and all of them have beautiful windows. Our windows are terrible. Our window dresser is not able to do the job." So we changed the window dresser not only for her store but for all the stores in Toronto.

Next it was, "Mr. Konigsberg, it's winter and the floor in the store is filthy. My budget allows me to have our floors washed once a month. That does not work. In the winter, we need them washed once a week."

"Yes, Mrs. Keys."...and we changed our floor washing policy for all of our stores.

Now, what was happening here? I was supposed to be managing Mrs. Keys, but she wasn't letting me manage her. Mrs. Keys was *managing* me. She was making sure that I did what she needed me to do to allow her to maximize sales in her store. In fact, with the window dressing and the floor-washing policies, she was managing that I contribute to maximizing sales in all of our stores. Senior management was not on the front line. We did not, and we could not, know what was needed, what was missing, not working or what was needed to work better. But Mrs. Keys knew. In fact, she was the only one who had the opportunity to know. It was fitting that she managed me.

So, in answer to Proactive Communications' question, "What message do I want to give my store staff?", I responded "We need a lot more Mrs. Keys managing our stores. We need many more Mrs. Keys managing all of our departments and managing me and the company. My goal is to be able to tell this kind of story about more and more of our people as time goes by."

It was as a result of telling the Mrs. Keys story and internalizing what I was saying that the idea of Managing Up was born. I realized that the answer to my questions had been staring my in the face but I could not see it. I understood that everything that happened everywhere in the company funnelled through the store managers into the stores, and I knew that the store managers were the only ones who knew whether all the departments in the company were doing an effective job. They knew how the customers were reacting to the merchandise, the store environment and the company's policies and practices. They also knew how the staff in the stores — those on the front line facing the customers — were reacting to the company's policies, rules and regulations. Actually, *the store managers were the only ones in the company who really knew what was working, what was not working, what needed to work better, what was missing and what needed to be fixed across all fronts of the organization.*

The moment I understood that, it made sense to me that the store managers, collectively, should be given the responsibility to manage the company. This meant turning the organization upside down and creating upside down management. So we created a new management system which complemented the AMA system.

MANAGING UP

UNDER THE NEW SYSTEM, senior management and department heads continued to be responsible for setting direction, formulating policy, making rules and regulations, and developing and managing processes and procedures. They were also responsible for evaluating information, data, requests and suggestions, and making decisions.

What was new for senior management hinged on the fact that we had given over the responsibility for managing the company over to the store managers and all the other staff on the front lines. It was now senior management's responsibility *to support the front-line staff at all levels to manage the company!*

What was new for the store managers was that they were now responsible for evaluating everything they saw and touched that affected their stores. This included all the work done by all of the departments in the company, as well as the company's rules and regulations, policies and procedures, and management decisions.

Everyone on the front line was given the responsibility to evaluate whether everything worked properly and whether anything was missing, then make requests for clarification or corrective action to the person up the management line who was responsible for the particular area. Those who received such requests dealt with those requests or, in turn, passed them further up the line, if necessary, and so on.

Similarly, everyone else in the organization shared the responsibility to identify what was not working or missing in their area or department and to make requests up the line for corrective action or clarification. We called that process "Managing Up."

It was through Managing Up that we effectively gave the responsibility for managing the company first to the store managers and then to everyone else up the line. Now, managing up, along with the idea of the store managers and everyone else managing the company, requires some explanation. Consider the following.

Shirmax had a large Warehouse and Distribution Centre (DC). Its function was to receive, process and pack merchandise in the correct quantities, colours and sizes, for shipment to the stores so it arrived in good condition and ready for sale. The manager of the DC hired staff, assigned them their jobs and ensured that they received the necessary training. But, once they were working, he had no way of knowing or ensuring that the job was being done correctly every minute of the day. In short, the DC manager could not possibly manage effectively.

When the merchandise was received in the stores, however, the Store Manager(s) knew whether or not it had been picked, packed and shipped properly. If anything was wrong or not up to standard, it was the store manager's responsibility to "manage up" to the DC Manager by making a request and having him take corrective action.

If the DC Manager could not correct the situation because, for example, his budget did not allow him enough staff, it was his responsibility to manage up to whomever was responsible for allocating that budget and get more staff. That process continued up the line, and could reach the top, or at least until the problem was resolved. So, by managing up, the store managers ensured that the DC was doing an effective job. In effect, the store managers, collectively, managed the Distribution Centre.

Just as it was the function of the DC to serve the stores, it was also the function of all departments in the company to serve the stores. So, the same way the store managers managed the

Distribution Centre, they also managed every other department. In effect, the store managers, together with the staff at all other levels, managed the company.

This process may sound like what goes on in every company. That is, the store manager has a problem and reports it up the line hoping it will be resolved. The difference was that at Shirmax it was not just a matter of reporting, making requests and hoping. Everyone in the company was also given the *authority* to hold those they managed up to, *accountable* for responding to their requests.

Requests were handled in one of two ways. Either:

- The request would be granted (suitably dealt with), and the person making the request was told "by when", **or**
- The request would not be granted (not dealt with) and the person making the request was given a clear explanation as to "why not."

One of the major challenges of getting Managing Up to work was that it was very difficult for people to believe that they really had the authority and the power the system gave them. This was especially so with those who came to Shirmax from other companies; over time, however, virtually everyone was won over.

To ensure that the managing up process really worked, the responsibility to manage up was not simply a matter of "if you please", it was a condition of employment. Everyone in the company was responsible to manage up.

Now, this raises two questions: how could the store managers and other staff at all levels possibly manage the company, and; how could I, the CEO, and senior management give away that responsibility? The staff did not have the experience or the background of information that senior management had to make decisions.

Obviously, senior management could not give away its executive responsibilities and decision-making functions. So how could the staff manage the company if they could not make decisions? In other words, how could we give away management without giving away decision-making? We did this by distinguishing between, and separating, decision-making from management.

The idea of separating these two functions is unorthodox and requires some explanation. Look at it this way:

Imagine you are a manager. As the CEO of the company, I am the final decision-maker. Now, consider my brain to be a computer. That computer is programmed to make decisions based on the best information it has at the time. You have the responsibility to ensure (to manage) that my computer has the best possible information at all times so it can make the best possible decisions.

If you consider one of my decisions to be questionable, it is your responsibility to challenge that decision (by providing me with better information) and make a request for clarification or corrective action, that is, to "manage up" to my computer. By doing that you are ensuring that I make the right decision or that I change my decision when it is inappropriate.

Through this process, you are effectively managing my thinking and therefore you are managing me. It is then my responsibility to "compute" your request and the information you provide and make the best possible decision. I make the final decision, but you ensure that it is the proper decision. And that goes for everyone in the organization who serves you. You manage up to their "computers", and so you manage them.

Upside down management can work only when decision-making is separated from management. At Shirmax we succeeded in doing just that by making it possible for everyone to participate in, and influence, the decision-making process without giving away the responsibility for final decision-making.

I did this by developing a new management model titled Managing Up, which became the center-piece of the Shirmax Management Program. I presented that Program to all managers and prospective managers in the company along with the Discovery with the CEO Program. Those two Programs became the foundation of the culture at Shirmax.

No matter what management system is in place, things will always go wrong. However, with the Managing Up system they did not stay wrong. Through Managing Up, whatever went wrong was fixed. That's what creates an organization that works and a company that survives and prospers no matter what goes wrong. *Things get fixed,* and that is amazing power!

Everyone who works for a living has two prime motivators: a need for reward (to be paid) and a need to know they are contributing and making a difference. Managing Up gave everyone at Shirmax the opportunity to contribute, to make a difference and to participate at the highest level — the management of the company. That was the most inspiring and motivating thing we could have done for our people.

MANAGING UP IN ACTION

I SAID EARLIER THAT TO CREATE AN ORGANIZATION that works requires that everyone in the company operate at an extraordinary level of efficiency and effectiveness, have an extraordinary commitment to the organization's goals, and take responsibility for the outcome. More than anything else, it was Managing Up that inspired everyone to operate at an extraordinary level. One of the major challenges of getting Managing Up to work was that it was very difficult for people to believe that they really had the authority and the power the system gave them. This was especially so with those who came to Shirmax from other companies; over time, however, virtually everyone was won over.

In Part One, I told my King of Maternity story and how the Addition-Elle Fashion Outlet division came to be. Both of those events highlight the power of Managing Up. In the case of King of Maternity, by managing up, Howard and Philip were able to force a decision to start a new maternity division, which eventually converted Shirley K Maternity into Thyme Maternity, and which went on to be successful in a way that Shirley K had never been.

In the case of the Outlet Division, I had long taken the position with Walter Lamothe that, "...as long as I am the CEO, we will never go into the Outlet business." Eventually, because of the inventory dilemma we had been struggling with at Addition-Elle,

*Addressing a Management Group at a
Shirmax Management Seminar*

*With Walter Lamothe at one of the Shirmax
Management Seminars*

Managing Up came into play. In this case, the store managers and inventory managers who had to deal with Addition-Elle's excess merchandise made requests, pushed and prodded, and so managed up to their respective supervisors, who in turn made requests, pushed and prodded, and managed up to Walter, who in turn kept pressing me. He managed up to me and eventually persuaded me to change my position. So, it was as a result of the managing up process that the Addition-Elle Fashion Outlet division was launched. (So much for "...as long as I am the CEO, we will never...")

The principles of Managing Up contributed to a culture in which decisions were final only until new and better information became available. My position that, "We would never go into the Outlet business" was valid only until Walter built such a case that I had no option but to try it. The rest is history. The Addition-Elle Fashion Outlet division became the "goose that laid the golden egg."

Over the years, there were many other examples of managers, particularly store managers, who managed up and made huge contributions to the company. Our experience with Debbie Bowen was a case in point.

Debbie was the manager of our Addition-Elle store in Toronto's Eaton Center, which was our number one store at the time. When she took over that store, she increased sales dramatically. After managing that store for a few years, she became pregnant and gave birth to twins. After she came back to work, it was understandably difficult for her to balance the all-consuming job of managing the Eaton Centre store with those of her family obligations, so she decided she would leave Shirmax.

The Bloor-Yonge district in Toronto is one of the top shopping areas in Canada. We had tried unsuccessfully for some time to find a store on Bloor Street, but eventually we gave up and compromised; we opened a store on Cumberland Avenue, which is just off Bloor. We expected it to generate annual sales of $1 million and so we spared no expense when we built it. However, it turned out to be a mistake because, although it was close, it was not Bloor Street. In the first year our sales were only $300,000; it was a white elephant.

Rather than lose Debbie, we gave her the Cumberland store to manage. Because it was a low volume store, we were able to give her flex hours, and that allowed her to accommodate both the store and her family. About three months after she took over, Mike Kershaw and I toured the Toronto stores, and we visited Deb at Cumberland. She greeted us with the following:

"I haven't been able to make much of a difference since I've been here. However, I believe I can turn this store around, but you have to let me call the shots. You see, you've classified me as a "D" store in all commodities. As a "D" store I get a little bit of everything, but I don't have a great representation of anything. My customers here are business women, but half of my store consists of casual sportswear. I just don't have customers for that merchandise. So, I want you to take the casual sportswear out of my store and change my distribution on career merchandise to that of an "A" store. That way, I can give my customers a proper choice and satisfy them."

I responded, "I'm sorry, but we can't do that. Our system does not allow us to allocate a "D" store as if it was an "A" store in certain categories only.

"Gentlemen, with sales of $300,000 a year, how much money are you losing in this store?"

"Probably about $300,000."

"I'm prepared to say I can double the business in this store if you give me the merchandise I need. If we did $600,000, how much would the store be losing then?"

"Probably $100,000."

"So, I'm telling you that I can cut losses by $200,000. And you're telling me that you can't accommodate me?"

"But Deb, we're a national chain. Our system is geared to a chain. It cannot accommodate the special needs of one store."

"Gentlemen, I imagine it wouldn't cost you more than $30,000 a year to hire someone to override the system and re-distribute my merchandise so I get what I need so wouldn't you want to spend $30,000 to save $200,000?"

She made her point. She had us boxed in and we had no alternative but to try to accommodate her. As it turned out we managed to do what Deb asked without hiring an extra person.

Deb remained in that store for a few years and worked very closely with our distribution department to ensure that she continued to receive the stock she needed. She built the sales to $800,000. As her twins got older, her life eventually got back to normal and she went back to manage the Eaton Centre store. After she left, sales at Cumberland fell back to below $500,000 until we finally closed the store. Deb's shoes were very difficult to fill. She was an excellent manager empowered by the Shirmax culture. She used the Managing Up system as it was intended.

In order to work and "make a difference", Managing Up required players who were willing and had the confidence to take on anyone, including the President and the CEO, to get the job done.

I should not leave Managing Up without referring to a related issue that we dealt with in the Management program.

In most organizations, the communications flow is essentially in one direction — from the top down — and there is no effective bridge between senior management and lower level personnel. As a result, lower level personnel often lack information and there is much they do not understand, agree with or believe in. But they have no alternative but to live with it because the culture does not support anything else. A corporate environment where people operate out of not understanding, not agreeing with, and not believing, creates a lack of trust and a high level of frustration, which inevitably leads to complaining.

There was a time before Managing Up became part of the Shirmax culture, when I wouldn't go into the cafeteria at lunch time because the chatter was all about complaining...complaining about the company, about management, about other departments, etc. Complaining within a company is like a cancer; it undermines and sucks power from the organization. Complaining inhibits team and makes it impossible to have an organization that works. However, when Managing Up became part of the Shirmax culture, everyone had the responsibility, as well as the opportunity, to resolve all of their issues and there was no longer a need to complain. In fact, we became intolerant of any form of complaining. We responded to requests only, not to complaints, and we effectively asked everyone to make a commitment to what we called the "Shirmax Way."

After the Shirmax Way became part of the culture, complaining simply did not exist at Shirmax. Managing Up and The Shirmax Way also took a huge load off my shoulders. I was no longer responsible for everything that was wrong. Everyone had the opportunity to get things fixed, so blame was no longer an issue and that took the entire burden off me.

THE SHIRMAX WAY

When I am frustrated, I have an innate need to complain, yet I understand that complaining accomplishes nothing and makes no difference. What does make a difference is to make a request and hold accountable those to whom I make the request.

- I will not complain.

- I will follow the Managing Up process.

- I will identify what's working, what's not working, what can work better, and what's missing, and I will "manage up" by making requests to the appropriate person for clarification and/or corrective action.

- I am entitled to one of two responses to my request: a.) my request will be granted, and by when, **or**, b.) my request cannot be granted, and I will be given a clear explanation as to why not.

- I am responsible for and have the authority to hold anyone in the company accountable for an appropriate response to my request.

- I am accountable to fulfill my obligations to the company and cannot use the excuse that someone else did not fulfill their obligations to me. I am also responsible to go up the organizational line if necessary (as a last resort) to ensure that I have the support I need to fulfill my obligations.

- Not only will I not complain, I will not accept Complaints and I will coach others who complain to turn their complaints into requests and direct those requests to the appropriate party.

25

ENTREPRENEURSHIP

Managing Up in itself made an enormous positive difference to the way we functioned at Shirmax. But especially in the early years, we did not maximize the potential of the Managing Up system. Although we had given the responsibility for the management of the company over to those on the front lines and they were using the managing up system as intended, they were dealing from a position of "what is." By that I mean they were focusing on making something that already exists a little better. They were thinking small and not exploiting opportunities. They were not thinking and managing up from a position of "What's possible?"

Unquestionably, if the management of a company is not imaginative, innovative and creative, if people do not think from a position of "What's possible?", the company will stagnate, atrophy and die. From my perspective, if we were to maximize our potential, we had to change everyone's way of thinking: everyone had to be focused on maximizing potential. We had to get everyone at Shirmax thinking from a position of "What's possible?"

Most successful businesses are built and developed by entrepreneurs, and those businesses grow and develop because they are built on a foundation of entrepreneurial ways of being, ways of thinking and behaviours that drive the organization. I decided that if we were going to maximize our potential at Shirmax we had to bring entrepreneurial thinking and behaviours into the organization. That decision raised the questions: What exactly is an entrepreneur? What is entrepreneurial thinking? And, what are entrepreneurial behaviours?

Genuine entrepreneurs are people who create companies from nothing. They are visionaries and risk takers and they invent the future from their visions of the future, not from the past. They start with a concept, some capital, and maybe a few contacts, and they convert their ideas into viable businesses. They are usually outside-the-box thinkers with the ability to conceive extraordinary businesses and produce striking results.

At Shirmax, I was the only true entrepreneur in the organization. I was the only one who had taken a risk, started a business from nothing and made a success of it. But in the new reality of business, with heightened competition and a more demanding consumer, one entrepreneur, especially in a large organization, will not produce a successful enterprise. However, a company would be truly extraordinary if everyone in the company operated from a background of entrepreneurship and brought entrepreneurial thinking to their jobs.

Even though most of the players on the Shirmax team did not fit the exact profile of an entrepreneur, in order to make Managing Up truly effective, everyone had to learn and internalize entrepreneurial ways of being, thinking and behaviours and operate and manage up from a platform of entrepreneurship.

In order to accomplish this, I wrote a program on Entrepreneurship and presented it to all managers in the company. The objective of the program was to provide them with a background of entrepreneurship from which they could manage up. A background from which they could analyze what's missing, what's not working and what can work better, and make requests that come from entrepreneurial thinking. In writing the program, I took a hard look at myself as an entrepreneur in a attempt to identify the characteristics of an entrepreneur. The following are some of the characteristic ways of being, ways of thinking, and behaviours that I saw in myself and which I perceive entrepreneurs. have in common.

Entrepreneurs are:
- *Driven* by hunger and passion for success, accomplishment, achieving extraordinary results and a desire to do what has not been done before. Entrepreneurs also possess the will and tenacity to make things happen.
- *Explorers.* They live in the gap, in the world of "what's missing" and the "glass is half empty." They live in the world of possibilities and opportunities. They are preoccupied with exploring how to get better, and how to maximize potential.
- *Creators.* They create opportunities and have the confidence to pursue what they believe in.
- *Risk Takers.* They are usually willing to take risks when they believe in something and when they believe in something they go for it.
- *Revolutionaries.* They are impatient and driven by a strong sense of urgency. They want everything now and they are willing to do whatever it takes to make something happen, even if it means revolution instead of evolution.
- *Non-Conformists.* They do not live in the world of "reasonableness". They see opportunities that others do not see and they are driven to stretch boundaries and go beyond what is reasonable.

The qualities of entrepreneurship manifest themselves in the kind of questions entrepreneurs ask. In fact, the single most important difference between an entrepreneur and a good manager is the nature of the questions each asks. Entrepreneurs constantly ask, "What's possible, what's missing?" and, "How can we make things better?" They ask questions that call for action and are not focused on avoiding risk. Their questions focus on what they have to do to get the desired results, what kind of actions, programs and promotions would it take to maximize possibilities and opportunities, and what are the possibilities if...? Entrepreneurs ask different questions that lead to different answers, which cause them to take different actions, and so achieve different results.

When a manager focuses on, "How can I avoid risk", he/she is confined or restrained. However, focusing on, "What's missing, how can I make something better, what do I have to do to make something happen, and what are the possibilities if...?" all come from entrepreneurial thinking, which encourages the search for new possibilities and opportunities. Living in that world produces breakthrough after breakthrough and contributes to an organization maximizing its potential.

Empowering entrepreneurship at Shirmax was not a license to break the rules. It was a license to be creative and innovative in the context of Managing Up. It was about identifying what's wanted and needed and making requests from a domain of possibility. Over time, entrepreneurial thinking permeated all parts of the organization and, without question, added a new dimension to Managing Up. It made Managing Up more effective and contributed enormously to Shirmax's success.

Our Secret Weapon

In the late '80s and early '90s, when I was giving The Shirmax Management Program, we used to list the names of Canadian retail companies that had existed five years earlier but were no longer in business. We had participants from all parts of the country so we had quite a list and we saw that the number of failed Canadian companies was very sobering. Once that point was made, I told the participants that as more and more American companies came to Canada, Canadian companies would not be able to compete, and those of us who were then still around would have difficulty surviving for another five years.

Most major American retailers are much larger than Canadian companies and have the economies of scale that come with size. Also, many of them are second- and third-generation retailers and have the experience and retail sophistication that give them an advantage over most first-generation Canadian retailers. Wal-Mart is a good example of an American company dominating Canadian retail. It's very difficult to compete with Wal-Mart because of its size, economies of scale and retail "savvy".

As I continued to give the Shirmax Management Program, I always made the same statement: "Within the next three to five years, there will be very few Canadian fashion retailers left in this country. Many will be knocked out of the box." Unfortunately, my prediction was correct and in the early to mid-90s there was what amounted to a blood bath in Canada when many prominent fashion retailers went out of business. In fact, in 1993, Shirmax itself came perilously close to going out of business.

By 1996, when we were doing well again, I started to suggest that Shirmax would be one of the few Canadian fashion retailers that would survive and continue to prosper. Now, how could I make such a statement? How dare I say such a thing!

I always had the same answer, *"Shirmax has a secret weapon — its people! — the entire Shirmax team is empowered by entrepreneurial thinking, Managing Up and the Shirmax culture."* Our secret weapon was the combined power of people identifying what's not working and what's missing and getting everything fixed — 3,000 people thinking and behaving like entrepreneurs, participating in the management of the company. That was an unbeatable force!

When I was nominated for the "Entrepreneur of the Year" award, I am sure the judges were influenced by our spectacular turnaround, but I believe they were even more impressed by the Shirmax culture, our entrepreneurial thinking and our unique system of Managing Up. I believe those were the things that made the difference and why they chose me as the winner of the award.

26

TEAM BUILDING

If supervisors and workers could be taught to talk together regularly and continually about work and how it should be performed, and could do it without friction or suspicion, and were jointly proud of the results, the impact upon our society and upon our economy would be dramatic."

American Management Association

I SAID EARLIER, THAT THE PURPOSE OF THIS PART of the book is to identify and elaborate on the ingredients required to build "an organization that works." Those we have already identified are all powerful concepts, systems and ways of thinking and every one of them contributed to the dynamic Shirmax culture. That culture promoted outside-the-box thinking that empowered ordinary people to operate at extraordinary levels, which, in turn, created incredible workability. Yet, there was still something missing, the element of "team."

Success in business does not depend only on a good business concept or a great product. It also depends on the "ways of being" of the people in the organization and their ability to work together as a team, exploring, developing and learning together. It is the combined effort of a team of people or departments working together and supporting each other that makes the difference between outstanding and mediocre, between success and failure. It is *team* that enables a company to manage effectively and ensure that all of the things that need to happen to be competitive, profitable and successful *do* happen.

Even though we had turned our business around and had achieved a measure of success, everything we had developed as a company was being compromised because we were not a team. We had always had difficulty working together as a team. There had always been finger-pointing and blame and there was no culture of mutual support. We were not all pulling in the same direction supporting each other and I knew that as long as we were not a team we could never maximize our potential or create anything close to an organization that works.

Part of a manager's job is to make decisions, but clearly, not all of those decisions will be good ones. Even if a manager has a very good track record and makes good decisions 80 per cent of the time, 20 per cent of his or her decisions must be poor. But too many poor decisions will kill an organization. Therefore, to ensure success and maximize the potential of the organization, the number of poor decisions must be minimized. With two, four or six people working together as a team, there is a good chance that the number of poor decisions will be reduced significantly. However, team is very difficult to achieve because being a team player goes against our natural instincts.

Most of us are competitive and have a natural desire to stand out as individuals. We are motivated by our personal agendas and our own individual egos. These traits are inconsistent with being a team player. Yet, team is the number one criterion for success in business. It was clear to me that if we were going to be truly successful as an organization, we had to find a way to bring team into Shirmax. To that end, I developed a program on Team Building that was intended to break down the barriers that inhibit team and to get everyone thinking and working together as a team. I presented that program to all Shirmax managers.

To begin our discussion on Team Building and how we brought team into Shirmax, it is important to understand that:

TRUST IS THE FOUNDATION UPON WHICH TEAM IS BUILT
AND ON WHICH TEAM STANDS

Trust is crucial to team. It is trust that makes team possible. Conversely, lack of trust inhibits team; if there is no trust there cannot be team.

In Part One, I shared the experience I had during the Six-day course when we studied five principles — Responsibility, Commitment, Integrity, Impeccability and Support. I believe those principles are the foundation for creating trust, team and, therefore, workability. *They are the pillars upon which success stands.* The team-building program focused on those principles.

RESPONSIBILITY

RESPONSIBILITY IS MOST COMMONLY UNDERSTOOD as a commitment to honouring our obligations — to obey the law, take care of our family, etc. That is one aspect of responsibility, but there is another much more powerful aspect that begins with the willingness to be responsible for, or, *the cause of an outcome.* In the context of team, of course, responsibility is about honouring our agreements and commitments, but it is also about much more than that. It involves *taking responsibility for the whole*, not just for one's own part. It involves taking responsibility for the integrity and workability of the entire team. In other words, it means that as members of a team we are responsible not only for playing our individual positions to the best of our ability, it also means *we are individually responsible for winning the game!*

We have already acknowledged that the essential requirement for team is trust. For there to be trust, team members must be able to depend on each other. My team-mates can depend on me when they know I am responsible for my agreements and commitments and I will honour them even though I may encounter difficulties. Only then can my team-mates depend on and trust me. Only then can we be a team.

There is, however, another important aspect to responsibility as it applies to team, which is owning and taking responsibility for our attitudes. Our attitudes have an enormous effect on our ability to be team because attitudes either foster trust and support team or they create mistrust and destroy team. When we do not take responsibility to ensure that our attitudes support team and something goes wrong, we tend to point fingers, blame others and make them wrong. If I blame and make others wrong, my team members cannot trust me and that destroys team. However, if I bring an attitude of understanding and support to my teammates, that builds trust and fosters team.

Things will always go wrong, things will fall through the cracks, people will make mistakes and people will say the wrong things. In these contexts, the attitude we bring to the table affects our ability to be team. If we bring understanding and support, we will have a powerful team; if we bring blame, we will destroy team. Blame in an organization is a cancer.

No Responsibility $\longrightarrow$ Blame $\longrightarrow$ No Support $\longrightarrow$
No Trust $\longrightarrow$ No Team = No Success

And that brings us to the Golden Rule:
Do unto others as you would have them do unto you.

In other words, treat your team members as you would have them treat you.

The power and workability of an organization would be astounding if everyone in that organization honoured their agreements and commitments and were willing to take responsibility for the whole (winning the game).

COMMITMENT
WHEN I DISCUSSED MY SIX-DAY COURSE experience in Part One, I described an episode when everyone in the course was prepared to honour their commitments only as long as it "made sense" and "was comfortable." Commitment as long as it makes sense and is comfortable is a commitment to nothing. That's not commitment. Likewise, a commitment to "do one's best" is a commitment to nothing, because it is a commitment to no outcome. So, if that's how I hold a commitment — that is, as long as

it makes sense to me and is comfortable or that I will do my best, then you cannot be sure I will do as I say or as I promise, you cannot depend on me, you cannot trust me and we cannot be team.

No Commitment ⟶ No Dependability ⟶ No Trust ⟶ No Team = No Success

On the other hand, if I am committed to getting the job done, despite any obstacles I encounter — no ands, ifs or buts — then you know you can trust me, you can depend on me, and we can be team.

The power and workability of an organization would be astounding if everyone in that organization honoured their commitments, kept their promises and did as they said they would do.

INTEGRITY

INTEGRITY HAS TO DO WITH TELLING THE TRUTH. We have integrity when our actions match the words we speak. Others have integrity when they are committed to do what they say they will do.

Getting people in an organization to operate with integrity is difficult because integrity is related to the truth and, having already discussed the truth in The Formula for Success, we know how difficult it is for us to see and tell the truth. Also, we tend to perceive things as being the way we would like them to be rather than the way they really are. Our emotions and prejudices get in the way of our seeing what is real and true.

To add to this , what we speak is often what we believe we "see", but what we "see" is not necessarily what is really so. Often we make things up, then we speak what we have made up, and we believe what we say as if it were the truth. When what we speak is not true, there is no integrity in our information and in our speaking.

At Shirmax, we frequently fell into a trap that was a good example of people acting without integrity, seeing only what they wanted to see and bringing inaccurate information to the table. We had regular Monday afternoon meetings where we analyzed our strategies and operating results. If our performance was below expectations, we pondered the questions as to what was wrong and why were we not performing. Our people from store operations were focused on sales. Their job was to maximize sales, and since mark-downs helped to fuel sales, they were always pleased when we took mark-downs. Their response to, "Why are we not performing?" was frequently, "The competition took mark-downs. They are on sale and we are not." When we checked, we often found that that information was simply not true. The truth was that the competition may have had one sale rack with mark-downs at the front of the store, but the rest of the merchandise was at regular price.

I am not suggesting that our store operations people intentionally set out to mislead us. They just saw what they wanted to see and believed what they wanted to believe, so their information was without integrity. If we had responded to their information without verifying that the competition was in fact on sale, we would have taken mark-downs on all of the merchandise in our stores and that could have seriously affected our profitability for the season. That is how costly it can be when we rely on information that is inaccurate, has not been properly researched and verified. Such information is without integrity.

If there is no integrity in the information on which we base decisions, poor decisions will be made, opportunities will be missed and the organization will not maximize its potential. What makes organizations powerful and allows them to maximize their potential, is people keeping their word and speaking about things they have verified and know to be true. Power comes from integrity and we cannot be powerful if we lack integrity. If we do not have integrity, there is no trust and we cannot be team.

More often than not, when we lack integrity, it is in our speaking. That is, when what we speak is not the truth. Who we are, how we are perceived and whatever impact we have in the world, is communicated through our speaking. The way we come alive in the world, the way we are noticed and perceived, is through our speaking. Our speaking is our most powerful tool and we should value our words as if they really mean something.

There is integrity in our speaking if we think something through and look for the truth before we speak. When we speak from "Ready–Fire–Aim", there is no integrity. When we speak from "Ready–Aim–Fire", there is integrity. So, for there to be trust, there must be integrity in our speaking. Integrity in our speaking and in our actions inspires trust, and trust empowers team.

In all aspects of life, we take positions. That is, we make up our minds about something often based on a quick judgment, a perception or on some other sketchy evidence. It might be a about a person, a project, or some aspect of our job. It might be a position we take as to what's right or wrong. In fact, we take positions on just about everything all the time.

However, the moment we take a position that "this is the way" or "that is the answer", we get trapped in that position. We stop being open and we do not make room for other information. We will not look for and find evidence that supports another position; we will not see or hear, indeed, we will ignore any information that contradicts our position. We will not get to the truth and we will be without integrity.

Some time ago, I watched a TV program about police officers/ detectives being trained in investigative techniques. The program was noteworthy because part of their training stressed the importance of being very careful when entering a crime scene, not to make any snap judgments or take a position as to the circumstances of the crime. The instructors made the point that as soon as an investigator took a position, he would not look for, be receptive, or open to, any evidence that does not support that position. Indeed, he would ignore such evidence. The point is, if an investigator makes premature or unwarranted judgments (Ready – Fire – Aim) he will lack integrity and could head off in the wrong direction, come to wrong conclusions and, at worst, convict the wrong person.

If I am without integrity you cannot trust me, you cannot trust what I say, you cannot trust the information I bring and we cannot work together as a team.

No Integrity $\longrightarrow$ No Trust $\longrightarrow$ No Team = No Success

By having an ongoing conversation about integrity at Shirmax and by sensitizing everyone to the pitfalls and the costs of being without integrity, we created an awareness that literally forced our people to be careful with their speaking, careful with the positions they took and the information they brought. That contributed to creating an empowered and effective team.

The power and workability of an organization would be astounding if everyone in that organization was committed to act with integrity; that is, keep their word, do as they say, and say what is really so.

IMPECCABILITY

IMPECCABILITY HAS TO DO WITH A COMMITMENT to excellence. It involves attending to every detail so that everything is done fully, the way it should be done, and that whatever is spoken is known to be true. Impeccability is about being true to oneself. It is about going the extra mile and doing and saying everything right all the time. It requires a commitment to research, to analyze and to get to the truth. Impeccability in our speaking, in what we say, comes from a commitment to the truth and to providing information that is valid and true.

One of the greatest costs to an organization results from things falling through the cracks, and things fall through the cracks when we are not impeccable, when we do not go the extra mile and pay attention to every detail. Consider the following:

Shirley and I went to dinner with some friends at a beautiful Chinese restaurant. The environment was outstanding, the food was delicious and the service was impeccable. In the middle of my meal, nature called. I walked down a beautiful marble staircase to the lower floor where there was a door leading to an outside alley. That door was wide open and the alley was piled high with garbage from the restaurant. There were thousands of flies around the garbage and it looked and smelled awful. I did not go to the washroom. I turned around and went back upstairs but I couldn't take another bite. I have never been back to that restaurant. Although they did nine out of ten things right, they paid no attention to the tenth. They were not impeccable and they lost me as a customer.

Anyone who has ever bought a newly-built home, would probably agree that there is very little impeccability in the construction and building industries. Very few builders live in a culture of 'doing it right the first time'. They throw homes together without paying attention to details and without concern for deficiencies, then they have to come back over and over again to fix the deficiencies, at enormous cost and inconvenience to themselves and the homeowner. Wouldn't it make sense for them just to build it right the first time?

A powerful example of how a lack of impeccability can threaten an entire industry occurred when the North American auto industry was virtually brought to its knees by foreign competition. U.S. auto makers had no commitment to impeccability — to 'doing it right the first time' — and while they were having recall after recall at enormous cost to themselves and inconvenience to their customers, foreign auto makers, with their impeccably-built, high-quality cars were laughing all the way to the bank!

There is a built-in resistance to being impeccable because impeccability demands a commitment to detail. It is about not cutting corners. Initially, it takes more time and is therefore more costly, but over the long-term being impeccable saves time and money because it is unnecessary to go back over and over again to make things right.

Impeccability and integrity go hand-in-hand. There is no integrity if we are not impeccable. In the context of team, being impeccable makes us credible. If I am not impeccable in what I say and do, you cannot trust the information I bring, I am not credible and you cannot depend on me, you cannot trust me and we cannot be team.

$$\text{No Impeccability} \longrightarrow \text{No Integrity} \longrightarrow \text{No Trust}$$
$$\longrightarrow \text{No Team} = \text{No Success}$$

Impeccability gives us power. Not being impeccable is ordinary. Being impeccable is beyond ordinary; it is extraordinary!

The power and workability in an organization would be astounding if everyone in that organization were committed to their integrity and were impeccable in what they say and what they do.

SUPPORT

TEAM IS POSSIBLE ONLY WHEN TEAM MEMBERS TRUST each other and trust is possible only when team members support each other. There are two aspects to support: giving support and receiving support.

We do not automatically give support. As with trust, support must be earned and in order to earn support we must behave in ways that engender support. You will not give me your support if you do not feel safe with me, and I will not give you my support if I do not feel safe with you. I can expect your support if you know that you can depend on me to do what I say I will do, and if you feel safe with me. If we are mutually supportive, and we feel safe with each other, we can be a powerful team.

Team is possible only when we are "open for contribution" — that is, when we are willing to accept input and support from others without being defensive. And we only accept input and support when we are comfortable with ourselves and who we are. The greatest challenge to team, and the reason team so often breaks down, is because team members are unable to accept each others' support. Often, when we are offered support, we interpret it as, "You think I am wrong", "You think I am not good enough", "You think you are better than me" or "You don't trust me." With any of these interpretations we feel threatened, we become defensive, we shut down, there is no support and we are not team.

No Support $\longrightarrow$ No Trust $\longrightarrow$ No Team = No Success

On the other hand, if we can get past our negative interpretations and embrace input from others, we can become powerful members of the team.

As I said earlier, even if one makes good decisions 80 percent of the time, then the remaining 20 percent are poor decisions, and too many poor decisions will kill an organization. By working together as a team — everyone exploring, learning and developing together — there is an opportunity to reduce the number of poor decisions significantly and contribute to the company's success.

The power and workability of an organization would be astounding if everyone in that organization were open for contribution, and were committed to and supported each other.

It is generally accepted that the power of team is greater than the sum of its parts. The commitment and effort of two people working together and supporting each other produces far more power than the commitment and effort of each individual working separately. The power of 1 + 1 working separately equals only two. However, the power of 1 + 1 working together and supporting each other is far greater than two. The power of a team of ten working together and supporting each other multiplies accordingly. However, if we add to that the strength of a culture that is based on the principles of Responsibility, Commitment, Integrity, Impeccability and Support, the power of the team increases exponentially! These principles are inextricably tied together and if any one of them is missing, there will be no trust, no team and no success. I call these five principles the Five *Pillars for Success* because they are the foundation for team and for success.

When I wrote the Team Building program I addressed the five principles in a context of what gives organizations power and what destroys their power. I attempted to show how powerfully these principles contribute to team and how the lack of them destroys team. When an organization operates out of a culture that embodies these five principles it will move out of the realm of ordinary into the realm of extra-ordinary to become an organization that maximizes its potential — an organization that works.

At Shirmax, the fact that we had ongoing conversations about Team, Responsibility, Commitment, Integrity, Impeccability and Support, created a context that empowered our people to behave in ways that were consistent with them. Over the years, working as a team and being guided by these five principles, greatly contributed to Shirmax coming close to being an organization that works.

POSTSCRIPTS TO PART TWO

I began this Part of the book by saying, "I have claimed many times that Shirmax was an extraordinary organization...It was special, it was different, it exuded energy and excitement, it had spirit and all sorts of other qualities that most other organizations do not have ... I assert that Shirmax was an organization that was beyond ordinary and was therefore 'extraordinary'...This part of the book is intended to give readers a sense of what was involved and the ingredients that were required in our attempt to turn Shirmax into an "organization that worked."

I hope I have managed to give my readers a sense of what was involved in my attempt to build Shirmax into an organization that works. As I reflect on my business life, it is very clear to me that I have learned some valuable lessons and have developed many strategies for managing an organization effectively, some of which I have shared here. I also hope my readers found what I had to say interesting as well as useful.

In reviewing what I have written here, it must be obvious that I was zealous about such things as outstanding customer service, visual presentation, managing up, the truth, entrepreneurship, team, maximizing potential, building an extraordinary organization, etc. I am concerned, however, that my obsession with these things may paint a false picture of who I was as the CEO of Shirmax. I must make it very clear that although these were my day-to-day priorities, I had an overriding obligation to my shareholders and their interest was my first priority.

Shirmax was a public company. Shareholders expected and were entitled to a return on their investments. As the CEO my obligation was to maximize shareholders' value. Shareholders did not care about customer service, visual presentation, empowering culture, managing up, the truth, entrepreneurial behaviour, team, etc. and such notions as maximizing potential and being an organization that works. They cared about today's bottom line and our ability to improve that bottom line going forward.

At Shirmax we also understood that our obligation to maximize the bottom line called for a commitment to our customers and required that we put our customers first. We understood that satisfied customers gave us our bottom line, and that customers could be fickle. We knew what it takes to keep her and that if we did nine things right and one thing wrong we would lose her. So, all of our other priorities were secondary to our obligation to maximize profits. Our "other" priorities were the 'how tos' we had to focus on and have in place in order to achieve the bottom line and maximize shareholders' value.

As well, we understood that maximizing the bottom line was a balancing act between maximizing today's bottom line, while investing in tomorrow. We knew that if we did not invest in our customer today, she wouldn't be around tomorrow. If we did not invest in our infrastructure today, we would not have a tomorrow, we would not grow as a company and we would stagnate and die. We were committed to be outstanding in everything we did, to dot every "i" and cross every "t", so as to maximize the bottom line and the return for shareholders. Ultimately, maximizing the bottom line was the driver that drove every decision we made and drove who we were as an organization.

In the process of writing this book, I had two experiences that highlighted for me the true essence of what Shirmax was.

The first was drawn to my attention by one of my editors who observed that "Shirmax sounds like it was a pretty serious place, with all the emphasis on maximizing potential, an organization that works, formula for success, the glass is half empty, what's missing, etc. It certainly doesn't sound much like a fun place to work. I find it hard to understand why the people at Shirmax were willing to give so much to the company if they weren't having fun." I thought about that for awhile and was reminded that several years earlier, at one of our management retreats, the subject of "having fun at work" came up, and after much discussion we agreed that running Shirmax was a very serious business. Having fun was not one of the factors we took into account.

We were a public company and we had to produce results every quarter. We were constantly setting stretch targets, identifying what was missing and making changes. In fact, we lived in a state of constant change. As fun is generally perceived, I cannot say that Shirmax was a "fun" place to work. We were driven by winning. Winning was the primary motivating factor at Shirmax and we felt like winners when our strategies paid off and we achieved the results we were striving for. Working at Shirmax was not about having fun. It was, however, an exciting, stimulating and rewarding place to work. It was a place of learning, personal development, growth and satisfaction, and I know that our people truly enjoyed working there. The rewards were far greater than having fun. Having fun was simply not a factor we considered

My second experience occurred in 2005 at a breakfast meeting I had with Walter Lamothe. Walter was with Shirmax for over a decade and was Executive Vice President, Operations, when the company was sold. He was a strong supporter of my vision of management and as I developed the Shirmax management programs, Walter was always by my side; it was he who implemented the strategies. We were a great team. After the Shirmax sale, Walter joined MEXX Canada, as President of the company.

At our meeting I was telling Walter about what I was writing, particularly about building an organization that works. In the course of our conversation I said: "It's all about people. If we want to build an organization that is extraordinary, we've got to get people to operate at an extraordinary level. It's about the culture people work out of, about empowerment and about being able to call people to a higher calling."

Walter kept interrupting me with the same comment: "Yes, Max, but it's first about having the *right* people, having people who can do the job. There is no point inspiring and empowering those who do not have the ability to do the job." Every time he interrupted me, I answered: "Yes, yes, obviously", and then I moved on with my own agenda. However, before we parted, Walter suggested that I read a hot new business book, *Good to Great* by Jim Collins.

After I left our meeting, Walter's remark kept coming back to me, but it was only after I read the Collins book that I understood where Walter was coming from. I thought to myself, "He is right. How come I've written about culture and drivers, about higher calling, about the truth, management philosophy, managing up, and about getting people working together, etc., but I did not think to begin with the obvious — make sure that you have the right people. Why did I miss that?" and then I understood. I missed it because having the right people was not an issue at Shirmax. Looking back, I see that we had an abundance of talented and capable people who were driven by such drivers as: "Living in the world of the glass is half empty," "What's missing?" "What's not working?" "Every square foot of every store..." along with Managing Up. All of these drivers instilled very high standards and high expectations, which resulted in very high levels of performance. So, over the years, we built a team of outstanding people because the ones who couldn't work in that environment or at that level could not make it at Shirmax. That's why it did not dawn on me to address the obvious issue of first having the right people — it was just not an issue.

When I was deciding how to end this part of the book, I was reminded of an experience that still puts Shirmax into perspective for me. It was an incident that occurred at one of the last Management Programs I gave before Shirmax was sold.

Toward the end of the Program, one of the participants asked, "Max, all of us have heard the Maria Moutzov story, where you rated Shirmax as a two out of ten. How would you rate Shirmax today?"

The question caught me off-guard, but without hesitation I answered, "Today, on a scale of one to ten, I rate Shirmax a ten."

That answer was uncharacteristic and surprised me as much as it did anyone else because I had spent most of my business life living in the culture of the gap and I had always had a tendency to exaggerate the size of the gap.

I then went on to say, "How can I say that? Does that mean that everything is perfect? Certainly not. But you see, I'm not rating Shirmax on the basis of perfection. It's an ongoing journey. Is it a worthwhile journey? Yes. Are our goals and aspirations worthy? Yes. Do we collectively at Shirmax feel good about what we are doing? Yes. Do we have an environment in which people can thrive and maximize their potential? Yes. Are we respected by our peers and the community at large? Yes. Is Shirmax a place where people love to work, and are we considered an employer of choice in our industry? Yes. So, declaring Shirmax to be a ten out of ten is not about being perfect, but it is certainly about who we are. So yes, today, on a scale of one to ten, I rate Shirmax a ten."

Today I still stand by that claim. . .

PART THREE

LIVING LIFE
WITH POWER

27

MANAGING OUR QUALITY OF LIFE

So far, I have written the story of my life, which encompasses both my personal and business journey, and I have described what I believe it takes to build an organization that works.

In my effort to build an organization that works, it became obvious to me that the greatest challenges, hurdles and stumbling blocks had to do with people — the way people behave and relate to each other and their ability, or inability, to work together. In the process of trying to overcome those challenges, hurdles and stumbling-blocks, I became interested in what makes people tick — that is, how we live our lives, what motivates us, drives us and causes us to behave the way we do.

I also became intrigued with the concept of personal power and the sources of personal power, achievement and personal satisfaction, particularly in the context of large organizations. That led me to undertake an exploration and out of that exploration I learned much more than what it takes to build an effective organization. I learned a number of valuable lessons and gained some understanding of how we are affected by life's challenges, those things that dictate how we live our lives, and how they affect our Quality of Life (Q of L). I also developed several strategies for successfully managing my business and private lives and for managing my quality of life.

My purpose in writing this part of the book is to share what I have learned about *managing* as it applies to our quality of life in the hope of giving my readers some insight into the possibility of living a fulfilled and richer life, that is, living life with power. If I can share what I have learned about managing my Q of L, and if I can communicate that knowledge so it has the same impact on my readers as it had on me, then I hope I can make a significant contribution — make a difference — to their lives. However, before I begin this exploration, let me set a context for why we should consider the concept of managing our Q of L and what is to be gained from doing so.

Some years ago I was in Georgetown, in Washington DC, and I saw a t-shirt in a store window with a message on it that read, "Life's a Bitch, Then You Die." I thought it was funny at the time but I later came to understand that the message is not at all funny. It is a reality of life; life is indeed a bitch, then you die.

The following is a prayer we read in our prayer books on Yom Kippur:

When I consider Your heavens, the work of Your fingers; the moon and the stars that You have established: what are we, that You are mindful of us? What are we mortals, that You consider us?

We are feeble; we live always on the brink of death. Scarcely ushered into life, we begin our journey to the grave. Our best laid plans are ever at risk; our fondest hopes are buried with us. Ambition drives us on to high exertion; indulgence makes us waste the powers we have; and evil seduces us to heap misery upon others. Success and failure, love and hatred, pleasure and pain mark our days from birth to death. We prevail, only to succumb; we fail, only to renew the struggle.

Our days are few and full of trouble.

The eye is never satisfied with seeing; endless are the desires of the heart. We devise new schemes on the graves of a thousand disappointed hopes. Like Moses on Mount Nebo, we behold the promised land from afar but may not enter it. Our life, at its best, is an endless effort for a goal we never attain. Death finally terminates the struggle, and joy and grief, success and failure, all are ended. Like children falling asleep over their toys, we relinquish our grasp on earthly possessions only when death overtakes us. Master and servant, rich and poor, strong and feeble, wise and simple, all are equal in death. The grave levels all distinctions, and makes the whole world kin.

When I read the prayer after my Georgetown experience, I realized it says just about the same thing as "Life's a bitch, then you die," except in a more serious vein.

If we were inclined to take a serious look back on the sum total of our lives and were really prepared to tell ourselves the truth as to how much time we have spent being happy, fulfilled, joyful and turned-on *versus* the amount of time we have spent feeling indifferent or unhappy, I believe that most of us would find that we have spent around 15 per cent of our lives being happy and 85 per cent being unhappy! I call this the 85/15 per cent ratio and if, in fact, this *is* the case and we spend only 15 per cent of our lives being happy then, again, I say, "Life is indeed a bitch, then you die."

I allow that some readers may question the idea that we spend 85 per cent of our lives somewhere between indifferent and unhappy because the notion is so disempowering. Nonetheless, if anyone disagrees with my figures and would prefer 20, 30, 50 or even 60 per cent, then so be it. But it doesn't change the fact that we spend far too much of our time being unhappy.

Whether we go to a synagogue, church, mosque or temple, or even if we have no particular religious affiliation, most of us acknowledge the existence of some universal 'power' or 'force', that many of us refer to as God. When I am in the synagogue listening to or reading the prayers, I am aware that our prayers are all about praising and honouring God. For most of us, Mankind is God's greatest creation. Now, if we are God's greatest creation, does it not follow that to truly honor our God, we must honour ourselves? I believe that the greatest affront to our God is not to honour ourselves and not to take care of our well being so if we waste one moment of our life living somewhere between indifferent and unhappy, then we are not honouring God's greatest creation and we are certainly not honouring our God.

If there were a way to increase the percentage of the time we are happy, wouldn't it be incumbent on us, indeed wouldn't we have a moral obligation, to do so? Well, I know it is within our power to increase that percentage substantially. If we truly want an enriched Q of L, it is in our power to have it. It is within our power to manage that we have it. However, we must first have access to that power, and in order to gain access, we must understand who we are as human beings, what drives us and how we live our lives. And that's what this part of the book is about — getting in touch with the power we have to manage our Q of L!

As we begin our exploration, it is important to understand that our Q of L is affected in two very different ways: first, *by events and circumstances themselves* and, second, *by the way we allow those events and circumstances to affect us.*

Let me explain:

When I started writing this book I told some of my friends that one of the sections would deal with managing our quality of life. Virtually everyone assumed I was writing about managing the things we do that affect our Q of L, such as spending more time with the family, relaxing, meditating, exercising, etc. These are all things we do and are in the realm of *doing*. They do, indeed, affect our Q of L, but that is not what I am addressing here. This exploration is about how we are *being* with life — that is, how we think, how we see the world and how we interpret and respond to the events and circumstances we encounter. It is about how we internalize, hold and deal with events and circumstances and how we allow them to affect us.

The reality is that our way of being with events and circumstances has a far greater impact on our Q of L than the events and circumstances themselves!

Before I took the *est* Training I had no understanding of the concept of 'being'. I was not conscious of how I was 'being', or could 'be' or aware that I might have any power or control over how I could 'be'. I was living my life out of what I call my "basic humanness" — as a victim, unenlightened and without power, at the mercy of events and circumstances, responding to life merely as it presented itself. Events and circumstances controlled how I felt, my moods, whether I was happy or unhappy, upset or angry. My entire well-being was controlled by external forces. I had no control.

Eventually, I began to understand that in order to overcome my basic humanness and gain control over how I allowed events and circumstances to affect me, I had to understand who we are as human beings, how we live our lives and why we operate the way we do in our basic humanness. Just as with a car, if we want to make it run better, we must first understand the mechanics of the vehicle, how it works and why it works the way it does. We cannot take appropriate action to improve the way it operates until we first understand how it works. In the same way, we cannot take appropriate action to improve our Q of L unless we first understand how we operate as human beings.

BASIC HUMANNESS

I KNOW "BASIC HUMANNESS" IS NOT A COMMON EXPRESSION, but I use it many times in what follows and it is central to this discussion. It is therefore crucial that we have a common understanding of what I mean by basic humanness.

Our basic humanness is the endowment we come into the world with.This includes our genetic inheritance, plus the additional conditioning and programming we absorb as we develop. It is generally accepted that all of us are products of our individual heritage and conditioning. Each of us has been shaped by our genes, our parents, schoolmates, education and training, experience, cultural influences and social environment. We have also been influenced by our experience of past events and by the decisions we made in response to those events. Consequently, each of us has his or her own particular conditioning or *wiring* and, in our basic humanness, that wiring determines our individual way of being, i.e., who we are, the way we think, the way we see the world, the way we behave and how we respond to life's events. As a result, in our basic humanness our reactions, behaviors and the way we respond to events are *predetermined*. They are automatic responses, they are not thought-out, carefully considered responses and they are not made out of choice. In effect, we are all slaves to, and victims of, our basic endowment and wiring.

The fact is, in our basic humanness we do not have a choice as to how we behave, react and respond; we operate like machines — mechanisms — that respond in predetermined ways to events and circumstances (stimuli). When our button A is pressed, we respond automatically in a predetermined way and we respond the same way every time our button A is pressed. The same goes for buttons B, C, D, etc. So, "who we are" in our basic humanness is...we are stimulus/response mechanisms that respond in predetermined ways, that is, *without choice*, to specific stimuli.

I have now introduced some new terms into this discussion — notably, stimulus/response mechanism, victim and choice. Let's look first at stimulus/response mechanism.

We will explore each of these in turn, but before we do, a quick review of *the truth* (which we dealt with in Part Two) is in order. In that exploration we saw how difficult it is for us to tell the truth, especially about who we are and what we are responsible for, and what we have created. We also saw how devastating it can be when we are unable to tell ourselves the truth.

In order to make something better, we must first acknowledge that it is not good enough or that it could be better. We must tell ourselves the truth as to what is really so, then take specific action to change it and make it better. However, if we are unable to tell the truth and we say something is good enough, even if it is not, we are prone to leave it alone. As a result, if we say that our Q of L is great when it is not, we won't take any action to make it better and it will not improve.

In summary:
- If we cannot tell ourselves the truth and we reject the validity of the 85/15 per cent ratio,
- If we cannot tell ourselves the truth and we reject the fact that we live our lives as stimulus/response mechanisms and as victims without choice,
- If we reject the fact that in our basic humanness we live our lives without power,
  then we will have no reason to take action to make things better, things will not get better and, at best, we will live lives of mediocrity.

Conversely, if:
- We are willing to accept the truth as it really is,
- We can accept that in our basic humanness we live our lives as stimulus/response mechanisms and as victims without the ability to choose,
- We reject living a life of mediocrity, and
- We make a commitment to have an outstanding Q of L,
  then miracles can happen!

Now let's get back to our central discussion.

STIMULUS/RESPONSE MECHANISM

I MADE THE CASE EARLIER that each of us has his/her own unique "wiring", which determines who we are and how we live in our basic humanness. As a result, in our basic humanness, our reactions (behaviours) are little more than predetermined, programmed responses to particular stimuli (events and circumstances). So our reactions are not carefully considered. In other words, we react or respond to events spontaneously, like machines — as stimulus/ response mechanisms.

When we live our lives as stimulus/response mechanisms — on auto-pilot, as it were — we live as victims of our past experiences and we do not have the opportunity to choose our responses. Therefore, we have no control over the way we respond to events and circumstances and we live our lives without power.

Unfortunately, in our basic humanness we are conditioned to focus on those things that detract from our Q of L. So, when we live our lives out of our basic humanness, most of us focus on the negative and that's one of the reasons why we live so much of our lives feeling somewhere between indifferent and unhappy. In fact, in observing people I know, it seems to me that most of us are committed to having misery in our lives. For examples.

Not long ago, Shirley and I had dinner with a couple who are close friends. During dinner they talked about a train trip to Toronto they were planning and the husband mentioned they had never before taken that trip by rail. He said, "I am really looking forward to the train ride. I'll take a book and read and relax. It's going to be great!"...to which his wife responded, "Sure, you're going to relax and even fall asleep, and I'm going to be sitting there biting my nails, waiting for the train to go off the tracks!"

Now, I don't believe our friend is really afraid to travel by rail. I think it was just her way of focusing on the negative. However, saying that she is waiting for "the train to go off the tracks" produces negative feelings and does not contribute to her well-being. Certainly, focusing on the negative and on things that can *possibly* go wrong does not contribute to her having much joy in her life. Now, our friend would probably argue that she was truly afraid or that what she said really didn't mean anything so what she said did not affect her Q of L. I would disagree on both counts. If she was truly afraid, I would argue that she caused her own fear and made it real by the statement she made. Also, if she insisted that what she said meant nothing, I would argue that the fact that she *spoke* of her fear made it real for her and that generated a sense of fear. Negative statements do not contribute to our feeling good, our sense of well-being, or to our Q of L.

We have another close friend who has had more than his share of mostly work-related challenges over the years. To add to them, he recently had some significant health problems that certainly affected his Q of L. We were at a wedding together and at one point I noticed him on the dance floor with his wife. He was dancing up a storm; he had a big smile on his face and he was obviously having a great time. Partly because I was focused on this book (and on managing our Q of L) at the time, I felt compelled to speak to him about his Q of L, something I had wanted to do for a long time. As he left the dance floor, I put my arm around his shoulders, drew him into a corner of the room and said, "I could not help but notice you dancing and that you had a big smile on your face. Were you having a good time?"

"I was having a great time." he said.

I then said, "You know, all of your troubles haven't disappeared. You still have some health problems and yet you were having a great time. Wouldn't it be great if we had a way to create or capture more good times in our lives? I believe we have the power to do that."

But before I could say another word he looked me straight in the eye and said, "That's unreasonable. You are not being realistic. Look at what's going on in Rwanda."

Now, I feel just as revolted, frustrated, and helpless as anyone else with regard to man's inhumanity to man, but that was another conversation for another time and place. I looked at him in shock.

"Where does Rwanda come into this conversation all of a sudden? Here we are at a wedding having a great time. I just wanted to explore with you whether we have the power to capture more of these happy moments and good times, and you have to travel to the other side of the world and find some misery to drag into this conversation"...to which he again answered, "You are not being realistic."...and that ended our conversation.

Sadly, that's what we humans are wired to do. If we can't find enough misery close to home, we'll dig it up wherever we can, even from the other side of the world.

In order to live a life of joy and have an outstanding Q of L we must manage to override our negative conditioning and get in touch with the power we have to do so. We must manage to override living our lives as stimulus/response mechanisms.

VICTIM

WE HAVE ALREADY MADE THE CASE that in our basic humanness most of us are conditioned and so we are predisposed to focus on the negative in our lives. Also, we seem to get a perverse pleasure from feeling sorry for ourselves and living as victims.

At this point, I must define victim as I am using the term here. The conventional view of a victim is a person who has somehow been wronged by an injustice, a crime, an accident, etc. All of these are beyond one's control and although they do make one a victim, that is not the definition of victim I am addressing here. I am using the term victim in the sense of *how we make victims of ourselves*, that is, how we hold, internalize, respond and react to events and circumstances. We can deal with events and circumstances from a position of strength and with power, or we can deal with them from a position of weakness, from feeling sorry for oneself. *That* is the victim I am addressing.

In most cases, living as a victim is characterized by the "poor me" syndrome. As victims, we whine, complain and look for attention and sympathy. Now, we may think we are getting attention and sympathy when we put on our victim act, but the truth is that most people have little tolerance for whiners and complainers and instead of sympathy, whining tends to elicit contempt.

Living life as a victim can be very comfortable because it allows us to avoid taking responsibility; we can always find something or someone else to blame. However, living as a victim is self-destructive because it robs us of personal power, and when we operate as a victim without personal power, we have no control over how we react and respond to events and circumstances. In other words, we can be a victims of, and crippled by, our conditioning and programming. In that case, we have no choice but to react in a particular way to a particular stimulus, and that, too, robs us of power. The following illustrates this.

Some years ago, Shirley and I met a young couple in Jamaica, with whom we became quite friendly. The young woman, Amy, was about the same age as our elder daughter, Esther. We invited them to spend a weekend with us the following summer at our country home in St. Donat. Our house is on a lake and there are two excellent ski hills just ten minutes away. You can see the ski hills when you are on the lake.

Shirley and I took our guests out on our boat and when Amy looked at the ski hills she told us she hadn't skied since she was a teenager and that she would love to ski again. So we invited them to come back to St. Donat for a ski weekend during the winter. That was in July. From then on, we were in frequent contact planning our ski weekend. Amy bought a new ski outfit and new ski equipment, and she was very excited at the prospect of coming back to ski.

When the time came — it was a Friday — we picked up Amy and her husband at the airport and went straight to St. Donat, planning to ski on Saturday and Sunday. At nine o'clock on Saturday morning we took off for the ski hill. We arranged for our guests to have a ski lesson in the morning and planned to meet for lunch and ski together in the afternoon. So, our friends took their lessons, we had lunch together, then we proceeded back to the hill. At that point everything was fine and Amy was very excited about continuing her skiing.

A short time later, Amy was struggling on one part of the hill where the incline was quite steep and I went over to her and said, "Amy, let me show you a technique that will help you. When you want to turn to the left, touch your right knee with your right hand. That forces your weight onto your right leg and causes your ski to turn to the left. After you've completed that turn, touch your left knee with your left hand and you will start another turn to the right. It's a very easy technique and I am sure you will find it a big help."

Amy said, "OK, thank you," then proceeded to ski down to the bottom of the hill.

When we were ready to go up on the lift again, she turned to us and said, "I think I've had enough. I am calling it quits for the day. You go ahead and ski without me."

"Amy, what happened?" I asked, "You were so looking forward to skiing and you are doing well."

Her reply was, "I just don't want to ski any more today."

So we all quit, went home and went out for a walk.

At breakfast on Sunday morning, Amy announced that she wasn't going to ski that day. She said "I just don't feel like it". We coaxed her to reconsider and tried to encourage her but she would have none of it. She was not going to ski. We were bewildered and could not understand what had happened to make everything fall apart. Anyhow, no one skied that day. We went for another walk and occupied ourselves with other things.

In the late afternoon the four of us went into the sauna together and, while sitting there in close quarters, the conversation somehow turned to Amy's background. Apparently, she had lost her mother when she was very young and her father had remarried. She never had a relationship with his new wife and to make matters even worse her father never approved of anything she did. In fact, her entire relationship with her father seemed to be about him being critical of her. Then, suddenly, she burst into tears.

"Amy, what's the matter? Why are you crying?", we asked.

"You won't believe what I just came face-to-face with", she answered. "You know when you came over to me yesterday on the ski hill and told me how to make a turn? I associated you with my father criticizing me, telling me that I can't do anything right and that I am inadequate. There was no way I was going to put up with that so I quit. I am very sorry I spoiled the weekend for everyone just because I got stuck on something from my past that I related to the present."

What had happened was that Amy reacted out of her past conditioning and programming. I had pressed a particular button and she reacted accordingly. She reacted out of her basic humanness – as a stimulus/response mechanism – and as a victim of her conditioning and past experience. As a victim, she was helpless, and she compromised not only her own Q of L, she affected all of us. That was the "bad news", the good news was that by understanding what had happened she was able to talk about it and get past it.

Certainly, living life as a victim does not give us power and it does not contribute to our Q of L. In order to live a life of joy and have an outstanding Q of L we must manage to override our negative conditioning that makes us prone to operate as a victim; we must take control and live life with power.

CHOICE

IT IS GENERALLY ACCEPTED that "who we are" is determined largely by our conditioning and programming — our wiring. That wiring shapes the vessels we are and causes us to react automatically, like machines, in pre-determined ways to specific stimuli. When we react automatically, we have no alternative but to react the way we do. That means we do not choose our reactions; *we do not have a choice*. A choice is only truly a choice when we have the option to choose something else. When we have no other option there is no choice. So, many, if not most of the choices we think we make are not really choices at all; they are just automatic conditioned responses.

Our inability to make real choices affects all aspects of our lives. There are literally thousands of different combinations of events and circumstances that we are exposed to and we have our own pre-determined responses or reactions to every one of them, and we cannot choose to respond or react differently–so there is no choice involved. Consider the following example.

I love all kinds of food–but there are two things that I cannot eat: snails (escargots) and frogs legs. At certain times of the year in Barbados there are snails slithering around on the ground. When I was a boy, I walked around barefoot and often stepped on one of those slimy, gushy, yukky creatures and they grossed me out. I hated snails. We also had a proliferation of frogs jumping all over the place and our house-keeper told me to avoid them at all cost because if one of them peed on me I would get warts. So I also hated frogs. To this day that's how I feel about snails and frogs and it goes back to my early youth. Now I know that I have been conditioned by those experiences, and even though escargots and frogs legs are considered to be delicacies, I cannot bring myself to eat either of them. One could argue that I choose not to eat snails or frogs legs, but I say it is not a choice because I cannot choose differently. I simply cannot eat them.

This is a simple example of not being able to choose that has no real consequence for my Q of L. Although I could be selling myself short and missing an exquisite culinary experience, the fact is that whether I eat snails and frogs legs or not has no real impact on my Q of L. However, there are hundreds of other situations where we don't get to make choices that do have significant consequences. For example, I loved my father dearly and there was nothing I wanted more than to have his approval, but I could never seem to please him. I always felt inadequate in his eyes and that caused me great pain. That was part of my early conditioning and programming. Based on that conditioning, when it came to my own children, I could have reacted (subconsciously) in either of two ways: to be like my father, or not to be like my father. But either reaction would have been an automatic response to my conditioning. Neither would have been a choice because I could not have chosen to react differently.

When I reflect on my relationship with my own children, it is clear to me that, subconsciously, the way I responded to my conditioning was not to be like my father. In retrospect, I know that because of my relationship with my father, I was programmed not to inflict the same kind of pain on my children as I endured from him. As a result, I was more indulgent of my children. However, my response to be not like my father was not a choice because I could not choose otherwise. Shirley used to complain that she did not get my support with the children and consequently she had to be the sole disciplinarian. Nonetheless, my conditioning was so strong I could not be different. I had no choice in the matter.

When we live our lives as stimulus/response mechanisms, unable to make conscious, deliberate, calculated choices, we live life as victims and we have no personal power. Some may find it difficult to accept that the choices we think we make are automatic responses and are not choices at all. However, if we can accept that many of our choices are not really choices, then we can override our conditioning, begin to make conscious, deliberate, calculated choices, be in control and live our lives with power. So, in order to live a life of joy and have an outstanding Q of L, we must override our conditioning and begin making conscious, deliberate, calculated choices.

In summary, when we live our lives out of our basic humanness — as stimulus/response mechanisms — we live as victims of our conditioning and programming and the choices we think we make are not choices at all. As a result, our Q of L is determined by the whims of the events and circumstances we encounter and we live our life without control and without power. In order to live a life of joy and have an outstanding Q of L, we must manage to override our basic humanness, override our stimulus/response mechanisms, stop living life as a victim and make conscious, deliberate, calculated choices — that's living life in control and with power.

The balance of this exploration is about getting in touch with the power we have to manage our Q of L, override our basic humanness, and make true choices. Living Life with Power requires that we manage our Quality of Life, that is, manage our way of being. That involves learning to override our basic humanness. It also requires a commitment to having an outstanding Q of L and an intolerance to living one moment being unhappy. None of these is easy.

Now, let's explore managing and management in the context of Quality of Life.

28

HOW TO MANAGE
OUR QUALITY OF LIFE

In simple terms, management is the process of taking action to ensure that the things we want to have happen do in fact happen. Things do not happen just because we want them to happen. They happen only when we take action to ensure that they happen — if we manage that they happen. Usually, when we refer to "management" and "managing," we think in the contexts of business, organizations and groups. In these contexts, managing has to do with directing and influencing people, processes, procedures, and resources in order to achieve certain objectives. However, few of us think of managing in terms of managing our well-being and our Quality of Life. Yet, what can be more important than managing our well-being? That is, managing our way of being — managing how we are with life, how we think, how we see the world, how we interpret and respond to events and circumstances, how we internalize, hold and deal with events and circumstances, and how we allow them to affect us.

For most of us, the idea of managing our well-being (and so our Q of L) is not part of our reality. We do not believe we have the capability or the power to do that. So, we devote an enormous amount of time and effort to managing our growth and development in terms of our schooling, work life, business, and profession, and we pay no attention to our Q of L, let alone to managing it! However, if we hope to live happy and fulfilled lives, it is essential that we manage our way of being. That is the secret to living a life with control and with power.

Four elements determine our way of being and dictate how we think, how we see the world, and how we allow events and circumstances to affect us. They are:

- The attitudes we bring to events and circumstances,
- The way we perceive events and circumstances,
- The way we interpret events and circumstances, and
- The judgements we apply to events and circumstances.

I fondly refer to these elements as our "*As, Ps, Is* and *Js*."

The way we allow our As, Ps, Is and Js to affect us, determines our Q of L. And managing our As, Ps, Is and Js so they contribute to, rather than detract from, our Q of L is fundamental to having an outstanding Q of L. Unless we manage our As, Ps, Is and Js so they contribute to our Q of L, we will be victims of happenstance and will live our lives without power.

I will get back to our As, Ps, Is and Js in due course, but at this point I must introduce the term "paradigm".

Paradigm

I understand a paradigm to be a "core belief"; it is a belief that has the status of certainty. The sense in which I use paradigm here is when we hold something to be sacred, A paradigm is a certainty; it is something that is really so. A paradigm is not about "I think so" or "it may be so". It is about "it is absolutely so!" and we live in that paradigm until something shatters it and creates a new one for us.

For example, in the 13th century, everyone knew that the world was flat. There was absolutely no doubt about it. Everyone lived in that paradigm. There was no "maybe" or possibility that it could be otherwise, then Columbus shattered that paradigm once and for all when he sailed west and did not fall off the end of the earth! He created the new paradigm we now live in; the earth is round.

Most of us live in the paradigm that we are the way we are, we are affected the way we are affected, we react the way we react, we feel the way we feel and there is nothing we can do about it. Now, one of the most difficult things for human beings to do is to break down a paradigm, but in this exploration we are going to try to do just that – break down the paradigm that we are the way we are... and there is nothing we can do about it. We will explore whether we can create and live in another paradigm that allows us to continually improve our well-being and live an enriched life. We will make the case for a new paradigm that we have the power to manage our Q of L.

Now, let's get back to our attitudes, perceptions, interpretations and judgments – that is, our As, Ps, Is, and Js.

I have already claimed that managing our As, Ps, Is and Js is fundamental to improving our Q of L. In order to manage our As, Ps, Is and Js, we must understand these terms and how they affect our Q of L. But before proceeding, let me make it clear that I am addressing As, Ps, Is and Js only from the perspective of managing our Q of L. It is not a comprehensive survey of the terms.

ATTITUDE

OUR ATTITUDE IS A PRE-DETERMINED POSTURE — a way of being — and is at the centre or *the cause* of the way we behave and respond to events and circumstances. Our attitude speaks to the world through both our speaking and through the way we present and project ourselves. Our attitude is part of who we are. We do not choose our attitude. It is formed out of our conditioning and is shaped by the past and our past experiences. Our attitude is one of the things we "bring to the table," to relationships as well as to events. Our attitude also acts as a filter through which we see the world. So, the way we see the world and the way we relate to events is determined by the filter of our attitude.

Our attitude has an enormous effect on our Q of L and causes us to see the world from either a positive or a negative perspective. When we see the world from a negative perspective, it does not contribute to our Q of L or to living a life of joy. If we are committed to living a richer, fuller life, we must be intolerant to any negative attitude and manage our attitude so it contributes to our Q of L.

Several years ago I received a flyer from a local personnel agency promoting their services. It caught my attention because it supported my view of attitude and how it affects our quality of life.

THE POWER OF ATTITUDE

"The longer I live, the more I realize the impact of attitude on life. Attitude, to me is more important than facts. It is more important than the past, than education, than money, than circumstances, than failures, than successes, than what other people think or say or do. It is more important than appearance, giftedness or skill. It will make or break a company...a church...a home. The remarkable thing is we have a choice every day regarding the attitude we will embrace for that day. We cannot change the inevitable. The only thing we can do is play on the one string we have, and that is our attitude...I am convinced that life is 10 percent what happens to me and 90 percent how I react to it. And so it is with you...we are in charge of our attitudes."

Clearly, events and circumstances do contribute to, or detract from, our Q of L but the "attitude" we bring to those events or circumstances has a far greater influence on our Q of L than the events and circumstances themselves. The above piece says it all: "...the longer I live, the more I realize the impact of attitude on life ...I am convinced that life is 10 percent what happens to me and 90 percent how I react to it."

I live in Montreal, where we have four seasons. Our winters are relatively long and cold, so it is impossible to ignore winter in Montreal. Every Montrealer has an "attitude" toward winter. Some of those attitudes contribute to, while others detract from our well-being and Q of L. Many of us adopt a negative attitude and focus on, "I hate winter, I hate the cold, I hate having to put on all these clothes and boots, I hate wearing a hat and having hat-hair." Now, if I am not a snow-bird and must live in Montreal through the winter, and I focus on "I hate winter", that attitude will only bring misery into my life. It does not serve me. Now, it is important to understand that my attitude is my own creation, it is mine and mine alone. So if my attitude does not serve me, since I have the power to create it one way (I hate winter), then *I certainly have the power to change it and create it another way.* I can manage my attitude so that it contributes to my Q of L.

I can create an attitude that focuses on "I live in Montreal out of choice, not because I have to or because I am a victim." I can focus my attention on all of the good things about the holiday season and the positive things that winter brings — on the joys of celebrating Christmas and Chanukah, the New Year festivities and the winter wonderland when the snow falls and everything is white. I can focus on all of the wonderful things about living in Canada and that Canada is acknowledged as one of the best places in the world to live. Clearly, I can *manage* my attitude and focus on those things that contribute to my well-being and Q of L.

Personally, I allow that there are some things about winter that I don't like. For example, I have a little Shitsu dog named *Tchai.* In winter, when I walk Tchai at 6:45 in the morning and again at 4:30 in the evening, we walk in the dark and I don't like the short days and the lack of daylight. I could focus on; "Woe is me! Poor me! I am out here walking in the cold and in the dark and I have no option because Tchai needs to be walked." I choose not to focus on that because that attitude certainly would not contribute to my well being. Instead, I focus on how much I love Tchai and the pleasure I experience when I see her scampering around in the snow. I actually sing to her while we are walking and I have an experience of total joy. That attitude certainly contributes to my well-being and Q of L. We have the power to do that — to manage our Q of L.

One may think that in discussing something as important as attitude examples such as coping with winter in Montreal and walking my dog are trivial. However, simple examples are often the best way to make important points. The fact is that our lives are influenced by hundreds of trivial experiences that, collectively, shape the quality of our lives. Having said that, the following is certainly not trivial.

On the second day of Rosh Hashanah last year, Shirley and I were in synagogue and after the service we fell into a conversation with a young woman. We had seen her in synagogue many times, always with a smile on her face, but we had never spoken before. During our conversation she complimented us on our family and the way we were always in synagogue together. Because she spoke of our family, we told her about our children and I mentioned that our daughter, Esther, is a physician and that she practices integrated medicine. So the topic turned to medicine and she told us that she had survived ovarian cancer 15 years earlier, when she was in her early twenties. She added that not many women survive ovarian cancer, especially at that young age. She went on to say that she felt very lucky because the cancer was discovered early.

Shirley asked her how they had discovered the cancer and she told us that there had been no symptoms and that the discovery of the cancer was a fluke; she had just been diagnosed with lupus, and it was during one of her examinations for the lupus that her doctors discovered the cancer. I then asked, "What were the symptoms of the lupus?" and she said, "If you can imagine how you feel when you're coming down with the flu, that's how I feel on a good day." Then, with a big smile she added, "...and I love my lupus".

Obviously, she loves her lupus because it saved her life.

Unquestionably, the circumstances this young woman has to deal with on a daily basis includes having to live with the effects of the lupus and it certainly affects her quality of life. But what has a far greater effect is the attitude she brings to her condition. It is how she thinks, internalizes and deals with the lupus, and how she allows it to affect her. That is what determines her Q of L. Her attitude and her way of being with the lupus have a far greater impact on her Q of L than the lupus itself.

It is very clear that she is an empowered woman who does not allow herself to be a victim. She has the power to manage her attitude so it contributes to her Q of L and she knows how to use that power.

PERCEPTION

PERCEPTION IS ABOUT THE WAY WE SEE THE world and the way we perceive events and circumstances. This is a product of our conditioning and programming and each of us has his/her own unique way of seeing the world and perceiving events and circumstances. As a result, our perceptions act as filters and we "see" what we expect to see or what we want to see. No two people will observe or perceive the same event the same way. Consider the example of two people who witness the same accident. Each will perceive the accident differently and tell a different story. So neither story can be relied upon to be an absolutely accurate account of what really happened. Both stories will be "as perceived" through the individual's unique filters and will not necessarily be "absolutely" true.

Our perceptions cause us to see the world, either positively or negatively, as in the example of living in Montreal in winter. The riddle of "the glass is half empty" vs "the glass is half full" is another example of perceiving the same condition either from a positive or a negative perspective. Half empty focuses on how much is missing and is usually a negative perception. Half full focuses on how much is in the glass and is usually a positive perception. Half full puts a positive "spin" on one's outlook and that contributes to our appreciating what we have, whereas half empty is about not having enough, and that creates dissatisfaction. The half full perception contributes to our

well-being and Q of L; the half empty perception detracts from
our well-being and Q of L.*

So, if we are committed to living a life of joy, we must be
intolerant of any negative perceptions and change them so that
they contribute to our Q of L – we must manage our perceptions.

INTERPRETATION

INTERPRETATION IS THE PROCESS OF ASCRIBING meaning to events and
circumstances. Those meanings or interpretations are determined by our conditioning and since we all have our own
individual conditioning, our interpretations are our own
creations. As with our attitudes and perceptions, our interpretations
also act as filters through which we see the world and influence
the way we respond to events and circumstances.

Each of us interprets events and circumstances in his/her own
particular way, so no two people experience the same event and
interpret it in exactly the same way. For example, when two people
hear the same speech or read the same newspaper article, based
on their individual conditioning and personal filters, each comes
away with a different understanding and interpretation of what
was said or read.

Once again, our individual interpretations of events and
circumstances can be either positive or negative. When they are
negative, they do not contribute to our Q of L. So, if we are
committed to having an outstanding Q of L and living a life of joy,
we must be intolerant to negative interpretations, and change
them so they contribute to our Q of L. We must manage our
interpretations.

For example, when it is raining, dark and dismal outside, I can
apply a negative interpretation such as: "Woe is me! The weather is
awful, I had planned to be outdoors. Now I am confined to the

---

* This example of half full and half empty pertains to our personal lives and should not be confused
with what I said in Part 2 about Shirmax being very effective living in the world of the glass is half
empty. That was in a business context. This explanation is strictly in the context of our personal lives.

house. What a bummer!" That interpretation does not contribute to my feeling good, my well-being or my Q of L. On the other hand, I can apply a positive interpretation: "The rain is here, spring is in the air, the streets are being cleaned and the new grass is being watered. I can stay indoors, curl up in my favourite chair, relax and catch up on some reading. What a pleasure!" That interpretation certainly makes me feel good, contributes to my well-being and to my Q of L.

Our interpretations can be the source of great pain in our lives and are often the source of difficulty we have in relationships. When one party says or does something, if we think about it, it is not what is said or done that causes hurt, pain, anger or upset, *it is how we interpret what has been said or done.* Psychiatrists' offices are full of troubled patients trying to figure out the source of their difficulties in life. Often they have to try to understand and come to terms with their relationships with their parents. Many of us carry baggage, hurt and grudges with regard to our parents — what kind of parents they were/are, if they were caring, giving and supportive or non-caring, hurtful or even selfish. The fact is that parents do what they do and say what they say, mostly with the best intentions. But whatever they do and say, it is rarely their actions and words that scar us and cause pain. It is our interpretation of their actions and words that do us damage. If we can understand and internalize the truth, that our interpretations of events and circumstances have a far greater effect on our Q of L than the events and circumstances themselves, and that our interpretations are our own creations, it will give us the power to be aware of our negative interpretations and override them. It will give us the power to *manage* our interpretations.

The secret to having an outstanding Q of L is knowing when our interpretations do not contribute to our Q of L, and *changing* them!

JUDGEMENT

JUDGEMENT IS THE PROCESS OF EVALUATING merit with respect to events and circumstances based on our personal values; it is the constant evaluation of things as being right or wrong, good or bad, acceptable or not acceptable, etc. We judge things to be good if they agree with our values, or bad if they do not agree with our values.

Our judgments manifest themselves as a constant chatter in our mind and most of that chatter has to do with ascribing meaning to events and circumstances, then evaluating (judging) those meanings to be right or wrong, good or bad, etc. Now each of us has his/her own set of values that has been formed out of our conditioning and programming. Our values also act as a filter through which we see the world and make judgements. Actually, human beings are judgement machines. Judging is part of the human condition and is the most insidious of our As, Ps, Is and Js because it never stops; our judgement chatter goes on and on. In the process of judging we cripple and rob ourselves of the opportunity to really be with what's going on around us. Because we are always judging, we can never be in a relationship "clean". We are constantly hearing and seeing each other through our judgement filters.

At this point, let me share another personal experience:

Rosh Hashana, the Jewish New Year, is an important annual event in my life. It is a time when our family gets together. Our children and grandchildren come to Montreal and part of our celebration is to go to synagogue together. Our entire family, including my brother's family, sits together and we are a noticeable presence in the synagogue. (If the truth be known, I enjoy this event more from a family and social perspective than from a religious perspective.) I place great value on this tradition and I look forward to the togetherness and having everyone there.

My granddaughter, Alana, has been having some difficulty with the concept of religion and would prefer not to attend synagogue. Last year, however, to please her parents and grand-parents, she agreed to attend, but her heart really wasn't in it. She brought along a book to read during the service and she sat quietly in her seat oblivious to us and to what was going on around her. Now there are times in the service when the congregation stands. Noticeably, everyone stood — except my Alana — and my judge-ment chatter consumed me.

Also, my daughter Rachelle and her husband were making a special trip from Toronto to celebrate the New Year festivities with us. I went to the synagogue early and waited for them...but they didn't show up. More judgement chatter in my head!

Rosh Hashanah is a time when we are supposed to appreciate family, feel love and enjoy the holiday. However, I was certainly not feeling joy or love. The chatter going on in my head was upset-ting me terribly. Eventually, I realized how this was affecting me. Given my commitment to my Q of L, I turned off that chatter and replaced it with a new conversation:

"These are my judgements and they are based on my personal values. My personal values are the result of my upbringing, my own conditioning and programming. My children and grandchildren are entitled to their own values. Who says that my values are the right ones or the only ones? In fact, I go to synagogue only twice a year and that suits my values. Those who go to synagogue every Sabbath could judge me harshly for attending only on the high holidays. The fact is, I have different values from theirs, so isn't it fair that Rachelle and Alana should be allowed to have their own values too?"

So, I said to myself, "Max, you are being a human judging machine. Get off it! Change your conversation!" My mood changed immediately and I spent the rest of the holiday the way I wanted to — elated, joyful and full of love.

So what happened here? I was judgemental and that certainly made me unhappy. I rejected being unhappy, created a new, posi-tive conversation and that changed my Q of L.

It should be clear at this point that it is our As, Ps, Is and Js that determine how we are being with life, how we think, how we see the world, how we interpret and respond to events and circumstances, how we internalize, hold and deal with events and circumstances, and how we allow them to affect us. It follows, therefore, that our As, Ps, Is, and Js, determine our Q of L and that if we want to have an outstanding Q of L, we must manage our As, Ps, Is and Js so they contribute to, rather than detract from our well-being and our Q of L. That leads us to the question, "Do we have the power to do that? Do we have the power to manage our As, Ps, Is and Js?" We will consider this in the section on Personal Power, but before we do I would like to introduce a new concept — Enlightenment.

ENLIGHTENMENT

I KNOW THAT ENLIGHTENMENT IS GENERALLY thought of in the context of Eastern religious philosophy and is interpreted by many as being the path to wisdom. I have no quarrel with that but I must make it clear that I am using another interpretation of enlightenment.

Enlightenment, as I use it here, is a heightened level of awareness that gives us the power to manage our Q of L. Enlightenment is the ability to be an observer in one's own life, able to function as both the "actor" and the "observer" simultaneously. Being enlightened allows us to observe ourselves in play — reacting and responding to life around us. Becoming an observer in our life allows us to see ourselves as a programmed stimulus/response mechanism in action. It also makes it possible for us to reject those reactions that do not contribute to our Q of L and to choose other reactions.

Becoming an observer in our life calls for another level of awareness that puts a check on our usual programmed reactions and responses. It enables us to ensure that our reactions and responses contribute to our Q of L. It is only when we become observers in our lives, and we can observe ourselves reacting in ways that do not contribute to our Q of L, that we can override the stimulus/response mechanisms that we are, choose other reactions and responses, and live our lives with a measure of control.

Looking back at our friend Amy and her ski experience, when she was able to observe her reactions and realized that she had associated me with her father and had interpreted my coaching as criticism, she had an "ah-hah!" moment — a moment of enlightenment that allowed her to override that reaction.

I had a similar experience that had to do with my mother.

My mother was a simple lady and was very focused on food and eating. Every time I visited her, the first thing she did was run to the refrigerator and start hauling out things she had prepared for me to eat. This always irritated me and I always reacted negatively when she tried to push food on me.

When I was in my 50s, a grown man and supposedly enlightened, I used to visit my mom in Florida. Because she knew I was coming, she prepared all sorts of dishes for me that she knew I liked. From the moment I arrived, it was eat, eat, eat and eat more. At the time, my mother was going on 80 and every time she started with her food routine my reaction was the same and it bordered on the violent. I was completely hooked and disempowered. Even when I really wanted to eat more, I would push my plate away. Every time she pressed me with "Are you sure you've had enough? Maybe I can get you some more?" etc. I would throw down my knife and fork and yell, "That's enough!"

I visited many times when she had already prepared a meal that I loved and I would say, "No, we're not eating at home tonight, we're going out for supper." I knew that hurt her, and the irony was, I couldn't help myself, even though I loved her (and her cooking) dearly but I was so hooked that every time she pressed my food button I was powerless. I had no choice in the matter. I could react only one way – badly. Those reactions definitely did not contribute to a nurturing relationship with my mother and they certainly did not contribute to my Q of L.

Fortunately, this story has a happy ending because one day, in the middle of one of our food routines, I had an "ah-ha" moment. I observed my reaction and behaviour and that triggered a conversation with myself. I asked, "What are you doing? What do you want from this poor, unenlightened old lady? She's just doing what comes naturally to her. You are being intolerant and more unenlightened than she has ever been. Your mother is precious to you and you are hurting her. Max, you have the power to choose a different reaction. Get in touch with that power, appreciate your mother, and choose to make her perfect exactly as she is. Eat what you want, leave what you don't want, and just love her."

(As I was writing this, Shirley pointed out to me that part of the reason why my mother was so focused on food with me probably stemmed from the time I was a baby and she didn't have food to feed me.)

My conversation with myself transformed my entire relationship with my mother. Although she continued her food routine and my initial reactions were always the same, I was able to observe what was happening, override my programmed reactions and move beyond them. I am grateful that I saw the light when I did because I did not have to deal with any guilt later when she passed away.

It is important to understand that as enlightened as we may become, everyone suffers from the same human condition: we have specific responses to specific stimuli and we cannot avoid having those responses when the stimuli are applied. Our conditioning is deeply rooted in our psyches, so when our buttons are pressed we react. We cannot avoid the initial reaction, but we can observe it, reject it and choose another reaction.

That's enlightenment.

Personal Power

Throughout this exploration I have used the term "power" in the context of managing our well-being and our Q of L — that is, not being a victim of our stimulus/response mechanisms, able to make real choices and live life with power.

Personal power is having the capability to manage our Q of L; it is the power we have to override our negative conditioning and programming, to override our negative As, Ps, Is, and Js and change them so that they do contribute to our well-being.

Personal power comes from understanding:

- How we react and respond to life's events when we live our lives out of our basic humanness
- How our conditioning and programming, and our As, Ps, Is and Js affect our Q of L, and
- That we have the power to manage and override our conditioning and programming, and our As, Ps, Is, and Js so they contribute positively to our Q of L.

It is certain that the universe will throw obstacles in our way, that fate will bring us personal challenges and that some bad things will happen to us. But we have the power to shape the As, Ps, Is and Js we apply to them.

Human beings have the potential to be amazingly powerful. However, few of us realize that we have that power. It is simply not part of our reality. However, we do have it — but we first have to get in touch with it. Once again, I must make it clear that I am not suggesting that events and circumstances do not affect us; they do. What I am saying is that we can deal with them from different perspectives–from weakness or from strength, either as a victim or with power.

Losing a child is probably the worst thing that can happen to a parent. When some parents lose a child they simply cannot deal with it. Their lives are destroyed. Yet, for others, even though their loss is just as devastating, they handle it very differently. For instance, some parents who have lost a child in a car accident have become crusaders against drunk driving; they do not fall apart. The same terrible event happened to both sets of parents yet, despite their pain and grief, they are able to go on and make a difference in the world. For one, life practically ended, and the other finds the power to go on and live a meaningful life.

Personal power turns on two principles, commitment and intolerance. Commitment is to an outstanding Q of L, and intolerance is to living one moment being unhappy. It is only by being intolerant to having anything except an outstanding Q of L that we will be vigilant and override our automatic spontaneous responses. In fact, these two principles, commitment and intolerance are key to having an outstanding Q of L.

Here, it is worth telling how I first came to understand the concept of personal power. But before I can do that, I must introduce another concept that I first encountered in my est Training. To illustrate:

In our culture when someone dies it is devastating for those of us who are left behind. We ascribe a meaning to the death that it is the end of everything and we grieve terribly. In some other cultures, people celebrate the event when someone dies. They ascribe a totally different meaning to the death, believing that the person is going to a better place. Clearly, each culture creates and ascribes its own meaning to the event. Now, even though the two interpretations are fundamentally different, the members of each culture believe the meaning they ascribe to death is the true meaning. So which is the "true" meaning? Each has created its own truth: death is what they say it is. As an event, death is the same everywhere. It is simply an event, but different cultures ascribe different meanings and interpretations to that event. With this example as a background, let's continue with personal power.

Late on the third day of my est Training, the course leader introduced the concept, "Life is empty and meaningless until we show up and give it meaning." That statement struck me as being negative and disempowering and it made me very angry. After all, we had just spent three days trying to make sense out of what life is all about. The more I thought about it, the angrier I became, and I challenged the course leader. "How can you say that? If life is empty and meaningless, what am I doing here? Why have I been struggling all my life? What's this all about?"

And he answered,

"Consider the context of what I said. In our personal universe, life and life events in themselves have no meaning; they are simply events and they mean what we say they mean. They mean what we create them to mean."

That started us on a lengthy discussion with examples but yet I cannot say I really understood the concept when I finished The Training. Despite the course leader's answer and our subsequent exploration, it took me many months to overcome my anger and it took almost three years before I understood the significance, indeed, the immense power, of that statement. Today, I don't consider that statement to be at all negative or disempowering. On the contrary, I see it as one of the most empowering concepts that shapes my life.

Let me explain.

Throughout our lifetime, our every waking moment is dominated by events. Now, as in the case of the meaning ascribed to death, what does any event mean? If each person ascribes his or her own meaning to an event, and the meaning each ascribes to that event is different, then what does the event really mean? The reality is that the event in itself is just something that happens; it has no meaning. It means only what we individually create it to mean; what we say it means. Whatever meaning we ascribe to the event depends entirely on the interpretation we apply to it.

So, events are simply that; they are events, and they have no meaning until we show up and give them meaning. And since our lives are dominated by events that have no meaning, if we add up all the events that have affected us, and if we apply this reasoning to each of them (that we, individually, have applied the meaning to every event we have experienced) then we are the creators of the meaning of everything in our life. And so, it follows that "life is empty and meaningless until we show up and give it meaning."

Now, how can I say that this concept is so empowering? It is empowering because if we understand that an event in itself has no meaning and that we create whatever meaning is ascribed to it, then it follows that if that meaning does not contribute to our Q of L, as the creator of that meaning, if we have the power to create the meaning one way, we also have the power to create it another way, so it does contribute to our Q of L!

Throughout the ages civilizations have searched for the "secret to life." Intellectuals have debated, scholars have pondered and books have been written on the subject. For me, in the context of our Q of L, the secret to living life, and so the secret to life, is understanding that events are simply things that happen, and that in themselves they have no meaning. Individually, we create and give meaning to everything in our lives. Therefore, understanding and internalizing the concept that life is empty and meaningless until we show up and give it meaning gives us the power to ascribe meaning to everything in our lives so that those meanings contribute to our Q of L. For me, that is the secret to life.

Most of us are aware that we have the power to take care of our physical well-being but, sadly, we are not in touch with our personal power and we do not understand the concept of taking care of our inner selves, our emotional and intellectual well-being, and so we don't! Yet, over a lifetime, our emotional and intellectual turmoil causes us much more suffering than any physical pain we may endure. The reality is that by not managing our emotional and intellectual well-being, we live without power and that is why so many of us live so much of our lives being unhappy, victims of the 85/15 percent equation.

If we want to change those percentages we must:
- get in touch with our personal power,
- manage our As, Ps, Is and Js,
- manage the interpretations and meanings we apply to everything in our lives,
- manage the way we allow events and circumstances to affect us, and so,
- manage our Q of L.

We have that power.

That's personal power!

On a personal note, I mentioned earlier that I have a degenerative eye condition known as macular degeneration. Usually, the condition occurs in people who are in their '80s. However, at the time of my diagnosis I was not yet 60 and I was the CEO of a major corporation. I was told that within a short time I would be legally blind and severely handicapped. Obviously that condition was going to make my job more difficult and life more challenging. I was in shock and understandably upset for a few days. But because I was committed to having an outstanding Q of L and I was intolerant to not having it, I could not allow myself to continue being upset. I knew I had to manage my As, Ps, Is and Js relating to my condition, and I knew I had the power to do that. I then had a conversation with myself that went something like:

"I have seen a lot in my life, but there is also much I have not seen. I am sure that my diminished eyesight will sharpen my other senses and that will give me the opportunity to learn other things. I am confident I will be able to deal positively with this handicap and, in fact, that I will turn it into an opportunity."

It has now been more than ten years since I was diagnosed. I no longer drive, I can no longer read or write, and I have to sit very close to a television set. Unfortunately, I also often walk by people whom I know but whom I cannot recognize at a distance or in poor light. Other than that, I function normally and my doctors hope I will not deteriorate any further. Being in touch with my personal power has served me well through this adversity. I continue to operate from a position of strength. I do not focus my attention on life's adversities or see myself as a victim. I focus on all the blessings in my life and I continue to have an outstanding Q of L.

Let's now move on to explore some "how-to" techniques that are available to us to manage our Q of L.

29

HOW-TO TECHNIQUES

AT FIRST IT MAY SOUND LIKE AN UNUSUAL QUESTION, but I ask it nonetheless: "Where do our ideas live?" The quick answer is, "In our minds." If I then ask, "Where does 'our way of being' and 'how we are being with life' live? Where does 'how we see the world, interpret and respond to events and circumstances live? Where do our As, Ps, Is and Js live?" The answer is the same — in our minds! All of them live in our internal conversations in the constant chatter that goes on in our minds. So, if we want to manage our way of being, etc. we have to learn to manage the chatter that goes on in our minds; we have to manage our minds.

MANAGING OUR THINKING

THE MIND, IN THE CONTEXT I AM ADDRESSING here, is where our thinking occurs. It is the home of our thoughts. Now, to a large extent, our Q of L is determined by how we feel intellectually and emotionally, and those feelings are determined by our thoughts. So, in reality, managing our Q of L, or the way we feel, is a matter of managing our thinking.

Most of us think we have thoughts, but that is not so. The reality is that thoughts have us; we are thinking machines. If we try and stop ourselves from thinking, we can't! Our conditioning will always trigger specific thoughts in response to specific stimuli. We cannot stop them. However, if we can become observers in our lives, we can observe our thoughts and if our thinking does not contribute to our feeling good and our well-being, we can redirect it; we can focus on something else. Since our thinking dictates how we feel, and how we feel directly affects our Q of L, in order to ensure that we live happy, fulfilled and empowered lives, we must manage our internal conversations, we must manage our thinking.

As in the example of Alana in Synagogue and Rachelle not showing up, my thoughts were upsetting me terribly and were certainly not contributing to my Q of L. However, when I observed my thoughts and what they were doing to me, I managed to change them by focusing on new thoughts that did contribute to my Q of L. That's managing one's thinking. Now, I am not saying that we can manage our thinking moment by moment, all the time. But with a commitment to our Q of L and an intolerance to having anything but an outstanding Q of L, with practice, we can become very skilled in managing our thinking, and so, improve on the 85/15 percent equation. That's the ultimate achievement in personal power.

MANAGING OUR SPEAKING

AS HUMANS, WE HAVE THE ABILITY TO REASON and think logically, and that separates us from most other animal species. But it is primarily through our speaking that we "come alive" and have an impact on the world. A person walking down the street makes no difference to anyone. It is through interaction with others, mostly through speaking, that he or she has any impact. So, our speaking is the single most powerful tool each of us has with which to influence the world around us. However, it is important to understand that our speaking also has an enormous influence on our own thinking, and so, on our lives.

Thousands of thoughts go through our minds in a day. They enter and fly away like feathers in the wind. Generally, the ones that stay with us are those we articulate. We give life to thoughts by speaking them, and through our speaking, a thought becomes real. And that's the progression:

Speaking $\longrightarrow$ Thinking $\longrightarrow$ Feeling $\longrightarrow$ Quality of Life.

Since we have the ability to reason, most of us believe that we think logically. We have a thought or an idea, we check it out, decide if it makes sense and whether or not we believe it, then we speak it. We believe that's how the process works. However, more often than not it is the exact opposite. We do not speak what we believe; we believe what we speak! Let me explain.

We say things for all sorts of reasons. It may be that we want to make an impression or we want to fit in or, perhaps, we want attention, sympathy, admiration or acknowledgement. So, we speak things that support those motives. Often we speak without giving much thought to what we say, so often what we speak is not necessarily true. But once we speak, we believe what we say. That's the way our psyche works: once we have made a statement, that is, once we have spoken something, we have no option but to believe what we have said. If we did not believe what we say, our sense of personal integrity and self-worth would suffer. So, once we say something, we believe what we have said, and we get trapped in that belief. (Remember the story of cannibalization in Part Two, and how I could have been misled by something that had no factual basis, but once I spoke it, I believed it to be so). Let me illustrate.

Bob is at a cocktail party and the topic of conversation turns to politics. One person in his group says something negative about the Prime Minister, then another person, who wants to participate in the conversation, follows the first remark with another slur. The conversation goes around and everybody has something negative to say about the Prime Minister. Bob is not at all au courant with politics and he knows even less about the Prime Minister. He has no idea whether or not the remarks he has just heard are true, but he doesn't want to be left out; he wants to be thought of as knowledgeable and as having something to contribute to the conversation as well. So he adds his two cents' worth and says something else uncomplimentary about the PM. Now, once Bob has spoken, his negative remark becomes real for him and he believes it. For no reason other than wanting to impress his listeners, Bob has spoken something about which he knows nothing and, because he spoke it, it has become a truth for him.

We do not realize it, but this scenario happens all the time. For all sorts of reasons we often say things that we have not thought through or verified, that we know nothing about or that we do not know to be true. As a result, more often than not, when we speak we are not speaking what we truly believe or know to be true. Rather, we believe what we have spoken, and we get trapped in that belief!

Here is another example from closer to home.

Shirley is a great traveller and tourist. Once she is on a trip she revels in the experience; nothing is too hard or too onerous for her. She is adventurous, sees the beauty in everything, loves exploring and adapts easily to different cultures. She is an absolute pleasure as a travelling companion, but she has a conflict; she is also a great home-body. When the subject of another trip comes up, her defences go up; she makes up a story and speaks it, and once she has spoken it she believes it to be true, then she gets trapped in that belief.

For example, many years ago, she heard a one-sided account about India that focused on the poverty, dirt, chaos and spicy food, and she decided she would never go to India. Over time, whenever the topic of India came up, she embellished the facts, and the more she talked about India, the more she believed what she said. She got trapped in her belief and eventually declared that India is beyond her tolerance. Since then, our two daughters, other family members, friends and acquaintances, most of whom are less adventurous than Shirley, have told her that India is an amazing and wonderful experience. But she is now so trapped in her belief that she will not even consider another side to India. Despite all our traveling, we have never been to India.

So, to manage our Q of L in order to live a fulfilled and joyful life, we must ensure that what we speak contributes positively to how we think and to how we see the world. If what we are inclined to speak does not contribute positively to our Q of L, we should not speak it. Therefore, to manage our Q of L, we must manage our thinking and to manage our thinking we must manage our speaking.

Consider another example.

I have a good friend whom I have known since we were children in Barbados. When she was 16, her parents decided to send her to the United States for a visit. She was very excited about her impending trip because it was a big deal to leave the Island and visit North America. She had never been off the Island of Barbados and had never flown. For a couple of months before the trip, she shared her excitement with everyone. She talked about it incessantly but after a while the lustre wore off and people no longer shared her excitement. Now, I know she did not intentionally set out to do so, but when everyone started losing interest in her trip she looked for another way to get attention and she changed her conversation to, "Oh my God, I'm afraid to fly!" When she couldn't get attention one way, she looked for it another way through sympathy. ("Please feel sorry for me.") She talked about how afraid she was to fly so much that by the time she was ready to get onto the airplane, she was literally a basket case. That became her ongoing conversation about flying and she was terrified to fly for many years.

I know that my friend's fear and the pain it caused her were real. But I am certain that she created her fear by speaking it, and kept it alive by speaking it over and over again. Her speaking had such a powerful effect that it turned her fear into a phobia and her Q of L around travel into shambles. On several occasions, I tried to get her to stop speaking about her fear and to stop verbalizing and reinforcing it. I did not suggest that she say something positive, such as, "I'm looking forward to my trip", although I believe there is a lot of power in that. My intention was simply to get her to stop talking about her fear.

I cannot be sure that my efforts had any effect, and I suspect that when she reads this she will say they did not, but I do know that she now travels frequently and that flying is no longer an issue for her. Is that because she has done a lot more flying? Maybe, maybe not, but I know she has changed her conversation. She does not speak about her fear any more, and that certainly contributes to her Q of L.

So, by managing our speaking, we manage our thinking, and so we manage our Q of L. When we have a fear, or anything else that disempowers us, we should just not speak about it; we should not reinforce it! Or, on an even more powerful note, we should change the conversation and create a new conversation that will contribute positively to our Q of L. We have that power.

In summary: we do not speak what we believe; we believe what we speak. It follows, therefore, that the way we think and our As, Ps, Is and Js are influenced by our speaking. Our speaking determines our thinking, our thinking impacts our state of mind, our state of mind determines how we feel, and how we feel determines our Q of L. Everyone has heard about the power of positive thinking. The power of positive speaking is eminently more powerful!

GUIDELINES FOR MANAGING YOUR QUALITY OF LIFE

The following checklist covers everything we have discussed here, and can be used as a guide to help us override our conditioning and programming, make real choices and not live our lives as victims — a checklist that can help us *manage the quality of our lives*.

1. Understand how we operate in our basic humanness.
   - Understand and accept the fact that in our basic humanness, we operate as stimulus/response mechanisms and as victims of our conditioning and programming.
   - Understand that we respond to events and circumstances (stimuli) in predetermined ways and that we do not get to make choices.
2. Reject living your life out of your basic humanness.
   - Reject being a victim.
   - Be intolerant to spending one moment of your precious time having anything less than an outstanding Q of L.

- Set a context for and make a commitment to living an empowered life and making real choices that contribute to your Q of L.
- Make a commitment to manage your attitudes, perceptions, interpretations and judgements so they contribute to your Q of L.

3. Create a vision for your Quality of Life.
  - Create a vision of how you would like your life to be, e.g., joyful, happy, fulfilled, etc.
  - Harness that vision and make a commitment to live your life consistent with making that vision a reality.
  - Reject and be intolerant of any attitudes, perceptions, interpretations and judgements that detract from your vision and from your Q of L.

4. Use the personal power techniques that are available to you.
  - Manage your thinking. Direct your thoughts so they contribute to your Q of L and away from whatever may have a negative impact on your Q of L. "Don't go there," when "there" does not contribute to your Q of L.
  - Manage your your speaking. Use your speaking to manage your thinking. Stay in touch with the power of your speaking and speak only what contributes to your Q of L.

Throughout Part Three I have tried to make it clear that there are *two* distinct components that affect our Q of L.

First, events and circumstances over which we have no control happen and do have an impact on us.

Second, and more important, is how we deal with and allow those events and circumstances to affect us.

This entire exploration has been about the second component only. It's about how we can deal with life's events and challenges and the power we have to manage our Q of L. I hope I have made my point and that I have made a reasonable case to support my claim that we have the power to manage our Q of L

Some Final Words

From the outset, this part of the book has been the most challenging for me because I am, at heart, a story-teller. As such, I have been concerned that what I have to say about "Living a Life with Power" may come across to the reader not as a story, but as a lecture, and I have no desire to lecture anyone. It has been difficult, too, because much of what I have to offer is about the human psyche, the traditional domain of philosophers and psychologists, and in these areas I admit to being very much an amateur.

Nonetheless, I know that what I have to say has value, because I have lived through the experience of learning how to live a life with personal power and I am certain it is possible for others to live powerful lives as well.

I truly believe that my "messages" can not only change your life, they can also enrich it! There are no pre-conditions. All you have to do is understand that it is within you to live a powerful life and make a commitment to start living with power and be intolerant to living even one day of your life without power!

Now, be good to yourself, go out and live your life to the hilt. You have the power within you.

Good Luck!

EPILOGUE

EPILOGUE

When I decided to write this book, I thought it would take a year to a year-and-a-half at most to finish it. Now, four years later, the end is at hand and, frankly, if I had known how difficult it was going to be, especially given my failing sight, I wonder if I would have started it. However, with the benefit of hindsight, I must say it has been an incredible and very rewarding experience. I learned a lot, not only about the craft of writing, but also about myself, what I value and what I believe in.

I have been told that authors seldom feel satisfied with their "finished" work. I now share that problem. I found it very difficult to be satisfied with what I wrote; there was always an overwhelming urge to "fix", change, revise, modify, improve, adapt, rewrite and polish — much to the exasperation of my editors. Still, all good things must come to an end, and so must this book. If it has flaws, if it is incomplete, if it has anomalies, so be it.

The book is finished.

I hope my readers will accept it in the spirit in which it was intended: to give them something of value.

ACKNOWLEDGEMENTS

ACKNOWLEDGEMENTS

IMUST FIRST ACKNOWLEDGE and thank my wife Shirley for her unstinting help and support in my endeavor to write this book and for the countless hours she spent with me verifying facts and refining text. I could not have done it without you and I am deeply grateful for your loving presence in my life.

I want to acknowledge Harvey Horowitz for his wisdom, patience, understanding and generous availability. As a consultant, advisor, all-round sounding board and friend, he was always there for me.

Pauline Kabbas and Gail Fairbanks deserve my special thanks for their patience, tireless efforts and good humour in assisting me with the agonizing process of writing, working and re-working dozens of drafts.

I especially want to acknowledge my editorial team, Eunice Thorne and Ed Matheson, for their four years of commitment to this project and for helping me make this book a reality. Although Ed and I brought two very different sets of expertise to this project and we had many differences of opinion with regard to editorial style and other details that go into the making of a book, despite our frequent tugs-of-war, there was never any doubt as to our mutual goal. I can say, honestly, that our journey together in achieving that goal was an extraordinary adventure — and that we both learned a lot from each other along the way.

Finally, I want to thank my guardian angel, who has always looked out for me, the "universe" for always delivering for me, and all the people at Shirmax with whom I have been associated over the tears. It was only through each and every one of them that I was able to fulfill my dream to build something extraordinary.

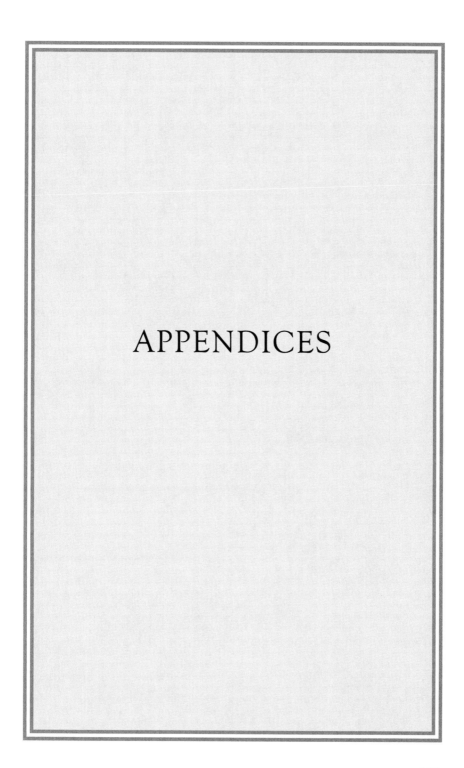

APPENDICES

APPENDICES

THE SHIRMAX MISSION STATEMENT

Our Mission is to:

- Surpass the expectations of our customers
- Be the premier marketplace for the markets we address
- Be a professional organization that uniquely and creatively meets the needs of our stakeholders, customers, employees, suppliers and shareholders
- Operate within a philosophy of cost effectiveness
- Make sufficient profits to ensure the ongoing health and growth of the enterprise
- Create a workplace within which each employee sees himself/herself as a part of a community of people who are mutually supportive and who function in an atmosphere of integrity, trust and mutual acknowledgement
- Pursue excellence and high quality

STATEMENT OF COMPANY VALUES

Our Company Values are:

- Total customer service
- Employee opportunity to achieve work and personal goals in a winning environment
- Teamwork
- Commitment to innovation
- To be adaptive (Adaptivity)
- Proactive communication
- Excellence
- High quality

STATEMENT OF TOTAL CUSTOMER SERVICE

Every Shirmax customer is entitled to:

- Complete satisfaction, so she will be a loyal, long- term Shirmax customer and will speak highly of our retail divisions.

- Merchandise that addresses her needs regarding fashion leadership and quality and that clearly shows it has been bought with an understanding of the needs of our customers.

- Merchandise that is consistent with her social and economic needs

- Professional service by professional staff who understand the merchandise, the needs of our customers and who at all times present themselves as being knowledgeable about fashions and able to provide the highest quality of service.

- Visual presentation that displays packaged and coordinated merchandise in the store so it is easy for the customer to understand the merchandise, be visually impacted by it (?!) and feel she is in dealing with a fashion-first organization.

- A physical environment that reflects a professional organization and is in keeping with the highest standards of the industry and which creates an atmosphere that will attract customers into the store.

STATEMENT OF EMPLOYEE ENTITLEMENTS

Every Shirmax employee is entitled to:

- Work in an atmosphere that is nurturing, enlivening and satisfying.

- Work in an environment in which everyone can communicate fully, openly, honestly and supportively in the pursuit of their personal and professional goals.

In addition to these core documents, each department had its own mission statement, as represented by the Mission Statement of the Human Resource Department which follows.

MISSION STATEMENT
DEPARTMENT OF HUMAN RESOURCES

Our Mission is to:

- Contribute to the well-being, success, profitability and growth of Shirmax by having it known that the company honours its people and recognizes them as its most valuable asset.

- Foster a culture of team, trust, integrity, mutual support, empowerment, opportunity to grow, participation, respect and personal acknowledgement.

- Contribute to the empowerment of employees in creating raving fans*.

- Lead corporate human resources activities by constantly bringing new, creative and innovative methods into the company to attract, develop and retain employees that encourage them to maximize their full potential.

- Manage all human resources programs and activities cost effectively.

- Actively pursue excellence and high quality.

*RAVING FANS: are defined as customers who acknowledge and are affected by an outstanding environment where they feel nurtured and taken care of, and are so valued that they rave about their experience to everyone.